Damn the Pressure,

Full Speed Ahead

Tom Pado

This is a work of nonfiction. The events and experiences detailed herein are all true and have been faithfully rendered as remembered by the author, to the best of his abilities. Some names, identifying characteristics, and circumstances have been changed to protect the privacy and anonymity of the individuals involved.

Cover design by NuMedia Marketing

Library of Congress Cataloging-in-Publication-Data has been applied for.

ISBN 978-1-73-4297058-9

Dedication

This book is dedicated to Thomas (Tom) Francis Pado, my cousin. Tom is older than me by about fifteen years. When I was growing up, I only knew him from stories my family told me. He was smart and learning about him as a child gave me hope that maybe my family was not as dysfunctional as I saw and maybe I could be like him someday.

Tom received academic honors in high school and college. He studied architecture at the Illinois Institute of Technology under the famous modernist, Mies Van der Rohe.

Figure 1 My cousin, Thomas Francis Pado, and me.

Tom worked on numerous projects that took him all over the world. His projects included high-rise office buildings and other structures such as airports, schools, manufacturing facilities, retail stores, housing and others. He spent three years as a captain in the Air Force Strategic Air Command doing architecture and planning. I have come to learn that we share interests in sailing, swimming, and pyrotechnics.

His example inspired me throughout my life. I am very happy to now be privileged to finally be able to know him personally and call him family.

Acknowledgements

Although I have lived the life reported in these pages, I have not been alone in committing my story to paper.

Many thanks to Gus Pearcy whose first writings showed me what my story could become. He was the start of bringing my stories to life.

Finding Elaine Whitesides was serendipity. She understood what I was saying and kept me on the right path. She wore many hats beyond writer during this adventure and couldn't have been a better partner. She was, at times, an editor, a therapist, and now a great friend. Thank you for taking this journey with me.

I want to thank Ronnie Kazmerski. A life-long friend, his camaraderie helped me to pull together many of the threads of my early life. We laughed together, we learned together, and his input has been invaluable.

I want to thank all the people who read the initial drafts and provided valuable suggestions and feedback. I also want to thank all the people who have become friends over the years. Each of you has played a part in making my life rich far beyond my dreams.

Most importantly, I want to thank Cindy, my wife. She was my first love and I am blessed to have her next to me again. This book would not be what it is without her by my side encouraging and supporting me every day along the way.

I am a better man for knowing each and every one of you.

Table of Contents

Foreward

I knew about Tom Pado long before I ever met him. His reputation preceded our introduction. The first time I heard him mentioned was from the people working on the Chevron ARMS Bell contract off the West Coast. I finally met him in 1982 in Australia on the Diamond M Epoch semi-submersible drilling vessel.

Ocean Systems had one of the first Remote Operated Vehicle (ROV) drill support contracts working for Philips. He showed up on the rig to take pictures and video of the first Dual Hydra ROV system to help promote ROV's to a drilling industry dominated by manned diving. He had a passion for the industry, and it was evident how hungry he was to know and understand everything about it. Part of the desire to know, I think, was driven by his curiosity. Another part was his humanity. At the time of the transition from manned diving to ROVs, divers were being injured, or dying at extreme depths in the pursuit of underwater oil drilling. Tom saw ROVs as the means to prevent that from continuing.

Tom not only brought his expertise and experience with ROVs to drill support contracts, God gave Tom an unabashed triple share of enthusiasm and the gift for gab. It was never dull around Tom. He could entertain people for hours. He accepted people as they were and made the best of bad situations. All these qualities came together to make me believe that Tom Pado is the best, most extraordinary salesperson I have ever met.

After he left Oceaneering, Tom went on to start his own business. It wasn't long before he was bidding against Oceaneering for contracts. The next time I ran into him was in the early 90's in Singapore. His company had won contracts against Oceaneering in Vietnam with his Toolpusher ROV. It was a robotic version of the ARMS Bell and worked well in high currents. His personal experience and technical understanding of ROVs and drill support operations kept his products on the cutting edge of the industry.

Tom was a tough competitor over the following decades, and I tried on a number of occasions to convince him to come back to Oceaneering to market for us but without success. He had his face turned toward innovation and controlling what and how he was going to do it was important to him.

The technology evolving at the time was important to Tom, but so were the people in the industry and the relationships he built with them. Because of that, competition was always intense with Pado but so were people. He'd be strong and ambitious in the battle to win contracts but meet up with his rivals for drinks and dinner later in the day. Despite being in competition many, many times, we managed to stay friends over the 38 years we've known each other. That is no small feat, in our, or any other industry.

The early days when the ROVs came on the scene were interesting times. If you liked to solve problems and invent technology to solve the problems, the ROV industry was the place to be. Tom applied his knowledge and skills and had an impact on underwater drill support operations, helping to change the oil industry as well. He was on the front lines, deep in the trenches every day. I'm glad to see Tom tell his side of the story about the part he played in it.

Kevin Kerins, Senior Vice President ROVs, Oceaneering, ret.
Marco Island, Florida.

Introduction

When I retired, after more than forty years living and working abroad, I returned to the United States with the love of my life, fully believing I was ready to rest and live the "quiet life" in rural Indiana. I knew very few people outside family, so I joined the local Rotary Club and started meeting people. These new friends would ask me questions about where I came from and what I had done for a career. I started with the fact that I was originally a Hoosier, from northern Indiana. Then to give them answers to their questions about my business and life, I began telling stories about my life full of submarines, diving, world records, family, rockets, inventions, entrepreneurship, hardships, life-threatening situations, and finally, success.

Figure 2 Here I am, Tom Pado, still happy after all these years.

My stories captured the interest of many. Some laughed about the fun, others were amazed at the sciences that fed my work, and others who, I think, honestly believed my stories were too extraordinary to be true. They encouraged me to write a book. I know that is a common phrase thrown around conversations, so I did not take it seriously.

Then, once I realized that my life's experience was, indeed, unique, unbelievable, and difficult to comprehend by many, I started listening to the reasons people were asking me to speak to different groups and organizations. What was it they saw in my story that I took for granted?

As I collected the stories into this book, I uncovered several threads had been woven throughout my life.

One was about my personal story. Where I started, how I managed those beginnings, who had given me guidance, and what traits and skills I developed that helped me reach goals throughout my entire life.

Another was about my business experiences. The trials, challenges, and successes. The lessons I had learned. The mistakes I made and what I did that made other attempts successful.

Probably the biggest thread woven through my life concerned the people I surrounded myself with and the influence they had on my decisions and the outcomes of those decisions.

I saw that my story could be instructive and save others from learning as I did, through the School of Hard Knocks. If they could be aware of pitfalls, emulate my strengths, and understand what it takes to be an entrepreneur, they would have a leg up early in their endeavors. They might be able to shortcut time wasted and use my experiences to avoid having to learn from their own experience.

I was part of launching a huge, technology-driven new industry that changed the lives of every single person in the world. Perhaps, knowing what I did and how I did it will provide people with some of the knowledge, skills, and tools so they can innovate and follow their dreams to make great changes in the world, too.

It is not easy to navigate life. We all face challenges in life, both personally and professionally. To me the two are so intertwined that all aspects of one affects all aspects of the other. If my story provides useful to others, perhaps it will be my greatest success. I dream that it helps people who follow in my footsteps to pursue entrepreneurship on their own.

Bear in mind I tell all my stories based on my perception and interpretation of situations, the places they occurred, and the people involved. Some of the people I talk about are alive, some have died, and the names of a few have been changed to respect their privacy. Even though a name might be changed, my story is accurately MY story. All the places, and events can be authenticated through public information.

Everyone's life is lived within the context of the times and history. I was absent from the United States and my daily life was lived mostly among Australians and other cultures of the world. While American pop culture was probably very different than what I experienced, I believe everything is relevant because business is business and people are people all the world over.

I am truly a regular guy, who, just like everyone else, had doubts, fears, and obstacles to overcome. Honestly, I believe that if I can make, as Steve Jobs said, "a dent in the universe," then so can you. It's your choice and I want my experiences to give you a reason to believe – in yourself, your abilities, and your dreams.

Read on and good luck in creating the life you love!

Section One - What Grows in the Shadows?

Part I - Growing Roots

Gary, Indiana,
Gary, Indiana,
Not Louisiana, Paris, France,
New York, or Rome, but
Gary, Indiana,
Gary, Indiana,
Gary, Indiana,
My home sweet home.
Gary, Indiana, Music Man,
written by Meredith Wilson

With the exception of that song, the Jackson family, and the steel industry, Gary, Indiana is not the sort of city many people today remember fondly as home, sweet home. I know, because it was home to me for most of my early life. By the time I left the city, it was anything but sweet to me. In fact, I, like so many others, couldn't wait to get out and as far away as possible.

Gary, Indiana grew casting a long shadow in the steel industry. U.S. Steel was co-founded by J. P. Morgan and Elbert H. Gary in 1901 by combining three steel companies, Carnegie Steel Company, Federal Steel Company, and National Steel Company, and other holdings into the world's first billion-dollar corporation. The steel mill was built in Gary because of its close proximity to Chicago and a transportation hub where shipping routes, train tracks, and roads traversed by trucks all converged.

Iron ore came from Minnesota. Coal came from the south and east, and there was a plentitude of limestone quarried in the area that could easily be trucked to the mill in Gary. U. S. Steel had a prime location for the construction of a port to ship the final product through the Great Lakes to the rest of the world.

Nowhere was the long steel mill shadow cast longer than on the streets of my hometown neighborhood. It was a welcome shadow enveloping a mass of mostly eastern European immigrants and their families providing clothes and food for many, and none more so than mine.

Figure 3 My grandpa, John Pado

My grandfather, John Pado, was an immigrant who arrived on America's shore around 1913 from what I believe was the Kingdom of Hungary. Grandpa and Grandma came from an area of the world with shifting borders, governments, and loyalties. It's hard to pin down exactly where my ancestors originated. They could have lived in what, at times, was the Austro-Hungarian Empire, Hungary, Slovakia, Czechoslovakia, Romania, or one of many other political regions. I believe they were Slovak in heritage, which, in most iterations of the region, were a minority group who were often not even allowed to speak their own language. At other times, even if they could speak their native tongue in public, they were also required to learn and speak Hungarian fluently or some other language.

The economy was raging in the Austro-Hungarian Empire at the turn of the century with the onset of the Industrial Revolution. The railroad, telephone, and auto industries combined with the agricultural wealth contributed to the surge. The plight of different races and ethnic groups as well as the politics of contending factions encapsulated in the broad Austro-Hungarian Empire kept everything in a constant state of upheaval. With the threat of World War I on the horizon all the time, my grandparents made a calculated decision to test their fortune in America.

Grandpa came to the United States with his brother, Mike, leaving behind my grandmother. I think Grandpa felt he would face the dangers of immigration so he could create a path that would be less treacherous for her. Grandpa and Mike ran through cornfields hiding during the day making their way to the port and a ship to bring them to America.

Figure 4 Mike Pado, John Pado, and Mary Pado

They arrived having already developed skills in the trades and together they made their way to the Heartland in search of work and a future. As an electrician, Grandpa quickly found work inside the walls of the new U.S. Steel mill in Gary and toiled hard to build something in this new land for his family.

He spent seven years in Gary on his own laboring at the steel mill before he was joined by his wife, my grandmother, Mary, and other family members. Grandpa worked hard and by the time he was joined by his wife and relatives in America, he had purchased a home from the (U.S. Steel controlled) Gary Land Company on Virginia Street. It was a place within the shadow of the mill where he hoped they would build a life that was safe, stable, and prosperous. Brother George also arrived in America at some point, but he was always on the fringes of our lives. I believe the reason for that was because he came to America illegally and was always just a few steps ahead of the deportation squads most all the time. How or when he came was a secret just like the life he had here.

Figure 5 John Pado, John Edward Pado, Annabell Pado and Mary Pado

Stories of my grandparent's early life in America fascinated me because they often seemed to live on the edge and that was exciting to me. For instance, there came a day the authorities knocked on the door of Grandpa's house looking for George. The family had gotten wind that they would be coming, so they had tucked Uncle George under a stack of firewood in the back corner of the basement. The immigration officers searched the house. They didn't find George in the basement. They left, and George left shortly after them. He never stayed around long. Grandma and Grandpa were always very interested in doing the right thing and living within the law of the land, so I suppose they didn't encourage him to stick around.

Gary was founded as a company town by U. S. Steel in 1906 and never moved beyond being a one-industry town. Over the next several decades, the steel company flourished, and the town of Gary grew in step with the mill. This was a prosperous time for Gary, known as an "instant city."

Figure 6 (top from left) Annabell Pado, Unknown, John Edward Pado, (bottom from left) Unknown, John Pado, Mary Pado at Marquette Park Pavilion

By the time of the 1920 census, 29.7 percent of the population was classified as foreign-born, mostly from eastern European countries. By 1930, the population exceeded 100,000 people, and because of the steel industry, Gary was the fifth-largest city in Indiana. My family were strangers among strangers, and somehow, that made it somewhat easier, I think. Unlike the different ethnic groups in their eastern European home, the strangers in America melded together to make it work. Languages, cultures, and the trepidation of being a stranger in a strange land was shared by all. No one was on the top. They were all starting at the bottom together. The fear of the authorities and those in power was always in the back of their minds, too.

Figure 7 John and Mary Pado at Marquette Park.

What they saw happening in Gary must have amazed them. Construction was occurring on every street and corner. Many apartment buildings and homes for the workers must have seemed to sprout overnight. Then came three-story buildings, the Gary State Bank, the Hotel Gary, the Knights of Columbus hall, and the massive City Methodist Church. The City Hall, courthouse, parks like the 10-acre Gateway Park provided greenery and leisure space. It was understandable for Gary to be named "Magic City" and the "City of the Century" because of the rapid growth and opulence of the buildings and parks.

Gary was not like the homeland, it was better, according to Grandma and Grandpa. Gary held hope for the future.

Because they had lived in a land that was often being overrun and annexed by different countries and governments, many of the eastern European immigrants knew what it was like to live at the bottom of society. They came to America knowing how to make a purse, not necessarily a silk purse, but a purse none the less, out of a pig's ear. They knew how to salvage every scrap and turn it into something useful. They knew how to feed a family on scraps and whatever nature provided in the area. Grandma could cook … anything. She made fancy Slovakian cakes from scratch and noodles by hand. Everything she made was delicious and in her broken English, she would say to me, "Here, eat Sonny, eat Sonny. You no be healthy if you no eat." Then she would hug me, kiss me, and tell me, "I could just eat you up!"

Grandma and Grandpa were very strict Catholics, as were many of their immediate neighbors. There was never a weekly mass missed and evenings would find them on their knees saying the entire rosary one bead at a time. Although my dad didn't continue the practices they so fervently repeated, my Auntie Annabell, and eventually her daughter, Louise, did.

Figure 8 John and Mary Pado

Their life was centered on family and church, supported by daily labor and a lot of hard work. I understood from my extended family that there were two kinds of workers, both were based on the skills from the mother country. One group were farmers and lived in the counties surrounding Gary growing crops and raising chickens, sheep, goats, and whatever else they could find. The others, like my grandpa and Uncle Mike, who was a pipefitter, were skilled tradesmen. Their livelihoods were based on the hard, physical work in the mills.

That's not to say there wasn't fun, too. In fact, during the heyday of Prohibition, when my dad and his sister were youngsters, my grandparents were regular visitors to the speakeasies on 38th Street, known as Ridge Road. They would dress themselves to the nines and take full advantage of the liquor, music, dancing, and gambling. While I could never envision Grandma bedecked in the beads and fringe of a creamy white flapper dress and a hat with long, flowing feathers, she was in her younger days, apparently, quite the looker and party girl. She and Grandpa, according to my Auntie Annabell, loved to dress up and participate in the social life.

My church going, law-abiding grandparents who always wanted to do the right thing during the years I remember, were fully engaged in the unlawful drinking and gambling on the weekends in their younger years.

Alcohol was a part of daily life for my grandparents, at least for Grandpa. Just like everyone else during prohibition, Grandpa found less legal ways to get the alcohol he wanted besides patronizing speakeasies. The family next door had their own distillery in the basement and supplied friends, neighbors and whoever else wanted it, with liquor for a price, of course. Grandpa kept a small supply, one little jar, in the back of a cupboard. No one thought much about it because everybody did it and besides, no one was getting hurt by it, except maybe Grandpa, and he was willing to take the risk.

Grandma and Grandpa got used to people coming to their door by mistake asking to buy liquor. They simply directed them next door and went about their day.

Early one morning just after the sun came up, there was banging on the door. Grandpa answered and a swarm of agents from the Prohibition Bureau demanded entry for a search. They claimed they had been tipped off that the family at this address had a distillery inside their house. Grandpa knew, of course, why the mistake had been made. No matter what he said, he couldn't get the agents to either understand or believe him. Grandpa insisted he was not producing alcohol. It was true. When the agents found his little jar in the cupboard, they arrested him and carted him off to jail. Grandma and Annabell followed with Grandma crying and saying "Otec (Slovakian for father) is going to jail!" Because Annabell spoke English better than Grandma, she went with her and together they were able to get him out of jail by the end of the day. Grandpa never told the authorities who the family was that was distilling the alcohol nor where the neighborhood source was located. He paid the fine for the liquor he had, and knowing Grandpa, went and bought some more. He said he was pretty sure those agents weren't going to be coming back.

Figure 9 Louie Rosnowski and John Pado

The neighborhood was filled with immigrants who continued many of the communal traditions established in their native lands just like Grandma and Grandpa. The men worked in the mill and the women worked together to share what they had so all the families could get by. It was a joyous day when the families who combined their resources took receipt of a railroad car of grapes, half white and half red. The fruit was divided amongst the families and each made their own wine. Cabbage, gained in the same manner, would fill casks combined with brine and stink up the basements of houses up and down the streets.

The Slovak people gathered together on a regular basis and eventually they purchased property in the Tolleston area of Gary. The group was first established in 1913 by a group of Slovak men from the Holy Trinity Catholic Church who wanted to preserve Slovak heritage and traditions. Originally, the group called themselves the Slovak Political and Educational Club.

I remember we would go to, what seemed to me, just large open fields near Merrillville surrounded by chain link fences. The boys and men would play soccer in this park. It was also the location where they held a traditional Slovak form of a barbecue. The day would be spent filled with family, sports, song, wine, and huge amounts of food. Lambs were cooked in fire pits to roast slowly. When the lamb was cooked through, the carcass would be lifted from the pit on the spit and the meat cut up with a band saw. I can close my eyes and still hear the sound – zzziiippp, zzzzippp – of the blade cutting through the meat and bone. The juicy slices were divvied up into little paper boats and served with homemade bread. My grandparents, father, and his sister loved it, and when I was old enough to attend, I loved it, too. It was heaven for us. Not for Mom. Mom hated it and refused to eat the lamb and food that filled the little paper boats. She'd wrinkle up her nose as we ate it with our hands and asked for more.

My Auntie Annabell and my father, John Edward Pado, had both been born and grew up within sight of the U. S. Steel mill in Gary. One of the entrances to the mill was a straight shot down Virginia Street. Like so many other immigrants, Dad's family enjoyed the fruits of life in America, but were always a little wary, too. Perhaps it was because of the conditions they left in Europe, or maybe it was because of the language barriers presented with English and so many other country's languages represented in Gary.

Figure 10 Annabell and John Edward Pado

My dad had lived a sheltered life, pampered by his mother and sister while his father walked the same route every morning and every evening to and from a hard day's labor in the mill. Even to a kid like me, it was evident that Dad liked being the center of attention. He went along with the coddling, unless there was something he wanted. Then he finagled his way around the protective nature of his family. During his time in school, he would tell me about bringing home the papers from school about events or fieldtrips and have to explain to his parents what the papers said because they could not read English. Time

Figure 11 My father, John Edward Pado

came around for football and Dad wanted to play. Grandma refused because she did not want him to play a game so rough. He was determined, so he brought home the permission slip and told his mother that it was for a fieldtrip and she signed it. He played football and I'm not sure Grandma ever knew it. I for sure never mentioned it to her.

When Dad reached the end of his school years, and therefore, adulthood, he didn't immediately step into the mill like his father. No, instead he was sucked into the vacuum created by World War II.

Figure 12 My father, submariner John Edward Pado

He voluntarily entered the Navy on June 22, 1943 and joined a celebrated group who became submariners. He was sent to New London, Connecticut where he attended submarine school and took the classes to become a submarine electrician. Electricians were the precursors to today's electronics wizards. During his time in the Navy, submarines ran on mechanics and electricity. I suspect that he developed an understanding of the mechanics as well. From his military records, I learned that my dad also had torpedo instruction for eight weeks in Newport, Rhode Island just before he was transferred to a submarine assignment on the *U.S.S. Boarfish* on September 23, 1944. Immediately thereafter, he was shipped out to meet up with the *Boarfish* crew that would be based in Fremantle, Australia.

It's not a commonly known part of the history of WWII that Pearl Harbor was not the only attack made by

Japan. Later in the war, they attacked the continent of Australia. Most of the population inhabited the areas around Adelaide, Brisbane, and Sidney on the eastern coast. The west coast was vulnerable and sustained several attacks, severe enough to pretty much devastate the town of Darwin. It is my understanding that the Australian government kept the severity of this bombing from the Australian people, even into the 1990s.

An inland harbor was built at Fremantle on the southern coast to serve Australian, Dutch, English, and American vessels, especially the submarines.

A retractable net actually constructed from anchor chain was fashioned across the mouth of the harbor. The net was lowered to let the submarines and vessels into the harbor, then raised to protect the Allied vessels from Japanese torpedoes.

The submarines' mission was to protect Australia from Japanese attack and to advance the war effort. While submarines did target and attack warships, their primary contribution was to attack and debilitate supply vessels. Dad would tell some stories about his service, mostly his social life between patrols. I learned more about his service from actual U. S. Navy records.

Submarine warfare was still in early development at the time. When a fresh boat and crew arrived, they spent the majority of their time running up and down the coast of Western Australia in maneuvers. The 70-plus man crew would practice diving, surfacing, and repairing the submarine for as long as it took for them to become proficient. Once deemed sufficiently skilled, they were sent off to patrol the South China Sea, searching for enemy vessels to destroy.

While waiting for the *Boarfish* to be finished, my father served aboard the *USS Cero SS 225*. The *Cero* was a WWI leftover and had actually moored for refitting at Midway in 1943 and patrolled the Truk-New Ireland shipping lanes for a time. During that time, she inflicted damage or sank many different tankers, freighters, and other cargo ships. WWI submarines were very small, and you would be hard-pressed to call them comfortable. Submariners had very little personal space, sleeping accommodations were minimal, and the air was not all that fresh. Submariners had to be a special breed to deal with the arrangement and the lengthy patrols out at sea that could be three to four months long. Combine the idea of being under water in the close quarters of little more than a tin can with the ever-present danger of combat action and you get an inkling of the stress submariners at the time endured.

The last patrol for *Cero* began in September 1944 when she set course for the Mindanao and Sulu Seas. While en route the *Cero* took on an additional fifteen tons of supplies and sixteen soldiers in Mios Woendi for behind-the-lines operations in Luzon. While so heavily loaded the submariners engaged in gun action, damaging two small craft and forcing them ashore. Once the submarine reached its destination in the Philippines, the crew unloaded and replaced the tonnage with four evacuees.

Afterward, Cero was attacked by a Japanese submarine. The Cero evaded the Japanese torpedoes and returned to port in Pearl Harbor.

The new, state of the art submarine, *USS Boarfish SS 327*, was moored in Pearl Harbor and Dad transferred to this new boat. This was the boat that my dad was trained to be on when it was ready to go to war. This submarine was larger and offered more room and more modern weaponry. Even if a sailor got an additional twelve inches in his space for himself and for sleeping, it could make a real difference in the comfort level. It was a step up for Dad.

There were just a few weeks of familiarizing themselves with the boat in Hawaii before they stood out of Pearl Harbor for the western Pacific. Within sixteen days after taking on provisions in Saipan, *Boarfish* engaged in an attack of several small convoy ships. Their torpedoes were not successful in hitting the targets. However, two weeks later, *Boarfish* engaged with two cargo ships, sending one to the bottom of the sea and leaving the second beached in a raging fire. American planes completely destroyed what was left of the enemy ship and *Boarfish* received partial credit for the sinking.

Figure 13 My father, John Edward Pado

From December 1 to December 31, 1944 Dad served as crews' galley hand on the boat. Everyone on the boat at some time or another in their career had to be a galley hand. This qualified him for additional pay. It is really difficult for me to ever have imagined my dad content as a crews' galley hand. The galley hand performed a variety of duties: setting tables, serving food or waiting on tables. A galley hand is also responsible for cleaning dishes and equipment, preparing coffee and beverages and even making the beds and cleaning the quarters of officers. He's an "all-around" man. In other words, he does whatever is asked of him by the Chief Steward.

By the first of the year in 1945, according to his records, he was back in his usual role, and I think he probably preferred that. He never made any mention of being a galley hand on the Boarfish. On February 5, 1945 the boat crossed the equator and he then qualified to be a "shellback." Here is the initiation greeting that would be spoken by a true shellback: "Is ye a Screecher, bye? Indeed, I is ye old cock and long may your big jib draw!" Fun and lore aside, I think the most significant of all the changes in roles for him must have been on April 14, 1945 when he qualified for torpedo duty.

Boarfish pulled into the harbor at Fremantle, Australia in February 1945 for refit. The next patrol sent *Boarfish* into the South China Sea where the crew engaged in attacking two convoys and carrying out two reconnaissance missions along the east coast of French Indonesia, eventually putting into the port at Subic Bay in April for a refit.

It was the third patrol after leaving Subic Bay that *Boarfish* saw action and damage that forced an early return to Fremantle. It began with the sighting of a junk in the Java Sea. After a search party found nothing on the junk, it was allowed to proceed. Just two days later, *Boarfish* encountered three ships along with two escorts. Torpedoes were launched and although an explosion was heard, the officer at the conn peered through the periscope to see not a sinking ship, but an escort charging. *Boarfish* immediately dove and grounded, knocked off the sound gear and made enough noise to be put in a perilous situation. The maneuver to hide betrayed their location and depth charges littered the sea as the *Boarfish* attempted to escape. Although the port propeller was hit, *Boarfish* was able to successfully return to Fremantle for repair.

The fourth patrol for *Boarfish* was in the Java Sea in a coordinated operation alongside *USS Blenny SS 324* and *USS Chub SS 329*. In addition to avoid being depth-charged from enemy planes, *Boarfish* performed lifeguard duties during an allied air strike on Singapore. After patrolling the Malaysian coast, *Boarfish* pulled into Subic Bay for refitting in August 1945. This was where the submarine was moored when the Japanese surrendered, and the war ended.

Another part of the early development included the use of torpedoes. In the beginning of WWII, torpedoes were highly unreliable. It was not unusual for a launched torpedo to veer from its intended target and end up striking the boat from which it was launched. The guidance systems were unreliable and dangerously inefficient because the gyroscope would wobble causing the torpedo to go off course.

Newer torpedoes were guided by sound. With the advent of these new weapons, the torpedo men would fire them, the captain would give the command "all stop" to shut down the submarine's propellers, and the entire submarine would wait in silence. It would be only for a minute or so as the torpedoes were rushing to the screws of the enemy ship, which would be the loudest thing in the water. The torpedoes hit the screws, the whirring propellers on the Japanese vessels, wounding the boat enough that the submarine could surface and finish it off with their three-inch deck guns.

I understand now that being a submariner during the war was a risky, but exciting, deployment. Although he wasn't engaged in hand-to-hand combat, his service certainly wasn't for the faint of heart. Not only was the sea trying to crush their vessel and them, they also had the stress of bombs trying to blow them up. Submariners had a reputation for being a cut above the rest and it was well-deserved. They were known to be hard-working, fearless risk-takers, and when they got on the beach, they lived life like it was their last day.

I didn't really understand it at the time and none of that mattered to a little kid like me. All I could see was that my dad was a great adventurer and warrior. Now, as a former U. S. Navy submariner myself, and learning more about his service, I have an even greater respect for him.

Later in life, when I lived in Australia, the locals would explain to me how much they loved the "Yanks." That close connection extended to all the people in town because all their young men were off fighting in the war with the British. The girls spent a lot of time with, and gave a lot of attention to, the Yank submariners. When a submarine and its crew was lost at sea in battle, the town mourned as if they had lost their own sons, brothers, and husbands.

The sailors loved Australia and the people, too. Dad said they were a fun-loving bunch. I loved to see how animated Dad would get when he told stories of the horse races and the betting there. The local farmers made their own fun, especially those who owned horses. They would build sulkies, two-wheeled carts, using a set of car tires and wooden planks. They would then square off against each other in harness races. The farmers were having fun and making money since the races attracted young healthy submariners with American money ready for some excitement.

Sitting on the edge of the couch in our tiny house in Gary, Dad would recount the races and how he would parley his wagers into winnings. His eyes would light up like he was reliving it in its retelling. Mom would get up and go into another room or go outside as he regaled me with his stories. I figured she'd heard them before. For me, they never got old and I would ask for more and more.

True to the reputation of American servicemen, his time off the boat in Australia was filled with drinking, racing, gambling, and, of course, carousing with the local girls. Later in life, during the one time my parents visited me anywhere, I paid for them to come to Australia. My dad and I returned to the Fremantle harbor, where he was stationed in WWII, and it brought back memories. He told me the story of when the five-o'clock bell rang to end the workday, everyone started planning for the evening. The train from Fremantle to Perth, nicknamed the Shack Master by the submariners, was their passage to drinks, music, and the opportunity to "shack up with" women. At the end of the evening, for those who didn't get lucky, the return trip to Fremantle from Perth was on the train they then called the Beast Master. It was nicknamed for the fights that broke out between the drunken beasts going home alone.

While we were walking around the harbor, he mentioned to some old-timers that he had been a submariner there during WWII. They started pointing out all the things they had scrapped from the war and those things with historical value that were set aside, such as the chain nets and the wench and capstans that raised and lowered the chain netting that closed off Fremantle harbor to keep the Japanese from firing torpedoes into the harbor to sink Allied submarines. Some of the original workshops were still there, now in use as a variety of things including a restaurant, schools, and craft shops.

At the close of World War II, Dad and the rest of the submariners were sent back to the New London base in Connecticut. It was in Norwich and New London where the sailors spent their free time, still drinking and carousing. Now they were out with the local Connecticut girls. Dad said he spent a lot of time in Norwich.

It was in Norwich that Dad met my mother, Shirley Malakov. My mother was from a family parented by Peter Malakov, of Russian birth and Polish heritage, and German mother, Edna Judge. Or, at least at the time my mother was born, everyone thought Grandma was German. Grandma Edna had been orphaned as a young child and had grown up in the home of a German doctor and his wife. Whatever her ancestry, she was the daughter of immigrants who left Europe for the United States, just like my dad's family.

It was shortly after Peter and Edna married that the young couple emigrated from Europe to America where they settled to build a new life and family. My mother had four other siblings, Harold, Jim, Ray and Flossie, all born in America and reared in the Anglican Church.

My mom, Shirley, was the life of every party. The one everyone simply described as "she was just Shirley," and went on expecting everyone to understand. She had friends everywhere and enjoyed them all, and they her. Or at least they put up with her antics and behaviors. Both of my parents were right on the cusp of 20 years old. When Dad met this vivacious female, he apparently decided she was the one, despite the fact that she was reared Anglican and had an upbringing very different from his own.

Figure 14 My parents, John Edward Pado and Shirley (Malakov) Pado

Within just a few months, Mom converted to Catholicism and they were wed. The young couple remained in Connecticut for about a year, during which time, I was born. By then Dad had been discharged from the Navy for about four months and wanted to return home. He missed his family and the Slavic traditions he grew up with in Gary, so, with his recently converted Catholic bride and young son in tow, it was back to the Magic City in Indiana. In addition to the familiarity of home and family, there was the draw of work in the steel mill, too.

Gary, like other towns and cities that relied on one primary industry, rode the waves of the steel business. By the time Mom and Dad returned in 1947, Gary was developing a well-earned reputation as a tough town fueled by rampant political corruption, racial violence and segregation, declining employment, and the filth and pollution generated by the steel industry. It seemed the wave had peaked and the industry, as well as the city, was on its way to crash onto the beach. Change was coming. Our family wouldn't feel the decline directly for more than a decade later. In that moment, however, Dad and Mom were ready to build a life.

Figure 15 My father, John Edward Pado and me, John Thomas Pado.

We initially moved into the house on Virginia Street with Grandma and Grandpa. The upstairs had been converted into an apartment with cooking facilities for us. Despite having our own space in the house, my mom explained later in life that there was little freedom for us. Grandma ruled the house within the rules of Catholicism and her native Slavic culture.

Mom wasn't much for the domestic side of life, and cooking, well, cooking mainly consisted of whatever she could throw together out of a can or box. Many times, Mom had told me about the Friday when Grandma came in and smelled meat cooking in the house. She said Grandma flew up the stairs to inform her that "You don't cook Sonny meat on Friday!" Although Mom had converted to the Catholic religion, she wasn't inclined to follow all of its rules like Grandma. It wasn't long after that incident that Mom was pushing Dad to do something about moving out and into a place of our own.

She was successful in pressuring him to take action. Our little family left my grandparent's house and moved into a 750-square-foot, two-bedroom house with a kitchen that was a block away on Louisiana Street. It was one of the worker's homes constructed by (U.S. Steel) Gary Land Company, and Mom said she felt, at least in the beginning, that she could breathe there. At $60 per month, it took years for them to pay off the $7,000 purchase price. The little house was theirs and she saw it as a foundation from which to build their life.

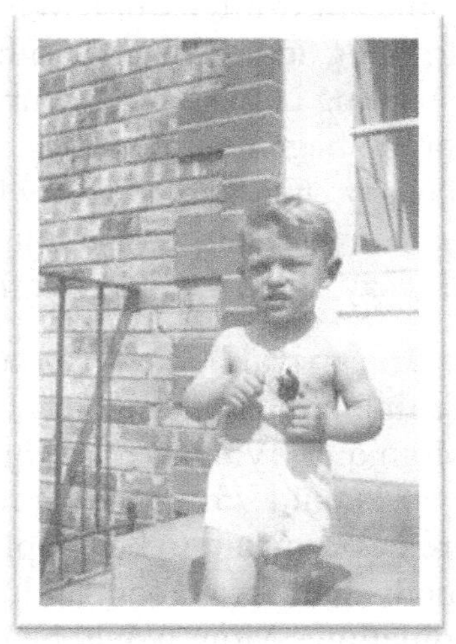

Figure 16 Me as a youngster.

She made friends with the neighbors. Dad had a job in the mill. He worked a rotation of shifts. Some weeks he was on from four to twelve, then the next week, midnights. As he moved up, he worked days. Meals were on the table when he got home of a night. Dad would come in, hand over his lunch pail, take off his jacket, sit down at the table, and we would eat together. Those meals were my first memories of that tiny four-room house.

Part II - Lessons That Launch

Those warm cozy suppers in the evenings grew more and more infrequent. It wasn't because Dad's work schedule changed so much. It was because Dad wouldn't come home after work. While he was out in the bars, drinking and carousing with women, Mom and I would be sitting at the table as our food congealed. Dinner time for me began with waiting for Dad with elbows on the table, my chin cradled in my hands, and my stomach growling. "Go ahead and just eat," Mom would eventually say, and I would gratefully do as instructed.

His arrival home grew later and later, and money kept getting tighter and tighter. It wasn't all that long before Mom quit trying to make meals and supper became whatever I could scrounge up on my own. To this day, foods are never meant to be simply breakfast foods or lunch foods. Food was food, and I ate whatever I found because sometimes Mom would be home to point something out. That didn't always happen.

Once Dad's presence at home became less consistent, it was replaced with something else that was consistent – the fighting. Every. Single. Day. If she heard the car pull up, Mom would wait by the door and it would barely open before she would pounce and start the screaming attacks. She would spew a river of words I didn't understand then like I do now. Accusations. Questions. Threats. Every. Single. Day. It would last for some time and then, often, be replaced by silence for the rest of the night. Or with one of them storming out the door. By the next day they were both back. When, or if, they ever returned home later at night, or in the early morning hours, I didn't know.

Occasionally, Mom would say to Dad, "Take your son somewhere. Do something with him." The look on his face told me he had no clue what that "something" might be. We'd climb into the car and off we would go.

His job meant he was either gone at work, or sleeping in bed, which meant there wasn't a lot of time to spend with me. I always had a great love for my dad and yearned for his time and attention. When Mom made these suggestions and I recognized an opportunity to spend time with him, I jumped on it.

A few times we went fishing near the steel mill. There was a tall chain link fence surrounding the steel mill property. People had cut an entranceway through it so they could get in to fish off the pier. That's where he took me, and we fished for perch. We'd catch a mess and take them home for supper.

A couple of other times, he took me hunting. He'd hand me a 22-caliber rifle and let me go. He'd go off shooting and eventually meet up with me carrying a few rabbits in one hand and his gun in the other. He must have been a good shot, although I never actually saw him shoot anything. I seldom hit anything. Just having the freedom to shoot at whatever I wanted was fun. In retrospect I see now that he handed me a gun and let me go to get me out of his hair. I never saw it that way then. At the time, I felt important that he had trusted me with a gun and the freedom to be responsible for myself.

Just about every other time, after we climbed into the car, we would drive to what I later figured out was the Gary bus station. He'd tell me to stay put and off he would go. As the sky morphed from day into night, I would huddle in the footwell of the back seat and wait until he returned. It's hard to tell how long it would be. Eventually, I'd hear the trunk click open, hear something being tossed in, and then there he'd be climbing back into the driver's seat.

Sometimes it was a trip to the Indiana Harbor bus station instead. Once I complained that the people who walked by scared me, so Dad told me to lock the doors and not open them for anyone. Oh, wow, that really made me feel safe.

Part of what scared me was that there were so many people who weren't like me. By this time, the Gary area we lived in was called "The Region" for its multicultural diversity and high crime rate. Still in single digits as far as age, I had little concept of the reasons for danger, only that I felt it.

Later in life I wondered why we would go to the bus stations. I learned that they were meeting places for homosexuals and offered a bustling trade in adult books. I can't say that really had anything to do with our visits there. What I can say for sure is that I also realized the bus stations were places where Dad could use the public telephones and I would see him spend time in different booths.

For some time, I really thought Mom was trying to get me and Dad to bond in some way. After she made it a habit to grill me on where we went, who we saw, and what Dad did while we were gone, I knew something was up. The truth is that she suspected Dad was cheating on her and she wanted the scoop. While I didn't provide much evidence, she felt her suspicions were founded because any time I reported he was on the phone, it would be met with, "I knew it! He was probably talking to HER."

The fighting continued to escalate. Mom continued to pounce as soon as Dad would open the door and step into the kitchen. The fights were longer, and more violent.

One night they were engaged at a fevered pitch and I heard a great Bong! Then a thud. Startled, I ran into the kitchen and saw Dad on his hands and knees rubbing his head and a pot laying on the floor next to him. Mom was just standing there scowling at him with her hands on her hips. She had hit him with a pot. If he didn't know it, I did. She was getting fed up.

During one argument Dad blurted out, "I wanted you to be different." I remember because she didn't scream back some response. She got very quiet. And for several days, she was quiet and didn't say much to him, or me. I think she felt she was the problem and maybe she could solve it.

Apparently not one to take this sort of thing in stride, Mom decided to make some changes. Three days after their big fight, she asked Dad to take her to the beauty parlor and then pick her up afterward. It was a strange request because with money so tight, Mom usually got together with her girlfriends and they did each other's hair. We were waiting in the parking lot when the door to the salon opened and out strutted this blonde-haired woman. Dad gasped and I looked to see who she was. No way was that my mom. She sallied right up to the car, opened the door, and settled in, not saying a word.

Things really changed after that. Mom started taking diet pills and lost a lot of weight. She started wearing tight shirts and those pants called stirrup-pants in bright colors, even some with leopard prints. In my mind, Mom was responding to that comment Dad made and was trying to change for Dad. After a while, she was spending a lot of time down at the corner gas station called Martin's getting cigarettes or a few dollars of gas in the car. It was evident she was also getting a lot of attention from the guys down at the gas station, too. With this change in their relationship, my outings with Dad stopped. Mom didn't complain so much about Dad being gone anymore either, probably because she was gone most of the time, too.

With both of them gone, I had lots of time to myself to think and explore. My thinking started out as thinking about what my parents were doing. I always wondered that if they both hated it so much, why didn't they just stop? Stop fighting, or stop being together. I fretted about it because it always left me with a very uneasy feeling. There was never any certainty for me in my childhood. I never felt stable or secure. The fretting led me to develop several tics. I constantly bit my lip, twirled my hair, and flicked my eyelashes. My mom would reprimand me by saying I was going to bite a hole through my lip if I didn't stop. I just wondered why she never stopped.

As if I was a miniature confidant, both of my parents would, at different times, confide that they were going to leave the family, or, more accurately leave their spouse and in both instances, that included me. Although I didn't realize it at the time, Mom made actual attempts. She would pack me up and take the train back to Connecticut where we would stay for a few months. Usually the money for the train fare arrived from her parents or her brother, Ray, and off we would go. To me it was a vacation and happened every few years. They were glorious times for me.

We would arrive and after a day or so at her parent's house, I was sent off to stay at my aunt and uncle's home where there were cousins to play with and no arguing every day. I slept on the couch and loved it. My cousin, Harold, and I were free to explore and let our imaginations run wild. Our explorations included poison ivy and itching was even glorious because of the special attention we got with calamine lotion and extra treats.

There were fields, creeks, and riverbanks where we caught lizards, turtles, and tadpoles. We watched snakes swim through the water and crawl through the grass on the other opposite bank. We bravely swam in the ponds and rivers and fished off the banks and piers. I loved to hear Harold cuss with his New England accent and goaded him into wild tirades that left me rolling hysterically in the grass.

One of our favorite spots was a shallow waterbed next to a high concrete wall with three pipes running out of it. We followed the river down to where it created a pond and considered it our own private hideaway. Our interest in the spot was amplified when we discovered treasure there. We'd find different things in the water like dog tags, jewelry or things from people's houses. After that, we always checked for new finds every day or so. One day we were knee deep in the creek combing the bottom when, all of a sudden, to our surprise, water came spraying out of one of the pipes. We watched as it fell into the creek and then I noticed something. "Hey, that's toilet paper. That's POOP!"

Our favorite spot was immediately spoiled. Funny how we'd never recognized anything – or any smell – before that moment. We weren't fools. That was the end of that for us.

During one of the Connecticut trips, I stayed at my grandparents for a few extra days. I remember little about staying in their home beyond the fact that I don't think I ever saw a cheerful face on my Grandma Malakov. I'm not sure I would recognize her face with a smile and the sound of her laughter would definitely be foreign. She pretty much seemed to go through all the motherly-type motions even though she wasn't very attentive or affectionate.

I will, however, never forget an experience with my grandfather. Old man Malakov was a railroad man and looked and sounded like it; big, both tall and wide, with a booming voice. He worked on the New Haven railroad freight train that ran from eastern Connecticut to New York and back every day and, on one occasion, I made the trip with him. It was an incredible experience for a boy with a virtual stranger in charge. Although I don't know what his particular job was, we were all over that diesel train as it sped over the tracks. At one point in the journey the train had to switch onto another set of tracks and wait for a passenger train to go by. He told me that passenger trains took priority over freight trains because they had people on them. Most of the time on the trip, I could put my arms out the window and feel the wind, but not as we sat waiting for the passenger train to pass. I was told to keep my hands inside. I found out why as the passenger train flew by within inches. Everything was timed to the second and I was enraptured that he could say the passenger train would be coming in 10 seconds, then count it down and there it went by! I was astonished at the power of the locomotive and the precision of the entire enterprise. This adventure made a lasting impression on a little boy who still remembers it today as an old man.

During these vacations Mom stayed with her parents. She spent her time out with old friends and made new friends as she resumed her position in the family and her social circle. I think these were happy times for her. Of course, they didn't last. Eventually I would be collected up from Harold's house, and we would take our seats on the train returning to Gary – and Dad.

Upon our homecoming, life would quickly return to what it had been. The fights grew longer and more violent. I learned to remove myself from the room – which was difficult in such a tiny house.

In the little house on Louisiana Street, which was only 750 square feet, I would escape to the basement. It became my laboratory, my workshop, my refuge. That was a place where I could think, experiment, build. Most of all, I could hide away in my search for peace.

Although his paycheck never made it home in full, it was not that Dad did not contribute to our home in other ways. Taking things from the mill was a common practice among employees, and Dad was no different. Of the many things Dad brought home from the mill over the years, things like rolls of asbestos insulation, tools, other leftover materials and excess supplies, he brought home a quantity of glazed tiles. He built a shower in the basement using those tiles. It was one of the only times that we used anything he brought home.

I'm not sure if he took things intending to use them, or just to take them. It might have been that it was the same with him as it was with me and Grandpa scavenging through the alleys of Gary to collect things. It might have been that when he saw leftover material from construction projects in the mill, he did as other people did. He loaded up his car and took it home. That way, nothing went to waste.

While it was theft, few saw it that way exactly. Anyone walking out with something knew it had to be done on the down-low, but it wasn't like it was a stealth operation. In fact, Dad laughed about a practical joke played on one of the managers. This particular manager had a Cadillac and he would pump his car full of gasoline when the construction teams left for the day. Everyone in the mill knew it. A group got together and replaced the gas tank from which he filled his car with a tank full of diesel fuel. Needless to say, by the time his vehicle made it to the exit gate, it was sputtering and the engine failed. He didn't find the joke funny. Everyone else did.

After one of the trips to Connecticut for the summer, something marvelous happened when we returned. A 12-inch, black and white television was placed in our living room. It was a miracle to me. Not only was it a mechanical marvel, it brought a whole other world into my home – and gave me an escape. *Felix, the Cat* was a stitch. *The Mickey Mouse Club* made me tilt my head and wonder what life was like for those kids. They did an awful lot of smiling, singing, and dancing. *You Asked For It* amazed me. I loved learning the answer to questions that real viewers submitted. I watched with my face just inches away from the screen. The television was only a few inches wide. It wasn't because of my vision that I got so close. I got close in order to block out everything else in my line of sight. If I could have crawled inside the box to escape, I would have.

Figure 17 Mr. Wizard and one of his student assistants on the TV show.

TV was the only friend I had at home and I took in everything it could give me, watching every show that we could receive. While I learned something from most all of them, it was *Mr. Wizard* that changed everything in my world. He would have some kid on each show, and they would do experiments with regular household chemicals like baking soda and vinegar. He would take things apart, too, to show how they were put together and worked. It was amazing. I started to figure out that I could do the same kinds of things at home.

I had very few toys and, after Mr. Wizard opened my eyes, I took them all apart. When I got a new toy, I took it apart. By taking it apart I mean I unscrewed every screw. I also broke those connectors that weren't meant to be taken apart. In my parent's eyes, I ruined everything I ever got and can't tell you how many times I heard, "I spent $5 on that toy for you and you just went and ruined it." Needless to say, the toys came further and further apart. That didn't stop me, or my interest in taking things apart. It simply meant I had to find other things to take apart, which wasn't difficult when my parents paid little attention to me and my Grandpa was teaching me to forage.

Scouting adventures with my grandfather were both fun and instructive. It was from him that I learned how to get stuff. At the earliest of ages, I would climb into my grandpa's big old Buick and we would cruise the alleys. My job was to be the picker. He would point to something and tell me to go get it. Boy, did we get stuff.

Grandpa had an eye for so many things. Every bit of clothing and shoes went into the back seat. Bits of metal, motors, wires, and anything that was considered mechanical went into the trunk. Grandpa was the king of dresser drawers. He collected every dresser drawer we saw. Three walls of his garage were lined with the drawers, each one labeled and housing neatly compartmentalized jars, bins, and boxes of nuts, bolts, screws, nails, fittings, and fixtures. Every motor was taken apart and each component part safely catalogued and stowed in the appropriate drawer.

Figure 18 My grandpa, John Pado

With his stash of hardware and parts, Grandpa could fix anything. It might not look the prettiest, but it would work. Anything that broke at home or in the neighborhood was taken to Grandpa's garage for repair. It was another part of his Eastern European life that came to America with him. Nothing was ever wasted and would eventually be used for something else. To say my grandparents were self-sufficient was a bit untrue. Everyone in the community gave to each other and did their part so everyone got by and this was what Grandpa contributed.

The clothes were a different matter. The home country was never far from mind for my grandparents. All the clothing, including socks and shoes, would be packed into big bags like pillowcases. Each bag would each be packed until it weighed just about one hundred pounds. Then it would be sewn shut and sent back to the homeland. Clothing out of the garbage cans in America was recycled by grateful citizens in a foreign land. Sometimes Grandma and my Auntie Annabell would sew letters and money into the hems of some of the clothing. They hoped it would reach family. Since they knew everything was inspected by the authorities before it arrived with relatives, chances were slim it would ever make it into their hands. That did not keep them from ever trying.

I loved time out in the car with Grandpa. So, whenever there was an invitation to go, I jumped at it. I never paid much attention to the amount of drinking Grandpa did. I didn't notice how clear it was to others that he was an alcoholic. He never seemed to show it. From the outside he always looked sober.

On one occasion after one of the big lamb feasts in the park, I jumped in the car with Grandpa to go home. One thing I neglected to mention was that just like so many women covered their furniture with plastic, Grandpa covered the car seats with plastic, too. As we flew around one of the curves in the park, a little too fast, I slid across the seat and fell into the door. Somehow, I accidently opened the door and flew out falling into the road. Fate (for Grandpa) would have it that Grandma and Auntie Annabell were following right behind us. When Grandpa slammed on the brakes, Auntie Annabell did, too. Grandpa felt the wrath of Grandma and Auntie Annabell that day and I was whisked away into Auntie Annabell's car immediately. I have no doubt how much my grand-parents loved me and being a favorite companion of one, and fiercely protected by the other, still makes me feel all warm inside.

Part III – Expanding My World

There was great celebration as my father rose from laborer to supervisor at the mill. It meant more respect for the son of an immigrant, and more money for the family. At least that was what I was told it meant. I know for certain that the one thing that changed had to do with what sat in the driveway. The barely running used cars we had were replaced. A used, but less used up, Studebaker took its place in our driveway. It wasn't just appearances that got a boost, it also meant we could take auto trips. Again, I saw these as vacations and great adventures, just like the trips to Connecticut.

Our trips weren't confined to weekends or summer vacations from school. The first of our trips was a relatively short jaunt. It was one I will never forget. It was just starting to darken one night as we climbed into the Studebaker and pointed its nose northwest. Eisenhower's network of highways was being built, so sometimes we were on these new ribbons of concrete. Just as often we were on the two-lane roads connecting one town to another. At night it was difficult to see all the changes in the landscape as we moved out of Gary and into the northern countryside.

Mom had slapped together some sandwiches and we stopped at a gas station where Dad got us each a bottle of soda pop. We ate in the car parked at the edge of the gas station. It was high living for me because I was on "a trip." We followed the map, Mom and Dad spitting and spatting over the directions, to South Bend, Indiana.

It was dark when we pulled into a motel parking lot with its big flashing light announcing vacancies. This was the first time I had ever stayed in a motel and I was impressed in our little home away from home. It didn't seem much smaller than home, just one less bedroom and no kitchen. It was a grand adventure for me and the fact that it was a five-dollar-a-night motel was of no consequence. It wasn't going to ruin the trip for me.

The next morning, we piled back into our magic machine, and we went to the Studebaker factory for a tour. There were only a couple other people with us as we passed through the door and onto the manufacturing floor. I was immediately awestruck. Machines as high as the sky were whirring and roaring, parts and pieces were hanging from overhead racks and rolling along conveyor lines, all moving in a syncopated pace with the sounds. It wasn't just the sounds, but the smells, too. I knew the smell of steel and recognized it right away. Here there were other odors, too, that I could not identify. Of course, every piece was important because they were building Studebakers, just like ours.

We got to the part of the factory where they were painting the chassis components. That particular day it was the big, rounded fenders. It wasn't the car parts that amazed me there, or the paint. It was how they were doing it. The fenders were hanging over a giant fountain-like bowl. The workers were spraying a dusty green paint on the fenders using spray guns fed by lines tens of feet long. Excess paint would flow down into the bowl and over the edges into another reservoir. They were recirculating the excess paint and feeding it back onto the spray guns. What I saw was a process that was efficient and effective – and like magic. It was amazing. Mom had to pull me out of the area into the next and I will admit, I can see that dusty green paint flowing over the sides of the bowl like water over a dam and smell it to this day.

We ventured south on a later trip to Louisville, Kentucky. By the time of this trip, it was our third, I knew we would be staying at a motel and that was just fine with me. I wasn't so interested in the accommodations. I was looking forward to the next day because I was going to see something remarkable. We were in Louisville to tour the Brown & Williamson Tobacco Corporation factory. The company was the first to introduce the menthol-flavored cigarette, the KOOL brand, and we were there to see how they were made. I was up early, dressed, and waiting. Mom and Dad were arguing about what we could spend for breakfast. I would have been happy with the leftover apple from our supper basket and some water, which wasn't much less than the toast and milk I ended up getting at a corner diner.

My nose was already in the air as we climbed out of the Studebaker in the factory parking lot because I could smell the menthol. It was a thrill because I didn't know what to expect and, damn, my parents were not walking fast enough, and chastising me for running ahead.

Once again, the syncopated symphony of the factory awoke the curiosity in my mind. We watched as the tobacco was shredded by one machine and dropped into a bin. Then there was white paper on huge rolls. I remember the guide saying that paper roll was four miles long and even though I wasn't sure how long that was, I was impressed. The roll of paper was being fed into a machine that cut it into tiny rectangles for each cigarette. The tiny papers met the tobacco as a measured amount was deposited onto each paper rectangle. Moistened slightly it was then rolled up into the cigarette shape and the filter attached.

Hundreds of rolled cigarettes fell into chutes where they would be jostled and fitted into the packages. Our tour guide, a woman, reached over and broke the filter off of one of the cigarettes and let the damaged cigarette fall back into the mix. I was appalled, curious why she did this. She just left it and walked on to the next part of the tour.

The sealed packages were being shimmied down another chute into cartons. All of a sudden one of the packs shot out into a separate bin. The guide smiled and picked it up. She pulled open the cellophane and smacked the pack against the palm of her hand. Then she pulled out the damaged cigarette. Whoa! How did she do that?

She explained that the packaging is all done by weight and if a pack did not weigh the proper amount, it would not be accepted into the final packaging. She called it quality control. I considered it a miracle.

Just as I had expected something remarkable, I was never disappointed. The handful of auto trips we took were all like this: five-dollar motels, meals in the car, and free factory tours. We went to breweries, whiskey distilleries, and factories that produced different products. While some people might find these trips pathetic, I loved them and know I benefited from them. Poor people might have poor ways, but these experiences were priceless for me. Although I could never have expressed it at the time, I learned that just about anything imagined could be achieved and it was possible through machines, parts, materials, and processes.

The fighting between Mom and Dad wasn't as severe during our auto trips. You couldn't say the relationship I saw between Mom and Dad was ever happy and fun-loving. They argued over directions and where to stop to eat. At least they weren't threatening each other with desertion or injury. Or, if they did, I was more focused on the adventure than I was on them.

Shortly after my parents moved out of Grandma and Grandpa's Virginia Street home, they decided that with all their children gone, they no longer needed a great big house, so my grandparents moved to a smaller house on Ohio Street. Auntie Annabell moved into a house on Ohio Street, too with her husband, Louie. It was just a few houses down and on the opposite side of the street from Grandma and Grandpa.

Figure 19 Louie and Annabell Roznowski

Every Sunday our family would gather at Grandma and Grandpa's house to spend the day with the family. My cousins and I would play, and our parents cooked and talked, and talked. All of us kids paid little attention to the adults. In retrospect I can only imagine how very long those Sundays were for my mother. At the time, I was more interested in finding adventures all around the yard and neighborhood with others nearer my age.

At least that's how it was at my grandparent's house on Sundays. When my cousin wasn't around, I had the grandparents to myself. Grandpa didn't say much. I think part of it was that he spoke little English. The other part was that he was content in the corner with a bottle of beer, and a big, old Dutch Master stogie. While Grandpa was quiet and not so involved with a little boy in the house, Grandma put all her attention and care on me. I reveled in the attention because it wasn't anything I was accustomed to getting much of at home. She would, I guess you could say, dote on me. She'd cook meals just for me and save pennies and nickels to give me so I could buy candy like my friends. When I was allowed to stay overnight, Grandma would rub my back with oil and then tickle me as she said, "I pinch you little fat stuff!" I don't know who laughed more – me or Grandma. At the time, I just felt it. Now I realize how much she loved me.

Figure 20 My grandparents, John and Mary Pado

Not only was Grandma's lap a cozy and comfortable place for me, there was a neighbor girl that I could play with sometimes. Her name was Barbara Warus. She lived right next door to Grandma and Grandpa and although she wasn't out much, when she was, we played together. To hear her tell it, our playing was mostly me tormenting her with bugs and snakes. She must have liked it some, because we are still fast friends to this day.

After Auntie Annabell and Uncle Louie moved into their house across from Grandma and Grandpa on Ohio Street, they had a daughter. My cousin was named Louise. She was a kind and gentle person. And I envied her because her mother doted on her, did everything for her, and got her everything.

It was a simple thing, but Auntie Annabell would fill out the coupons on cereal boxes and from the Mickey Mouse Club ads, tape a nickel or dime to it, and send it in for a variety of toys and trinkets. I coveted those trinkets. Of course, I had none of them and she had lots and lots of them. When I would go to her house to play, I would finger all of them and insist on playing with them. Louise, tired of them, would want to do other things.

One day, I slipped one of the toys into my pocket and took it home with me. I never brought it out at home, keeping it well hidden away from my parents. Auntie Annabell called my mom insisting, "I know Tommy has the toy." And demanded that it be returned immediately.

Figure 21 Me and my cousin, Louise Roznowski

My mother was mortified when I finally admitted my sin and produced the toy. Sheepishly, I returned the toy to Louise, who took it and tossed it on a shelf. Louise didn't care one bit about that toy. Auntie Annabell did. She went to the shelf and arranged it properly into the collection.

After that day my humiliation was replayed every time I visited Auntie Annabell's home to play with Louise. Before leaving, in the presence of my mother, Auntie Annabell would frisk me, "to be sure he hasn't stolen anything else."

Implications for My Future

There are so many parts of who we are that come from our families, good and bad. I know that I watched all my family work hard and I just came to believe that that is how we are to be as people. I took that lesson to heart in everything I did as a child and carried it with me long into the future.

My grandparents, especially my grandpa taught me to make use of everything around me. It was his resourcefulness and ingenuity that showed me to make do and shape what I wanted from what I had at hand.

I learned lessons, lots of lessons, about integrity and honesty as a youngster. Often it was from being made to admit my transgressions and live with the consequences of my actions. I was not so much troubled by punishments. I was much more affected by how it made me appear to those people I cared about around me.

I also learned lessons about the bigger world. The trips to manufacturing plants and museums flipped a switch inside me. These places were huge and amazing. Never once did I feel intimidated. I wanted to see and understand it all. These experiences opened a well inside my head where ideas took root. A ravenous hunger for more knowledge took hold and would prod me continuously in my future.

Even at such a young age I became intensely aware of the dynamics of interactions between people. I could not express what I understood and felt. I watched the relationships between my parents, between them and their parents, and between people in the community as they moved in and out of daily life. I heard what was said, and although I understood little of the words, I understood the meaning of the tone, the inflection, and the actions around the words. It was the way it felt and made me feel that was my lesson. Without realizing it, as a student of the nature of people, I was on my way to developing an ability to socialize and get along with people. Little lessons, inadvertently taught by the adults who surrounded me, developed one skill that has given me much of the success I have found in life. Who knew?

Section Two - School Years

Part I – Rough Academics

Books weren't anything we saw much of in our house. Stories weren't read to me, nor were songs sung with me. Academics were not anything I was familiar with at all. I didn't know letters and I couldn't write my name or anything else. And nowhere was that fact more impactful or obvious than when I started school.

Kindergarten at Emerson School was a surreal experience. In my mind, there were an incredible number of toys piled on shelves and there were so many people my size. Besides my cousin and a few children close by in the neighborhood, I had never been exposed to what felt like hordes of kids. Every day I could talk with someone new and make new friends. I took full advantage. I guess that's when I began to discover that I could talk with people. I was good at telling stories and I found it easy to make them smile and laugh. It felt good because when they were happy, I knew they would like me. My knack for socializing was one skill I made it a point to develop immediately. Besides playing with toys and socializing, we had naps in kindergarten. Being around so many people and making friends, well, that is what was most important to me at school.

Books and educational activities were never part of my childhood before school. In fact, I don't think I ever saw either of my parents break open a book and there definitely were not bookcases filled with books. I suspect that my mother may not have graduated from high school. Just like her, I was more social than academic. Combine that with my natural curiosity, I was always busy doing things, not sitting quietly reading or coloring.

The worst part of school was when we were expected to sit at tables for a long time. I didn't much like that. It was not just the sitting. It was also the handling of pencils and crayons to form letters and images that I didn't care to do. It was taking time away from my socializing, therefore, to be honest, my letters and images were made in haste and looked mostly like scribbles, if they were even made at all. These days much research has been done on different modes of learning, communicating, and approaching the world. It would have been obvious to everyone that I was verbal and loved relating to people. That has apparently always been the way I approach the world and it still is today. Knowing where I have been able to go in life, and what I have been able to do, I think the way I approached the world worked just fine. At the time, though, the adults in my life were not as positive about it.

One episode at school was so special that I remember it clearly to this day. The teacher, a kind woman by the name of Miss Kenwright, began a conversation with the class. She said we all had to have a name that we wanted to be called. She went around the group from person to person asking each, "What do you want people to call you?" When she got to me, she knew my name was John Pado, just like my Dad's name. She asked what my middle name was, and I said Thomas.

She said, "Why don't you call yourself Tom?" From that moment on, I was called Tom, or Tommy. Funny, I don't remember what I was called before then, other than Sonny by my grandma. It didn't really matter, because with Tom I had a name that separated me from my dad, a name that was mine alone. It made me feel special. Miss Kenwright had bestowed on me the name I would take forward into the world and from that moment on, she was forever imprinted on my heart.

First, second, and third grade were a blur as far as school was concerned. We had recess and milk afterward. I was good at wheeling and dealing so I regularly ended up with two chocolate milks rather than one regular, or white, milk. Academics weren't my thing at all, and I remember little, if anything, about those first few years of school having to do with that kind of learning.

Figure 22 We really thought the NIKE missiles would protect us.

Everywhere there was evidence of the Cold War. There was talk about it on TV and in the neighborhood. My dad, and most of the other fathers on the block had served in the war. Although I know I never voiced it, like most others, way back in the recesses of my mind and in the pit of my stomach I felt a nervousness.

The government had installed Nike missiles not too far from our home, maybe five or six miles. We would drive by the field where they were poised skyward in an open field of sorts. I think they were put there to make us feel safer. Now, as an adult, I realize that those missiles would not have been able to protect us if there had been some sort of attack or nuclear war.

At school we had those drills where we all climbed under our desks and put our heads down under the cover of our arms. It's ridiculous to me now how all these things made me feel safer and less nervous at the time.

One episode I do remember, which had nothing to do with school per se, was standing in line to have my blood type tattooed on my back. The gun vibrated and made lots of noise. It stung but all of us kids believed it was a small price to pay for our own safety. We believed it when the adults told us that transfusions saved lives. If there was a war and we needed blood transfusions, our tattoos meant we'd get the right stuff.

I was made to believe that the Russians were terrible people, bad people. People who ate their children. If I had really thought about it, I would have realized that my own family had come to America from that area of the world. That didn't come into my mind at that time. I just saw the Russians as the enemy.

Later in life, when I was traveling in the world and I had interactions with people from that area of the world, or had others describe it, I realized that the people there were just like us. They had families like us. They lived for the same things we did. The politicians in Russia might have been a problem, but the land was filled with good, warm-hearted people.

During most of those years, the Russians stayed in the back of my mind and school concerns were a nagging stress. In reality, I was much more concerned with what was happening every night in my house and worrying about where I would be the next day than whatever was on the curriculum calendar. I know I went to school because by the end of third grade, I was failing and that was a big, big issue for my parents.

Mom told my Auntie Annabell that she didn't know what to do with me. Auntie Annabell told her to send me to the Catholic school, St. Luke's.

What I knew about the Catholic school terrified me.

First of all, I went to Catechism at St. Luke's at night starting when I was in the first grade. My classmates were the same kids I went to school with during the day and the first-grade nun was nice. When second grade Catechism came with Sister Thedia in charge, everything changed. Her reputation was set and nothing I saw from her counteracted any of the stories. To me, and most of my classmates, she was mean and intimidating.

The second thing I knew about St. Luke's had to do with the afternoon release from school. When the doors of Emerson Public School were flung open at the end of the day, we ran out free. When the doors of the Catholic School opened at dismissal, the students marched out in double file and in step, like they were trooping. They weren't free until they turned the corner at the end of the block. We called it The Prison because it was obvious the students weren't kids. They were controlled inmates.

The other thing that set them apart from us at the public school is that they filed out at the end of the day with their arms filled with books. We didn't have anything to cut into our play time like they apparently did with all those books and most likely, assignments for homework attached to them.

Despite all my apprehension, arrangements were made, and off to The Prison I was sent.

On one hand, the transfer to St. Luke's Catholic School caused me a huge amount of anguish. On the other hand, I now understand how much of a blessing it was as well. Having to fail and watch my friends go on to the next grade, leaving me behind would have been devastating for me if I had stayed at Emerson School. It was prominent in my thoughts and I worried about it. Not being in the same school gave me the opportunity to repeat third grade without the stigma of flunking. No one at St. Luke's ever said I had flunked third grade. It was never mentioned. I was able to repeat the year more comfortably, except it was evident to teachers and students that I was far behind everyone else in the class. That fact followed me all the way through high school.

My first day at school immediately revealed to what degree I was behind my fellow students. I could barely write my name, let alone any other words. I could not compose phrases or sentences. I could not read. I had no interest in geography, history, literature, or most of the other academic classes in school. I watched as the St. Luke's students ran circles around me so quickly that all I could do was sit with my mouth open and stare. I was in the deep end of the intellectual pool here and I was drowning.

When I entered St. Luke's School, I discovered how seriously the students took their education. I mean, everything was very organized and on a tight schedule. When the students stepped into a classroom, they would sit down, pull out their books and get right to work. I didn't understand what made them want to do that. I needed to see a reason to do something. I didn't care about the Romans or geography of the world. I always asked why I needed to know any of that stuff. They wouldn't give me the reason why, so I wasn't interested in learning it.

Reading and writing were my biggest problems. I could do neither, which is why they sent me to Sister Isabel. That's when we all discovered just how far I was behind in my education.

Boy, I have to tell you, Sister Isabel was all business. There was no chatting, no small talk, no stalling, and no complaining. That first year when I had to stay after school while all the other kids were outside having fun. I knew it because I could hear them. I hated having to spend time with Sister Isabel and, at least in the beginning, I hated her, too.

Figure 23 Sister Isabel was all business.

I was intimidated by her. She was old and wore a formal habit with a coronet. The wingspan of that coronet also intimidated me, and it bothered me that all I could see was her face. I knew, because she was a human, that she had to have hair, but I have no idea what color it might have been. She stood behind me most of the time reading over my shoulder, and her demeanor made me believe that she never smiled.

Sister Isabel tutored me for five years. In that time, she patiently nudged me into reading. I realized that she believed I could learn to read and eventually she made me believe that I could read, too. She never insulted me or my intelligence, nor did she ever make me feel bad.

She would tell me I had to read ten pages and I would try to trick her by turning multiple pages at a time. She was not fooled. And she always got her way, pushing me harder and longer than most people ever had the opportunity to do.

Sister Isabel was a constant in my life when I needed a constant. Her tenacity and unwavering certainty in my abilities changed how I felt about myself.

My dad would see poor grades on a report card and reinforce my own belief that I was just stupid and would end up digging ditches for the rest of my life. That did spur me on – into believing he was right. Sister Isabel's response to poor grades was her belief that I could, and would, do better and be capable of great things.

Those five years under the wing of this formidable woman changed my life.

Besides what I considered being held captive in Sister Isabel's grasp for too much of my free time, something else was changing at home.

There are few events as memorable as the birth of a sibling. As a nine-year-old already struggling with a difficult home life and the social and academic transition to St. Luke's, the birth of my sister, Debbie, was a very unwelcome event. Everything was difficult and I felt I was failing at it all. I had spent the years I can remember in my short life to that point vying for the attention of adults, especially my parents, and now I had even more competition. And who can compete with a baby?

I was thinking of a new baby as just more competition. I have since come to believe that the new baby was a deliberate ploy by my mother. I believe Debbie was supposed to be an anchor baby. I think Mom hoped it would change something in my parent's marriage. Or, probably more likely, she figured having two children would prevent my dad from leaving. It must have worked, because they never divorced. In the end, though, I think we were both foolish. A new baby did not change my dad's behavior, toward Mom or me. In fact, it did not change the amount or kind of attention I got from either parent.

Figure 24 My sister, Debbie Pado, didn't deserve all the grief I gave her.

While I relished the special attention from my grandparents, I yearned for the same kind of attention and care from my parents at home. What little attention there was for a family, I had to share with Debbie, which in my little mind, just didn't seem fair. Making matters worse, Debbie would be left for me to care for while Dad would be working, and Mom would be out.

I must admit, much to my regret that I took it out on Debbie. Little sisters annoy even when they don't mean to, and when an older brother resents her very presence, it takes sibling rivalry to an entirely new level. I tortured Debbie mercilessly.

I am sure Debbie never felt too safe around me as a kid. I pushed her out of her seat relentlessly. I am surprised the poor girl didn't jump up every time I walked into a room where she was sitting. Not only would I take toys or things away from her, I would hide her favorite toys and make her believe that she had lost them or that someone had stolen them. When she would go to bed at night, especially on moonless or cloudy nights, I would make sounds and convince her that monsters were coming to get her, actually touching her to make her scream in fear. I locked her in dark closets for as long as I could. Not only did it satisfy my desire to torment her, it kept her out of my hair for a while.

One day, I was lying on the floor watching TV, and Debbie came in and plopped down on top of me. She leaned down and bit me in the ass. I mean, she didn't just make a little pinch, no, she had hold of my ass and she wasn't letting go. I know if I had had on anything other than my jeans, she would have drawn blood. After the screaming subsided and the pain went away in a couple of days, I had to admit she had gotten my attention. And I knew I deserved it from her.

She would plead with Mom and Dad to make me stop. Just like they were hands off with me, they were unresponsive to her pleadings, too. Poor girl, I just was not a model brother.

Part II – Personal home curriculum

With little success at school, beyond the social kind, which was apparently not sufficiently acceptable, I was more interested in getting home at the end of the day. At home I had parents who were still at odds with each other most of the time. That didn't mean they paid much attention to me. In fact, they pretty much ignored me past the basics of food, shelter, and clothing. I had found a place to immerse myself where I wasn't at the bottom of the heap. That magic television provided me with an escape and I totally immersed myself in the shows I watched.

Figure 25 Me and my first mobility equipment.

When a curious, self-sufficient kid like me is left without adult supervision, you should expect I would find something to do. The Mr. Wizard show was always on my mind, and after seeing him combine baking soda and vinegar into a fizzing frothy foam, I had direction. From the reactions my mom had to other things I had done I knew anything I did that was Mr. Wizard-like had to be done in secret. And that is what I did when I set up my own undercover laboratory that was open for business when Mom was out of the house. I knew we had vinegar and baking soda in our home, so I figured I could make my own fizzy volcano. It worked for Mr. Wizard, so it would work for me, too, and it did.

Once I did that, though, that thrill was gone. What else could I do? I began to pull chemicals out from under the kitchen sink. Mixing them together didn't do much and I was soon bored. Then I remembered Mr. Wizard heating solutions over a Bunsen burner. I did not have a Bunsen burner. I had Mom's stove. Using her pots and the chemicals under the sink, I started combining them and heating them. I really had no idea what I was doing. If Mr. Wizard had warned of any dangers, they went unheeded because I was far more interested in his results than the precautions he might have voiced or protections he was taking. I did not know that heat causes a reaction to be more violent. I just had some ideas and options in the form of under-the-sink chemicals and went with them.

All during the time I was actively pursuing my chemical adventures, I was aware that my mother would not approve. I knew I had to be sneaky.

One day I combined bleach, ammonia, and drain cleaner (sodium hydroxide) in a pot on the stove. This created a rather toxic concoction. It foamed over the sides of the pot and smelled just terrible. I mean really, really terrible. I later described smelling it was like when you eat too much horseradish. It kind of burned my nose and throat and took my breath away. It felt like getting hit in the back of the head with a hammer. The fact is that it is the same feeling you get when you smell mustard gas, which is pretty much what I had inadvertently produced.

Unbeknownst to me, this gas was toxic, and I mean that in a deadly way. The day I created it, it got on my skin and burned me. It caused large water blisters much like a second-degree sunburn. I inhaled some of it and it caused me to cough terribly for a while, making me sound like I had a cold or the croup.

When Mom returned home that night, the house smelled terrible and her son looked terrible. I was coughing, red, and blistered. She opened all the windows and aired out the house. Which, now I understand was very important. The gas I had created was toxic. So toxic, that it could have killed me, or the entire family if not dispersed.

She was screaming, "What did you do? How did you get this way?" The words that really struck home hit me like a boulder and stayed with me for years. In her exasperation, she asked, "What is wrong with you?" She grabbed me by the neck and marched me into the bathroom where she dressed my wounds and reminded me that, "when your dad gets home, you're going to get a spanking you won't forget."

I managed to survive my deadly lab day to go on to concoct other stinky inventions in the future. However, it was my mustard gas, intentional or not, that scared my mother enough that after that day, she locked the house when she went out and took the keys with her. She said that I would just have to wait outside until she got home. I did not care that she did that to me. I did try all sorts of ways to get into the house and back to my makeshift lab. I even broke a window once.

She saw locking me out of the house as a way to stop my activities, but I loved doing my experiments. Stopping was not what I had in mind. In my mind, no lock should ever impede scientific exploration. I realized that I had to really go underground now. I had to get better at being sneaky. I began to unlock a window before I left for school in the morning. That way, when I got home, I could simply climb in the window. I would do whatever experiment or project I wanted and scuttle out before she came in the door.

After the initial mustard gas episode, I realized the great potential in my discovery. I was so pleased with the stink that I made another batch and filled an eyedropper bottle with the liquid. The expansion of the compound ballooned the rubber tip to an enormous size, which acted like a timer that would eventually explode. I had created a gas bomb. I saw potential, real potential, in this.

I talked my friend, Diane Thompson, into helping me execute a secret mission. My plan was to take the stink bomb and drop it into the basement of a less-than-friendly neighbor's house as a joke. As the covert team leader, I enticed my cohort with the allure of clandestine adventure that would escape any sort of detection or consequences. We would be infamous amongst our peers for avenging the slights of cranky old people.

Of course, I had already scouted the target house and knew that two of the basement windows were always left slightly ajar. There would be no damage to the window since it was open and inviting. I selected the window that was opposite the kitchen and living room of the house. It was directly below the bedrooms. I knew because most of the tiny houses were similar, if not identical, in structure and it was just a few doors down from my house.

I prepared the weapon of choice. I hadn't quite worked out the timeline for the explosion, but that did not really matter. Our mission for this day was to get the bomb into the basement.

Diane Thompson met me at my front door. At first, I thought about taking our bikes so we could make a quick getaway. Since the target was just a few doors down, and we'd have to drop our bikes right by their yard, I determined that did not make a lot of sense. Instead we scrambled bent over or army-crawling our way along the two-foot hedges that surrounded my yard, slipping through them to find shelter behind the blooming lilac bushes or other shrubs until we had worked our way across the neighbor's yards and to the edge of the property adjacent to the basement window. We made sure that we left no footprints in the dirt under the hedge and bushes. The window was just beyond a concrete sidewalk and then stones around the house's foundation.

With Diane acting as the lookout, we sidled up against the house, so no one would see us from the bedroom windows. I slipped the bottle through the window and listened. There was a small clink and I pumped my arm knowing that the bottle had landed without getting broken. Silently cheering, we wiggled back through the hedge and ran all the way back into my yard, falling breathless onto the grass.

Then we laughed and cheered. That was short-lived as Mom pulled into the driveway. Diane's eyes got wide and her eyebrows went up. I swore her to secrecy, and she ran out of the yard before Mom came close. I felt strangely powerful all night.

The next day, news spread quickly at school, of course. We knew that no one would give us up after all the pats on the back and amazed plaudits from our classmates. We were heroes.

News of a stinky episode in the neighborhood also spread among the adults. The basement of the target house was not the only part of the house that smelled. The odorous gas had infiltrated the entire house. When the offending bottle was found, the gig was up. All the adults knew it was a prank.

There were many days that Mom had come home to a house filled with a stench and knew that it had been created by me. She knew I was getting inside the house, although she did not know how. I think it drove her crazy. I didn't care. In fact, I kind of enjoyed the subterfuge.

Of course, after the incident, my mom knew exactly who had committed the crime, and I was in big trouble again. You could say it caused a big stink with the neighbors. In any event, my stink bomb days finally came to an end.

That did not mean my days of sneaking back into the house had come to an end. Nope, not at all. In fact, it opened a whole new range of possibilities. I suddenly realized that when I was home alone, I could sit in what Dad called "my place" and do anything I wanted to do. I discovered I could look through their drawers and closets. One time, in their nightstand drawer, I found packets of balloons. I was confused but not deterred to carry on my explorations. I moved downstairs to go through boxes in the basement and then out to the garage. This gave me a whole new perspective on my place at home.

My mom was a good housekeeper. My buddy, Tom Kerlin, his mom would fiddle with her house. It would take her all day to clean it. My mom knew how to clean the entire house in short order, often in two hours or less. She also did the laundry pretty quick. In fact, I often felt that I would step out of my clothes, walk away, and they would be clean again, she was that quick. And she ironed a lot, too.

Mom was always pretty determined to keep up with the neighbors. Today, people want hardwood floors, hot tubs, and a backyard fireplace. Back then, it was a certain car in the driveway, French provincial furniture with plastic covers, and wall-to-wall carpeting. Mom's carpet was gray, and it was her pride and joy. Until I happened upon it.

One afternoon, I found a soldering iron in Dad's stuff. The best light to work with was in the living room so that is where I dragged the soldering iron, the solder, and the project I was going to work on at the time. I plugged in the soldering iron and walked away while it was heating up.

Needless to say, by the time I returned, it was hot. I was going to be in hot water. The tool had been laying on the carpet and burned it black. This was one time I got really lucky. After the punishment was over, Mom moved a chair to cover the burn. It was still there the day we moved out of that house. At least I didn't have to face it every day. We all knew it was lurking there beneath the chair.

The basement was a good-time place for me. It was a full basement under the entire house. About a quarter of it was taken up by the coal furnace and coal supply. There was always that coke smell in the house and I watched Dad work to get the fire started and then shovel coal into the furnace to keep it burning. I never got to shovel coal. The closest I ever got was being put to work carrying cinders and taking them out to the trash.

It was a blessing, for us all, I think, when the coal furnace was replaced with a kerosene heater. The heater was inside, and the kerosene tank was outside. That cleaned up a good portion of the basement. It was when the kerosene heater was replaced by a natural gas furnace that made the biggest difference in the house and basement. The house was always nice and warm, and the basement was all cleaned up and a place I could spend hours during the winter.

I roller skated across the smooth concrete floor. One time I caught a pigeon and named him Walter. I put him in a box and smuggled him into the basement. I would take him out of his box and let him fly around. He'd poop everywhere. That's how Mom found out about him and boy, was she mad.

The basement was my place and it just got better and better as I got older. It was full of centipedes and spiders.

I did not care one bit. My dad had built a workshop after the coal furnace was removed, framing up an area and filling it with a bench and tools. It became my space, where I could get out of their sight, away from the yelling, and work on things that were interesting to me.

Despite my academic failings, in hindsight, my intelligence did show itself in my youth. Maybe it was this love of science or a need for attention. Whatever it was, I was not afraid to try something and fail. I had time and a mind open to learning that allowed me to pursue answers that would satisfy my curiosity.

I took the Edison approach to inventing – and failure. Every failure was just another step closer to success. This quest for success – and my failings – had almost killed me and my entire family. It was also a driving force that stayed with me throughout my life.

Although my interest in chemistry had been subdued after the stink bomb incident, my interest in all things science never waned. My parents took me to the Museum of Science and Industry in Chicago. In fact, we went there a lot. I never considered if it was because I was so interested in science, or if it was just a way to keep me entertained and out of trouble. I never thought about it because I did not care, not as long as I could keep going.

On the trip from Gary to Chicago, we would drive, and Dad would always get lost. Mom would be screaming because of his penchant for always finding the "worst" neighborhoods. Once we arrived and went through the front door, I was let go and I would be free to run from exhibit to exhibit on my own. For me to be free in that place was really important. In fact, it was something that changed my life.

One of my favorite exhibits was the submarine. The first visit to this exhibit was immediately after it arrived in the Museum. The U-505 was a German submarine that had been captured during World War II and is the only German sub in the United States. It arrived via Lake Michigan amid great fanfare and news reports. TV reports chronicled the moving of the sub from the Lake across Lake Shore Drive to the Museum in 1954.

Because of his naval service, my dad was very interested. I was proud of my dad for being part of a special group in the Navy, the submariners, so actually seeing the U-505 was exciting. When the exhibit was opened to the public, I think we were some of the first visitors.

It was amazing. There was all sorts of information to be had and short movies to watch. We could even see through the periscope. I was absolutely fascinated by the fact that the space inside was so small and completely filled. There was no room to add anything else. Everything was organized, and each line, lever, gauge, and button had a purpose. There were so many different kinds of science and it all worked in a small space to achieve something fantastic. It was busy. A pipe was not just a pipe. It was fitted with a valve and a flange and elbows. Pieces were made of steel and copper and brass. It was shiny and beautiful.

The sub was not luxurious by any means. I could tell that it was built as a purposeful machine designed with function before form, and the humans that needed to go inside it to make it work were an afterthought. It was the human man next to me who knew all the parts, how they worked, and what they did. My dad spent hours explaining each part to me and I loved it. Over the years I cannot say how many times I visited that exhibit or how many hours I spent going from bow to stern over and over again, touching, thinking, wondering how it would feel to be under the sea in this magnificent machine, just like the movie, *20,000 Leagues under the Sea.*

On the way home, we always stopped at White Castle. I always got an orange pop, fries, and a bunch of sliders. Besides the afterglow of a day at the museum, I appreciated that for the short time we were at White Castle, Mom and Dad were not at each other's throats.

It was not just the physical sciences that caught my attention. I visited all the zoos in the area, and each was memorable in its own way.

In the last days of one school year at St. Luke's, we went to the Michigan City Zoo on a field trip. I remember it was small. We were let loose, being cautioned to stay out of the woods and by the creek. Of course, I went to the creek where I caught a snake. It didn't go home with me, probably because I didn't have anything to put it in.

The zoo we went to most frequently was the biggest zoo in the area, Brookfield Zoo. At the time visitors could still feed the animals and I loved tossing bags of peanuts to the bears. It was like they communicated with me through their eyes. We would look each other in the eye and the bear would raise his paw. After a moment I would toss the bag of peanuts to him and he'd catch them. I swear he would wink just before he stood down and ripped open the bag. We would spend all day and visit the different animals from reptiles to bears to camels and elephants. The houses each had their own distinct smell, even the buildings housing tanks filled with insects. One of the best parts of the visits to Brookfield Zoo was handing over my cents to the ice cream vendors. They had ice cream bars covered with coconut. Those were the best ever.

Although I liked the animals that lived in the sea, we only visited Shedd Aquarium once. It's funny that when it comes to ocean life, I enjoy it, but it's the technology to tame it that I really enjoy.

The visits to the zoos generated an awareness about how many different creatures there are in the world and the diversity between them. It wasn't long before I was seeking out living creatures in my own environment. I noticed that I had my own little zoo in my basement. It had a variety of creatures, including your standard spiders and the brown recluse spider. Just like the black widow spider, it is poisonous. I later learned that the brown recluse spider could give a person rheumatic fever. There was only one kid I knew that got that fever. I don't think we knew that it could have been from a spider bite.

The creepiest of all insects to me were the centipedes, with their excessive number of legs and wiggly antenna, they were one of the few creatures that ever gave me the willies. And there were lots of them. I just knew that the term creepy crawlies came from them. They gave me goosebumps and made me want to wiggle, just how the thought of creepy crawlies makes you feel. Just creepy.

On occasion we would also get an odd earthworm in the basement, pill bugs that rolled up like armadillos, and things that looked like beetles. I later discovered that those beetle-like creatures were actually cockroaches. Nice, right?

Part III – Community Experiences

U.S. Steel infiltrated many aspects of life in my Gary, Indiana neighborhood. It wasn't just relative to our home and my dad's livelihood. In the summer, the children of the mill workers had the opportunity to attend Good Fellow Youth Club Camp. It was a week-long residential camp in Porter, Indiana. It is now part of the Indiana Dunes National Lakeshore. The camp was initially built during the early days of WW II with an administration building, a caretaker's house, ten tent platforms, a washhouse and a dispensary. It was expanded five years later to include several more buildings, four concrete tennis courts, shuffleboard courts, a playground, a water filtration plant, a pool house, a steel footbridge, and, believe it or not, a stainless-steel swimming pool.

I am fairly certain my parents saw it as a week of relief from me and my antics. In the beginning, I didn't see it as anything I wanted to do. In fact, after arriving at the camp, I cried for the first couple of days. Finally, the counselor pulled me aside. He told me to wait until Wednesday. By then if I wanted to, I could go home. By the time Wednesday rolled around, I never wanted to go home again.

Figure 26 The U.S. Steel Good Fellow Camp stainless steel pool where I learned to swim.

There was so much to do and try. One of my favorite places was the biology area that was filled with all sorts of animals and information about them. Then there was the guidance counselor in charge of my group of eleven boys. She was a dream and I was in love with her. Never one to keep my ideas or feelings to myself, I shared it with one of the male counselors. I will never forget his reply, which in effect was advice. He said, "Yeah, she's pretty, but look at her legs. Her ankles are fat and that means she's going to be fat later." Not sure if that is truth that plays out in the end. He was right. She did have fat ankles.

I attended the Good Fellow Camp a couple of years. I learned a lot there.

The first year, I learned to swim in that stainless-steel swimming pool. I wasn't so sure I would be able to swim. Then the instructor boomed out a promise to us all: You will know how to swim by the end of the week. I took him at his word, and I did everything they said to do. I got through all the levels and learned all the techniques they demonstrated. He was right. By the end of the week, I was swimming. The next year I got the lifesaving certificate. At the time I never considered that swimming would become such a big part of my life.

I was away from my parents and under the guidance of people who taught me things. I liked it. I discovered when I liked something, I went after it with wild devotion. At this camp, I was part of a tight-knit group. We sat around campfires and sang about great green globs of greasy, grimy gopher guts. We ate together, sang, worked, and learned together. I really liked that and, as normal, I went after everything I could with enthusiasm.

As I was growing up, I noticed that most people had something that made them special. Everyone, that is, except me. I began to think that this had to be the reason that my parents didn't care so much about me. There wasn't anything special about me.

One day, just by happenstance, I was discovered for something that I just knew would make me special enough for them to pay attention to me and put up a little fuss about me. We were singing in the sixth-grade choir class and one of the nuns walked up behind me. I was a little mortified when she leaned down close to me. I shifted my eyes to look at my buddy, Ronnie, and raised my eyebrows. He just opened his eyes wider and kind of shrugged.

She asked me to stop by her desk after practice. I knew I had to have done something wrong and was going to get it for sure. Ronnie told me he'd wait for me outside and gave me a look that just said, "I'm sorry."

Instead of a dressing down, she said she noticed that I had a nice voice and wondered if I would be interested in trying out for the Bishop's Choir. Now that was a B-I-G honor for anyone in the Catholic neighborhood. I said I would find out what my parents said and let her know.

I knew full well I would go for it. A soprano songbird is what I would be. I practically flew out the door and grabbed Ronnie's arm dragging him in flight.

Of course, this was the kind of honor that my parents would be thrilled to show off. It was agreed my mom would take me to see what the Bishop's Choir was all about. The choir members got to wear special robes with wide cuffs we crossed our arms into and great big crosses on our chests. The choir participated in all the special masses. We would file in the church through the aisles singing to the front of the church after all the congregation was seated. It was special with a capital S. After trying out, I became a member and my mom started taking me to practices.

I could do this special flourish at the end of a run that was really high pitched, and Ronnie could do it, too. I suggested that maybe he would be interested in trying out and he agreed. One afternoon he and I went to see the director and Ronnie auditioned, adding in that little high-pitched flourish like I did. He got in. I had a buddy in the choir now and it was fun for both of us. I never figured out why the sister singled me out that first day instead of Ronnie. I was happy that she did and especially so after Ronnie joined me in the choir.

Finally, I thought I had achieved the special-ness I needed to be the beloved son. I had a best friend in Ronnie and singing became one of my favorite activities. Eventually, though, for my mom, it became another responsibility and I ended up catching rides with Ronnie and his parents most of the time.

Figure 27 Being in the Bishop's Choir was an honor.

I was at High Mass at eleven o'clock every Sunday morning singing in my robes. Dad seldom attended church. He was either working or sleeping. Mom would attend church occasionally, and neither of my parents attended any of the special events when I performed for them. It was not long before I realized that although this honor would be in the win category for me personally, it would not change my place in my parent's view. It wasn't enough, and I wasn't special enough by my participation in it.

Because money was an issue, Dad had taken a second job at the gas station that was next to the Studebaker dealership. Because he would be filling up the cars for the dealership, he got to know the owner. One day the owner mentioned that they were giving memberships to the YMCA to boys. He offered one to my dad for me. Dad was told to bring me by the dealership to get it.

Although Dad had explained we were going to get the YMCA membership from the dealership man, I did not understand what that really meant. All I knew was that I was going somewhere with Dad. He pulled into the Studebaker dealership, parked, and turned off the engine. I walked in with Dad and sat down at a big desk. The man handed me something. I took it and said thank you. A day or so later, I went to the YMCA and became a member for a whole year.

I wasn't exactly sure what you could do at the YMCA. It didn't take me long to figure out that this was another place where I could go for the win with enthusiasm.

For one thing, I had never been in a wood shop before. Just like I had always taken apart the toys I received to figure out what was inside and to make new things, I discovered I could cut things up, rearrange the wood and make other things. There was a man there who was the overseer. He was a wood guy. He was only there to answer questions and make sure we didn't kill ourselves. There were saws, belt sanders, drills, and other tools. When I asked the man a question, he would tell me what I needed to know and then I was on my own, just like an adult. I loved it because no one told me what I could or couldn't do and I went wild. I made all sorts of things from little boats to contraptions that had no names. Not one person told me it was stupid or wrong. I loved it.

Then there was the pool. I had already developed a love of swimming from my days at the Good Fellow Camp. Here they pushed me in new ways to develop competitive swimming skills. With my 'go for the gusto' attitude and a desire to show my parents that I could be good at something, it wasn't long before I was in the upper ranks in the competitions they ran. There would be teams and we would do all sorts of things like playing tag in the water and swimming relays. We would also compete in goofy relays where we would have one person on the team swimming in their clothes, and others doing other odd things. It was fun, and I was pretty good at it.

As a complement to the swimming skills I was developing, I was introduced to weights. It was a free workout room and gym and I had never seen anything like it before. I would see men in there with builds that were like something I had never seen, either. I told the trainers that I wish I was built like that and they assured me that I could have the broad shoulders and strength I saw on others, if I would work on it. I started to work out and lift weights in addition to the swim practices.

I talked about the YMCA at home, telling my parents what I was doing. I asked Dad what I had to do to be strong and he said, "Eat more spinach like Popeye." I told him about the weights and working out. He had a guy at the mill make a weight set for me to have at home. It was crude, but functional. I kept it in the basement and used it every day. He also brought home some metal bars, which I assumed he had stolen for me. They were long and heavy. They suited my purpose well.

I worked hard and put in long hours in the pool and gym. I grew strong which resulted in my being recognized as a top swimmer at the YMCA. I thought if I was able to achieve that, my parents would support me. For sure they would be proud of me. I learned that things don't always work out the way you think they will.

At the events where we competed in the games, some of the swimmer's families would show up. By this time, I knew that when there were functions at school, church, or the YMCA, other kids' parents might be there, but not mine. They would not promise to be there and then not show up. No, they just never seemed to even consider coming. Maybe part of it was that my dad worked different shifts. Whatever the reason, I was never disappointed, because I never expected them to come. I just considered it a fact of life and lived with it. I never fretted over them not being there. Without a doubt, I was envious of the kids whose parents were there, patting them on the back and saying how proud they were of them.

Some of the other parents would tell me how good a swimmer I was. That made me feel really good. I knew they weren't just being patronizing, because I did, indeed, win a couple of the events when I swam, and I wasn't their kid. A little bit of recognition went a long way with me, especially when it came from adults.

My experiences at the YMCA were another win – for me.

Part IV – Set Free in The Library

By seventh grade my reading had progressed, thanks to Sister Isabel. I don't think she could have done anything more that would be enough to keep my interest in reading classes. In frustration the sisters turned me loose in the library. The books that were within my reading abilities were not interesting to me, and there was no incentive they could give me to read them. They told me to just go find something I liked.

That was a turning point for me, and, in retrospect, for my life. Again, made possible because of all the time I spent with Sister Isabel. I discovered the science section of the library and it was like being given a million dollars in a candy store. Book after book on technical subjects fed my curiosity. Deep in a book on bottle rockets and rocket technology, I read about Wernher von Braun's work, the first and best example of a rocket scientist. It was a whole new world for me. I had already been experimenting with black powder, so I was aware of some of the stuff that could make a rocket go boom. With some cut-off matches, potassium nitrate charcoal and sulfur from the pharmacy, I had sent racing cars and used CO2 cartridges soaring for blocks.

Figure 28 My sister, Debbie and me.

As my curiosity and interest accelerated, I started to build a rocket with water as a binder and black powder. It was fashioned out of a couple of beer cans that I shaped like a rocket. It was eighteen inches high and weighed three-and-a-half pounds. I spent hours on my own in the basement creating a fancy aerodynamic fuselage, stabilizing fins, and a nozzle at the workbench.

Though I was itching to see my creation shoot to the sky, I first took it to school. The nun in science class showed it to the others, even the administrators, and everyone was amazed at the workmanship. They fussed over the metal rocket and placed it on a shelf of honor in the classroom. All the kids could see what I had created. That day, I finally found some positive attention for my creativity. I was hooked and knew where my passions lay.

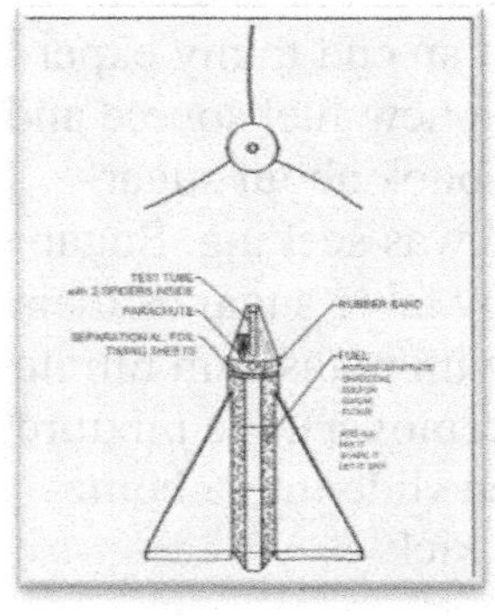

Figure 29 Schematic of my first rocket.

Fortunately, the rocket remained in its place of honor, never to feel the heat of a fuse in class. I know now that if it had been ignited, it could have exploded like a shrapnel bomb among the class of little seventh grade students eagerly watching. I did try to launch it later on in a field. There was no lift off, it just burned at the launch pad. That did not diminish the thrill I got from that rocket sitting on the shelf in my classroom.

Over the next four years I continued to build rockets, modifying the specifications to achieve a higher, longer shoot. Once, in what I called my "black powder stage" of rocket development, I stuffed a used CO2 cartridge with the fuel and launched a rocket from an old metal pipe. My friends, Jim and Louie Grosdanis, were standing nearby when the rocket unintentionally exploded, wounding Jim to the point of leaving a lifetime abdominal scar. Not only has the scar lasted a lifetime, so has our friendship. In fact, you can still hear him boast about the event (and show his scar) at the occasional party.

I started using the Pythagorean Theorem, protractors, and a stopwatch to better calculate height and speed. Even with better calculations, the scare of Jim's casualty caused me to rethink the fuel and put an end to my experiments with black powder. I needed a new fuel source and realized when I found an article in a book about sugar rockets, that it was just the solution I was seeking. Sugar rockets, as the name suggests, employ table sugar as their fuel. Mixed at six-hundred degrees with potassium nitrate (which is commonly used as stump remover), the mixture becomes a thick brown syrup that can slide into a homemade rocket fuselage. That stuff has kick.

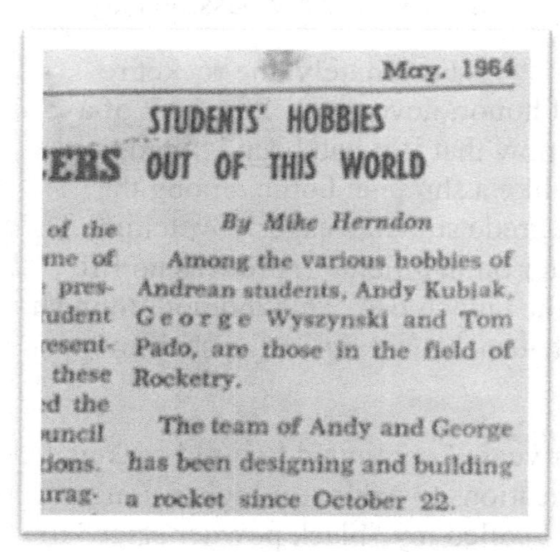

May, 1964

STUDENTS' HOBBIES OUT OF THIS WORLD

By Mike Herndon

Among the various hobbies of Andrean students, Andy Kubiak, George Wyszynski and Tom Pado, are those in the field of Rocketry.

The team of Andy and George has been designing and building a rocket since October 22.

Figure 30 The first article ever written about me

This was the first time in my life that I was the subject of a published article. I remember so clearly being approached by a girl who asked for a few minutes to interview me for an article. I thought, "Wow, she wants to write about me." The article came out fairly accurate, which I learned later in life is pretty much par for the course. Information published later in life contained errors and I learned not to care too much about that fact.

Part V – Fake Bully Makes a Friend

"Verily I say to you, in as much as ye have done it to one of the least of these my brethren, ye have done it to me." Matthew 25:40

I thought Allan Templin, one of my all-time best buddies, was the leader of a pack of boys that had the reputation for being bullies. Because my dad often slept during the day after working third shift, I was regularly shuffled out the door and told to make myself quiet or scarce, so he could sleep. That meant I was off and on my own. Usually I would end up at Allan's house. I loved the feel of his family. There were four children and they lived in a household that was governed by strict rules.

Lee Freel was a big boy who faced the challenges of Cerebral Palsy. Because of this condition, his speech was difficult to understand and although he could walk, he was slow and unsteady. His condition made him the target for bullies and left him lonely.

No one likes to admit they have ever been a bully, but I have to do just that. The positive side is that my bullying days were cut short by my victim, and my life changed in many ways because of it. Even though Allan and I were great friends and constituted the known ringleaders in the neighborhood, I thought I floated on the outskirts of that circle of terror when it came to bullying people. One day we were just hanging out and saw Lee lumbering down the sidewalk toward us. We started to mimic him and make fun of him. This wasn't a new activity for any of us. This time, he looked me straight in the eye and pointedly asked, "Why won't you be my friend?"

I think Lee, being a smart guy, saw that I was on the fringes of the group and that's why he singled me out for his question. I didn't have a comeback that made any sense to me. His question had stopped me dead in my tracks. I had never thought about the inner workings of his mind. I had only seen the shortcomings in his physical being. It made me feel sorry for him and I thought, "Why not?"

One day soon after, I followed him home and met his parents. They suggested we go downstairs. At first, I was wary. Then I saw all the "radio shit" everywhere. Lee was a real electronics guy. Geek. Nerd. Whatever you want to call him is okay, because he was brilliant.

I found I had a mind for electronics and would tear down transistor radios and other small appliances to understand how they worked. This natural inquisitiveness got me in more trouble with my mom than I care to discuss. I had even tinkered with a television and a few speakers, taking them apart. I never really understood how they worked. Lee understood how everything worked.

For the next several months, I was like Lee's apprentice. Lee was the master and I was the underling. I would help him do the mechanical work, and he would tell me what to do technically, explaining the arrangement of wires and magnets, and the how and why of electronics. Together, the two of us would rebuild radios using an oscilloscope and a voltmeter, while he provided an excellent tutorial on volts and ohms. We were working with tubes. The theory is fundamental, even in today's digital age.

My tutelage did not come without cost. I paid for my electronics education with stories. Glorious, and rather embellished, stories of life with girls. Lee had never had a girlfriend and my hot stories of love and sex made him shudder and drool with excitement. My stories were mostly tall tales (I was only in the seventh grade) but he loved them. He realized that his excitement was entertaining to me, so we laughed away many, many hours in this reciprocal self-awareness.

My friendship with Lee was one of my early courses in humanity. I could see that he was intelligent and fun. He understood his situation and lot in life. He seemed to always make the most of it. I learned to look past the physical nature of a person to see their mind and heart. In my case, I had to look past the infuriating as well. He was able to make me laugh more than I could entertain him and that is a tall order. He would exaggerate his disability with such buffoonery that I would laugh until my stomach hurt. We were truly great friends.

We lost touch and when I later sought him out, I learned he had died. The boy that so many of his peers bullied and saw little value in any friendship with him had achieved great success in his life. I was sorry to not be able to spend time with him as an adult and share what his friendship inspired in me.

Lee Freel's Obituary

Freel, Lee Gordon Age 66, passed away peacefully Saturday, December 18, 2010 in Elkhorn Wisconsin. He was born March 26, 1944, to Hazel and Chester Freel in Pulaski Co. His father, Chester Freel, preceded Lee in death in

1945. Lee's mother, Hazel married George H. Olmsted in 1950 and relocated to Gary, IN. where they attended the Eastside United Presbyterian Church. He attended Norton Park Crippled Children's school, and graduated Emerson High school, class of '65. He earned his Ham Operator's license while still in high school and enjoyed attending Hamfests with his friends throughout his life. He earned his bachelor's degree and first master's degree from Indiana University Northwest. He earned a second master's degree from Wheaton College in Illinois. He was employed by the Northwest Indiana Regional Planning Commission, Indiana University Northwest, Ivy Tech State College, and also served on the Gary/Chicago Regional Airport board. He was a member of the Evangelical Covenant Church of Portage, and most recently joined the family at Inspiration Ministries in Wisconsin where he fell in love with Wendy Fitch.

One memorable project Lee mentored me through was wiring a speaker to also be a microphone. I traded my BB gun for an intercom slave unit from Lee and set out to make it into a two-way communication device. I rummaged for the necessary parts and worked for hours trying to get the switching mechanism to operate. I was obsessed to the point of forgetting to eat, losing track of time.

When I had the speaker wired with the knife switches and extension cords, I began wiring my house, from the basement up. I stuffed speakers in the air vents from the heating system in all four rooms of the house--the two bedrooms, living room and kitchen. From the basement, I could tune into any room and listen to what was going on there. The speakers picked up everything down to shoes scuffling and clothing swishing.

My heart swelled with pride as I searched my mom's face for approval when I demonstrated the achievement to her. She turned away, disinterested, until I whispered from the other room and she could hear me. "Where do you have those machines?" she hollered. I answered that I had installed them in the kitchen, the front room, and the two bedrooms. And, after a pause, she tromped down the stairs into the basement and cried out, "How long have they been there?" I said that they had been there for about two weeks. She pursed her lips into thin lines and breathed in a big breath through her nose. "Get them out now!" she screamed. It never entered my mind, before or after, that mom may have been entertaining someone in our house when my dad took me out hunting or fishing.

It was in seventh grade, too, that I joined the football team. Football was my introduction to organized competitive team sports. I was part of the city champion Catholic Youth Organization football team.

No one at home said anything about football or me playing. It was during our neighborhood pickup games that my friends first suggested I try out for the team at school. Like most other things in my life, I said, "Why not?" and joined them at the audition scrimmages.

Figure 31 Me in my tough football days.

After the first few runs, the coach called me over and told me that I would go against "Big Bart." He was bigger than me and had played before on the team. In the very first face off, Bart came up and pushed me right in the face. I fell back to the ground. I got right back up and went at it again. After that first push, Bart never was able to hit me in the face again. I made sure of that.

Along with my buddies, Ronnie Kazmerski, Tommy Kerlin, and Mike Curjeski, I made first string as right guard. We were the Four Horsemen. Bart was the first-string left guard. For two years he and I held those positions. I played every single game and felt good about myself. I never missed a practice or a game.

While many of my teammates practiced in the evenings and on weekends throwing the ball in the yard with their dad, I did not. However, my parents went to some of the games. It is kind of hard to avoid when the whole neighborhood went to the games to watch their sons play. It kind of became the thing they had to do to keep up with the neighbors. At the end of the game when others jumped in the family car to go home with their parents, I did not. They had already left.

Figure 32 The Four Horsemen: (left to right) Mike Curjeski, Tommy Kerlin, Ronnie Kazmerski, and me.

One spectacular night I was the team hero. It was a night game against St. Mark's. St. Mark's was in the Hispanic neighborhood and the players were all big and tough. It was a challenging team and the score was zero to zero.

At the scrimmage line the St. Mark's guard growled at me and said, "We are going to go after you this time." All I knew is that because of the kind of helmets we had, with face guards, he would not be able to hit me in the face. His team had the old style of helmets that simply had a leather strap under his chin. I went straight for his face, just like Bart had showed me that first day. The St. Mark's guard went down and the next time we met at the scrimmage line he was not as cocky.

Later, in the same game, St. Mark's had the ball and they were running for a touchdown. We were all running trying to catch him yet not making up the distance. They were going to get the touchdown, score the first points and win the game. As I was running, there was a guy off to my right running after me. He clipped me, and I fell and rolled. Whistles blew, and I headed back to the bench. The coach ran up to meet me. He said, "Pado, you're a genius!" I was confused. What had I done? The coach explained that the touchdown was disallowed because of the St. Mark's player clipping me. That call saved the game as we tied them, and it put us on the way to an undefeated year and the City CYO Championship we won.

It was another win for me, and I must admit, I went after it with a strong appetite to win.

Seventh grade had been a big year for me, what with football, rockets, making a good friend with Lee Freel, the choir, and swimming at the YMCA, yet academics were still a struggle.

While I struggled along with reading and writing, math was a completely different arena for me. That was a difficult concept for teachers to understand in those days. I had been labeled a poor student and wasn't a poor student a poor student in everything?

At the end of seventh grade, the sister who taught us math put a challenge up on the board. Without ever having shown us the concepts of algebra, she wrote $6 = 2x$ on the chalkboard. "What is x?" she asked. No one, not even the smart kids, raised their hands. I was amazed. To me, the answer was obvious. "Three," I said rather timidly. Her eyebrows arched, and she wrote the answer on the board.

It was clear the sister thought I got lucky. When she wrote $3x + 1 = 10$, and I raised my hand to say, "X equals three," her face filled with confusion.

For some reason, I could just figure out how to solve the equations. I didn't know the names of the theorems or rules I just knew how to apply them. It was just in my head and I couldn't explain why.

The sisters got to the point during class that they would ask for "anyone other than Tom" to solve the problems. My friend, Barbara Warus, noticed how I could outshine the rest of the class in this subject.

As would be expected, my Catholic schooling included religious education, learning about God and the church. The nuns would often mention what an honor it was to have a nun or a priest in a person's family. The thought bounced around in my brain. An honor? By this time, I was in need of a real honor to get the positive attention of my parents. Nothing else had ever worked.

The summer of seventh grade, Auntie Annabel took Louise and me to a religious retreat in Wisconsin. I think it was the home where the Sisters of Notre Dame retired. There was an area with rows of booths selling religious items to raise money for the nuns. There were rosaries made from olive seeds grown in Israel, crosses with holy water amulets inside them, glowing plastic Jesuses and Virgin Marys, and hundreds of other bizarre ornaments for sale.

As I was walking down the aisles of booths, I passed one with a lone priest sitting behind a table. "What are you selling?" I asked. He replied that he was recruiting for the Basilian Fathers. In other words, my words, he was trying to get kids to join the priesthood. "Oh," was my reply, and I kept walking, still thinking of what he said.

About two aisles later I turned around and walked back to his booth. "I want to join the priesthood," I said, and I signed up to be a priest. At that point in my life, I felt I was going nowhere. Life at home was a mess, my grades were terrible, and I knew we did not have enough money for me to go to college without a scholarship and that was only if a university would even accept me.

From my years at St. Luke's I was actually quite devout at the time, so I thought, why not? I'll join the priesthood. They say it's an honorable profession, you're always around a lot of people that love you. Seemed as if it would be a sound decision for someone like me.

My conviction was soon tested. About that time, I started to notice that the girls were growing bigger in certain areas. It got my attention immediately. Until that time, I had been interacting with the girls at school mostly by chasing them, pulling their hair, and slugging their arms. Suddenly, they got curvy, and I started to consider different ways of interacting with them.

The recruiter in Wisconsin had sent word of my application to my school, so the priest at St. Luke's was following up with me. One day early in my enrollment, I asked him, "There aren't any girls in the priesthood, right?" It was my way of opening up the subject to let him know I had changed my mind about becoming a priest. I was just too interested in the way the girls were developing.

Apparently, that wasn't enough of a reason for the priest. He was a persistent fellow, and he came around to my house every other Thursday evening for the next six months. When he knocked, I would run and hide and tell my parents to tell him I wasn't home.

My parents went along with my ruse to hide from the priest. In fact, none of the family seemed all that joyous about the prospect of having a priest in the family. It might have been because my father's blood line would end with me. If I became a priest, there would for sure be no known little Pados in my future.

Eventually the priest quit coming by. I am not sure if he just gave up or if my parents convinced him that I wouldn't be a great candidate for the priesthood. They would know, right?

It wasn't just girls that were changing and taking my attention. By this age, every so often I would ask for some money. Every kid needs a little cash once in a while. Dad would give me a nickel or a dime. Eventually, I became aware that money was not plentiful in our household. It did not take me long to realize that if I ever wanted something, I would have to get it myself. There were not a lot of things I wanted, the occasional candy bar or toy were enticing sometimes.

Once I got to an age where I was mobile and independent around the neighborhood, I would visit stores other than grocery stores. Places like Kalaric's Hardware and the old type of Army and Navy stores where they had all kinds of military gear. I loved it. I would pore over the goods aisle by aisle and look at all the things I would like to buy for my own projects. If I wanted those kinds of things, I had to make more money than I had already saved.

That is when I learned that I could earn money by doing jobs around the house or neighborhood. Of course, I started at home. I got Dad to agree to let me mow the front yard for seventy-five cents and the back yard for seventy-five cents. I would get the same for organizing the garage or cleaning up the basement. Dad had a little notebook where he would record the date, the job I had done, and the amount I had earned.

That is when I decided to expand my territory and the jobs I could do. My friend, Allan Templin, had a paper route. I followed him every day for weeks, conspiring to be his "relief" carrier when he was on vacation or sick. It took some doing to convince him of the deal. I was able to keep a portion of the money I collected and all the tips. I also mowed grass, shoveled snow, and washed cars.

I had an old cigar box that my grandfather had given me in my room where I squirreled away every penny. I was shaking with excitement the day I realized I had saved up close to sixty dollars! I was rich. I could buy anything! I ran out into the yard to share the good news with Dad. He was really interested and when he told me he was a little short and asked if he could borrow – how much did I say I had? – Oh, yes, could he borrow say, sixty dollars? I was so honored. I felt like such a grown up that I could lend money to help out MY DAD. I ran to my stash, collected it, and counted it out into the palm of his hand. He politely thanked me, got in the car, and left.

I went into the house and shared my proud moment with Mom. She erupted, screaming that I was such a fool and I would never see that money again. It was in that tirade that I first heard the word, gambling. I walked away with my tail between my legs. I hated to admit she was right. Dad never paid me back.

Shortly after that, I ask my dad if he could get a steel box with a lock from the mill for me. A few days later, a 12-inch by 8-inch by 8-inch box arrived with a hasp on it that I could lock with my own lock and key. After that, I never told anyone, Dad or Mom, how much money I had saved and stashed, nor where I kept it. Believe me, it was well hidden and under my personal lock and key. Even though I kept cutting the grass in our yard and cleaning up the garage and basement, Dad never paid me any part of the money that was recorded in that little book. I had learned that gambling probably wasn't a good thing. At least not for me.

Jobs kept getting bigger and bigger and paying more and more. By the time I was in high school, I had saved a thousand dollars. I broke my own rule and told my parents and showed them the money. They were amazed. In my imagination, I knew my dad was thinking that he sure would like to get his hands on my money. I learned the truth in "once bitten, twice shy" and I stood my ground waiting for him to ask for it. He never did. And you know what else, I never hated my dad for not paying me what was due to me or for not repaying what I had lent him. Funny how that is.

Part VI – Changes Mean Moving Out and Up

Times were changing, and the fortunes of the mill were shifting. Competition from Japan and Brazil in the steel market had hit U.S. Steel hard. There had been several layoffs already. Dad survived the layoffs each time, but there was always a cloud of uncertainty hanging over us.

At home, even though Dad was in a management position, money was still always tight. Dad was very much a spendthrift and gambler because he always saw more money coming in. Mom made every penny work as hard as possible. She paid our bills the best she could.

We got by, until the day Dad came home with bad news. He had been stopped leaving the mill that day and when his car was searched, it was discovered that he had in his possession several items that were the property of U.S. Steel. His sticky fingers had finally caught up with him, and he was fired for stealing.

All I knew that day when I got home from school was that Mom said, "Don't go in the front room. Your dad is having a hard time."

It was warm weather and to get away from the fighting, I usually stayed outside or at friend's houses as long as I could and then come in just in time for bed. I was passing through the living room to go out the front door on my way outside. Of course, I peaked at him on my way out the door and saw him sitting in the chair with his hands hanging down, completely limp. He didn't look normal. He was very quiet, which was also out of the ordinary. I knew something bad had happened. I wasn't sure what it could be that would be worse than the way home life already was between their matches. It wasn't until later that Mom told me Dad had lost his job.

In those days, when you were looking for a job, you put out feelers and talked with friends. This was one time when I saw my parents really stressed but working together. It wasn't long before he found another job. Someone he knew let him push a broom in the tire department at the local Sears store. The new job did not pay as well as his position had at U.S. Steel. The talk was that Sears had a great retirement plan.

Suddenly we, like many other Americans at the time, became a dual-income family. Mom went to work at The Lure. It was a fast food hamburger joint. They were not saving up for a Caribbean vacation. No, they were working to pay for the basics. To me her absence wasn't anything new. I just had a better idea where she was and when she might be home.

I wasn't aware of all the issues over inheritance when Grandpa died. I did know that my dad had inherited my grandparent's house, because we moved out of our four-room home and into the home where my grandparents had lived. While I was sad about losing my refuge in the basement, I was going to have Barbara Warus as my neighbor. That was exciting to me and I didn't have any inkling how important she and her family would be in shaping my future.

In our first little home, I had to share a room with my sister. By the time of the move, there was a huge chasm between our ages, and I had outgrown everything having to do with a little girl just old enough to begin school. In Grandpa's house there were three bedrooms upstairs. Two of them were huge and had two closets in them. My mother and father took one, and I got the other. It was amazing to have so much room to myself. I didn't really care that Debbie was put in the small bedroom. I didn't care if she had to go to the attic, I was free of her in my space.

It wasn't that I was happy to have my own room. I felt living in this house gave me a new place in society. I finally had a house that I could bring girls home to, and at this time in my life, girls were becoming more important in some aspects of my life.

Even though it was all good for me, in the beginning, inheriting the house was kind of a mixed bag for our family. Not only did it mean more space for our family and reduction in housing costs for the budget, it also meant it came along with Grandma. Nothing had ever really changed in the relationship between Mom and Grandma through the years. Apparently, it was enough of an issue that when we moved into the house, Grandma moved in with Aunt Annabell and Louie in the house they had moved to in Merrillville. While that was a good thing as far as Mom was concerned, I missed the love and attention I had grown to enjoy from Grandma. Things would never be quite the same between us.

By this time, Dad was moving up into sales at Sears. When he started at Sears pushing a broom, he recognized that the guys in the tire department making real money were the salesmen. That made him put his sights on a sales position. Once he achieved that goal, he saw that the guys selling air conditioners and appliances were making even more, so he pursued that position. His next goal was selling televisions and electronics. He kept making more. No matter how much more he made in wages, it was not making it home. Many times, it was money from Mom's brother or her parents that kept our household running. Mother did all the mechanics to keep me and my sister alive. There was food on the table, clothes on our backs, and beds to sleep in, but neither of my parents were around to supervise or guide us through the day – or through life.

Figure 33 My father, John Edward Pado

Many of the houses on Ohio Street had big front porches and with no air conditioning, people spent a lot of time on them. Mother was talkative, and she'd meander up and down the street, smoking, drinking, and conversing with the neighbors. My mom was always the center of attention and would be called to join in with groups gathering on the porches and in the front yards. She was the one to laugh the most, and the loudest. That was probably her most endearing, and aggravating, quality. While she was out socializing, I was extending my interest in creatures.

Outside was a whole New World when it came to critters. Before this point, I had limited my collection to what I had found in the basement of our other house. Now it seemed a limitless possibility, just like the zoos I had visited.

The first things I noticed were the lightning bugs. To me they were incredible. They would come out just as the sun was going down day after day. Of course, another flying insect, the mosquito, would join the fireflies in the night air. In my learning about all the insects I could find, I later discovered that the mosquito is considered by many experts to be the deadliest animal in the world. I would read that huge numbers of people – like 2.5 million –were dying every year from mosquitoes. My mind raced because I thought other animals like sharks, hippopotamuses, lions, snakes, bees were more likely to be raging killers. No, there's that little mosquito that annoys you at night buzzing in your ear and carrying diseases like malaria, dengue fever, Ross River virus, heartworms for cats and dogs, and the list goes on. What a lesson that was for me in what you have to really fear. It's not always the big, scary things that can really hurt you.

After learning about the deadly mosquito, you can imagine how the fogger truck was received in the neighborhood. First, we would hear that distinctive noise it made and then watch for it to reach our street. All of us kids would run after it, breathing in that white fog. Now I understand that the fog was a mixture of diesel fuel and the super chemical, DDT. We didn't know what we were doing to ourselves in those days, and neither did our parents. Not that mine would have tried to stop me, anyway.

My interest in fireflies was much more magical. I was amazed at their fluorescence and the way they could turn it on and off. All of us boys found creepy ways to squeeze their abdomens to get the light-emitting chemical out of them. Then we would make rings and necklaces with it, and, of course, chase the girls and wipe it on them.

From other kids in the neighborhood, I learned about putting them in jars with a lid punctured several times, and grass for them to crawl on. I'd load up a jar and by morning, they would all be dead. Perhaps, I thought, I could keep other bugs alive.

One evening, while Mom was down the street socializing, I started collecting different kinds of insects and crawly things and putting them in jars and boxes. As dusk settled in, the lightning bugs came out in full force. It was not too long before I was running out of places to house them, so I figured I would stash them in the house loose. In other words, I would just open the front door of our home and throw the bugs in. Yes, you heard it right, I used our home as a big place to keep my bugs.

That worked until Mom walked into our dark house and the blink-blink-blink of the lightning bugs fluorescing lit up our living room and kitchen. Boy, was she mad! She made me get rid of what I could find, and I know she killed a bunch of them. My bug zoo was banned from the house. Nothing like that would quell my curiosity, nor stop my collecting.

We had these curbs in the street that collected a lot of rainwater. Inevitably, there were low spots in the street where puddles would collect and remain unless it was an extremely dry period. These water pools allowed certain kinds of water life to have its own little ecosystem. I was digging around in one of these ponds that had collected a bunch of rocks, dirt, and tree leaves.

Figure 34 Giant Water Bug (lethocerus americanus) photo by Eric Lyons, 2018

Suddenly, this three-inch water bug shot out from under some leaves. The only way I can describe it was that it looked like a three-inch surfboard with two-inch pincers on the front and lots of legs underneath. Oh, and it was black with muddy brown spots. If there was a monster movie, this insect would be a star. My heart started to beat fast and I immediately thought I needed to have this creature. There was never any consideration as to whether it was poisonous or dangerous in any way, I had to capture it.

I knelt and bent over. Using a stick, I started moving things around. It had been so unexpected when it shot out that I was surprised. I could not believe that something of that size would be living in a shallow pool of water in the gutter. This time when I uncovered it, I would not be startled. I would be ready to seize the moment and scoop it into the jar I held in my other hand. There was no chance I was going home to find something to use to scoop it up or trap it. I would use what I had right there. I didn't want to miss my chance. However, that did not mean I was going to touch the bug.

It didn't take long to find it again and my adept stick usage guided him into the jar. By the time I screwed the lid on tight and took it home to my zoo, sweat was running down my forehead and down the small of my back. I had done it. I had captured this alien creature.

Research revealed that it was a giant water bug, *Lethocerus americanus*. According to the information I found, the insect does indeed pinch and bite. Its prey included fish, frogs and sometimes even small snakes. Sporting hairy legs to help it swim, the giant water bug was known to hide at the bottom of ponds in the mud or under leaves. That was just where I had found it.

This insect became the star bug in my zoo. I tried to create a habitat for it to live in because I was not a catch-and-release kind of kid. It was mine – forever – 'til death us do part. My mom screeched the first time she saw it. I knew she would, and I had no intention of keeping it in the house. It was in my outdoor zoo until his dying day, which eventually did come despite my best efforts.

There was another reason this ugly bug was such a prized possession. It was great to use to chase the girls. They would run and scream, tears in their eyes. Life could not be any better for a boy than to have a bug like this one.

When we lived in our first house, one of the things I remembered seeing Dad bring home from the mill was a pair of welding gloves. I paid attention to the new items that would appear in the garage or basement from time to time. I found the welding gloves in the basement, and I also spied centipedes and spiders down there, too.

I kept the gloves with my stuff to use in my outdoor adventures and they really came in handy when we moved to Grandpa's house and my boundaries were expanded to Highways 12 and 20 to the north, the High line to the south and east and Virginia Street to the west. Me being me, the place I really wanted to go was just beyond the expressway and just before the U.S. Steel mill. Along this strip were all the big billboard signs. They were huge like drive-in movie screens, especially up close, which is where I wanted to be.

I had discovered a wonderful environment under these big billboards. When the advertisements on the billboard would be changed, the giant sheets would be stripped off, dropped, and left under the signs. The piles of old signs created the perfect place for frogs, tadpoles, turtles, lizards, and snakes to flourish.

By this time, I was aware of some dangerous creatures like Copperhead snakes and Cotton Mouth Water Moccasins in our area. I was braver, outfitted with the welding gloves. No, I would say those gloves made me fearless. I went after everything I could manage to grab or trap. I developed my own technique. I could put one hand on the board or paper I was going to lift and get my other hand ready so when I lifted the cover, I would quickly pounce and slam my hand down on top of whatever was there. I caught a few garden snakes and a lot of lizards. I learned you have to be careful with lizards. Sometimes I would grab one by its tail and it would break off, allowing the lizard to skitter away.

Needless to say, going beyond my boundaries had consequences. The punishments were sequential, and you might think were actually in the reverse order of severity. The first time I can remember the stick used to spank me. That was not exactly effective, so there was obviously a second infraction. After that I was restricted to the yard. That wasn't so bad, so you know there had to be more visits planned to the billboards. The last punishment was sitting in a chair in a room by myself for a long time. That punishment was absolute mental abuse for me. Sitting in that chair drove me nuts.

Undeterred by even that punishment, I collected as many of every creature I could find and brought them all home. In the beginning, I started collecting them into jars and housing them on the side of the house in a small area that was seldom accessed by anyone but me. Later I had to move into boxes. I was getting pretty good at keeping my captives alive.

After one of my forays, when I was punished with restriction to the yard, I had a brainstorm. I wanted to be out with my friends. I could not leave the yard to get to them, and, in those days, gatherings were prompted by dropping by someone's house on your bike. No cell phones, I did not even have a string and can. I put up a sign. Zoo Admission 25 cents. If my customers didn't have a quarter, they could at least come in the yard for twelve cents. If they wanted to sit in the tree for a spell, it cost another nickel. I spent the day with my friends, sharing my love of creatures and fun, and made $1.85. It was a great day and a great way to get punished, don't you think? I did learn something that day that has stuck with me for a long time. Not all my friends were interested in seeing my zoo on any normal day, but when I put a value on it and charged admission, suddenly, everyone wanted to come see. It was interesting to me then, and even today, I still find it interesting and worth noting when it comes to business practices and setting prices. Value matters.

Not everyone gets a girl next door. By some lucky chance of the draw, I did, and I got the best girl next door you could ever have. Her name was Barbara Warus, and as fate would have it, we were in the same grade together at both St Luke's and high school as well. We were both Polish and Slovak.

As far as girls next door go, there are a few types, and I would have liked Barb to be the girlfriend type of a girl next door. Alas, she appeared to have a long-time boyfriend, Ronnie Kazmerski, and he was one of my good friends. That meant I had to settle for the sister type girl next door. In the end, that was for the best. Our friendship lasted all through grade school, high school, and even today. This relationship changed so much in my life.

In my first home, the basement was my refuge from the battles being waged between my parents. Losing that tore a huge hole in my safety net. Lucky for me, I had Barbara and her family next door, and their home became my refuge. I don't know

Figure 35 Ronnie Kazmerski, Barbara Warus, and me.

if Barb shared with her father about my collection of creatures. Somehow, he knew about it. He encouraged me and would even bring home empty meat boxes for my ever-growing wildlife collection on the side of my house.

Barbara was amazing. With the volatility in my house, Barb brought comfort and sanity to my life, and the occasional meal, too. What I didn't know was that Barbara had her share of strain and tension at home, too. Her mother Lillian would get sick from time to time with terrible migraines, and Barbara would take over the mothering duties. Together, we made it through the trials of both our lives.

Our routine evolved into one that probably made us appear like we were two little married people. I would go over at the end of the day and tell Barbara everything that happened at least from my perspective because she was with me a portion of the day. She would share her news while she would be cooking at the stove. Then we would eat together. She was a great cook and great company. Later, in high school, the other kids found out about Barbara's place, and her well-furnished basement, filled with food, entertainment, and laughter, became our local hangout.

Barb's parents were businesspeople. They owned Warsaw Meat Packing Company, which distributed different kinds of Polish meat. The hams were amazing, and in my eyes the Warus family was well-to-do. After all, they had both a full grand piano and a large organ, the kind you'd see at church, in their living room.

Barbara and her mother played the instruments with complete competence. I would name a song and they would play it. Barbara had her seat at the piano and her mother was at the organ. There were many, many nights I had my own private concert.

One day, Barbara played a song called Moonlight Sonata. I loved it and I asked her if she could teach me to play it. She got me settled onto the piano bench with the authority of a serious teacher. Really, I just wanted to sit next to her. I didn't let on. She took a lead pencil and numbered the ivory keys. The patience and kindness she showed while I pecked at the keys is something I will not ever forget. I practiced playing the tune over the next couple of days and eventually coerced a melody out of the piano. I couldn't believe it. It actually sounded like Moonlight Sonata. I was so very proud. Sixty years later, I can still play that piece on a keyboard, and my gratitude is as deep to Barbara now as it was the day when she taught it to me.

Through the years I did a lot of odd jobs for Barbara's father, Johnny. Unlike my dad, he actually paid me for washing and waxing their car and cutting their grass. It was a great thing for a kid with no money. Even better, he didn't just pay me, he paid me well. I always did the best job I could for him.

Besides the meat distribution company, Barbara's family also owned an apartment complex four blocks north of Emerson High School. On occasion Johnny would take me over to the apartment complex to do maintenance work.

One day he asked me if I had a BB gun.

I said, "Yes, and I also have a pellet gun."

"Even better!" he replied. Pigeons had taken up residence on the apartment building roof, and he wanted them, along with their mess, done away with and I was just the guy for the job.

Armed with my pellet gun, I was happy for the job and excited about the urban warfare I would wage on the unsuspecting pigeons.

There I was, five stories up, lying flat on the apartment roof. I looked out over the rooftops far into the distance. I had never been that high up, let alone on a roof of such a tall building. I am sure if I had had other parents, I would not have been allowed to do such a job. In reality, I do not know if I even told my parents about this job. I do not think it would have mattered. One of the benefits of my upbringing was that I was left with lots of unsupervised time on my hands. I made a lot of my own decisions and choices, for better or worse.

By this point I was fairly adept at hunting and shooting things, which I guess is pretty much an American sort of pastime. This assignment was right up my alley. By the end of the week I was adroit at reaching my perch quickly and easily and had filled a bushel basket with my pigeon prey. I felt proud that I had been commandeered for such a mission and glad that I could be of service to Barbara's father. Of course, having such a new adventure, and getting paid for it, were huge bonuses.

I'm sure that being around Barbara's family and watching them run successful businesses subconsciously prepared me for the business world, precluding any intimidation or uneasiness in my future endeavors. After all, at 12 years old, I had already been a paid mercenary! If adults I respected, like Sister Isabel and Johnny Warus appreciated what I could do, well, then I could do just about anything.

My proximity to the Warus family helped me develop a mindset that I have never lost, and that has served me well.

It was not just in the neighborhood that Barbara had such an impact on me. Unbeknownst to me, she also changed my direction at school.

Little did I know my performance in seventh grade math class plus my friendship with Barb would save me the humiliation and loss of self-esteem of repeating the seventh grade.

Toward the end of that school year, Barb overheard the nuns talking about me and debating whether or not I should be held back for another school year. Barbara was mature for her age, so when she suggested that they rethink their decision, they considered her reasoning. As my next-door neighbor, she said, she noticed me reading stacks of books from the library. She reminded them that I had built my own functioning rocket just by reading, and that I had a knack for technical ideas, as shown by my innate understanding of algebra.

Figure 36 Me on the day of my eighth grade graduation

It wasn't until our class reunion when I had been overseas for 35 years already that Barbara told me about the conversation that unknowingly changed my life.

Because of Barb, and her interjection into that conversation, I believe I passed on to the next grade that year, and subsequently each year thereafter as I grew my skills. All I know for sure is that Barbara was an excellent student and the teachers all had great respect for her, and I was never held back again.

At the end of middle school, there was an entrance exam to get into the newest secondary Catholic school in the area, Andrean High School. I took the test, fully expecting to fail it. I had, inaccurately, assumed they let any Catholic in regardless of scores because I was sure I hadn't passed that test. It turned out, however, that my tinkering and experimenting were making their way into my academics, and I had actually passed that assessment. I had qualified for the quality education that I was about to receive. I enjoyed it. Amen.

I didn't have to go to remedial reading, we changed classes throughout the day, there were plenty of pretty girls, and there were sports. In grade school I had played football, and in seventh grade we won the Gary City CYO Championship. In eighth grade we came in second. Now, all the kids I had played against over those years were in the same high school together with me. I figured we would all be on the same side working together now. In my mind we would make a great team, so I went to the try-outs.

Being a private school, they had the pick of the cream of the crop. I soon learned I was not the part of the crop that was cream at the top. I would have been better suited for rugby. I was built like a brick. I could not run for anything. Immediately it was evident that Coach Doornbos was not going to be a fan of mine. In fact, I could tell he just did not like me. I did not fit his usual mold of a great football player. I was slow, I was short, and I did not come from an affluent area. So, that was that. I did not make the team.

Never one to be idle, when my friend Tom Kerlin suggested I try out for the swim team, it sounded like a good idea. All the time at the Goodfellow Camp and the YMCA really paid off for me. I was a freshman and I beat out the top breaststroker, who was a senior. I found myself on top again. I was a freshman on the varsity swim team.

The swim coach, Jerry Bradford, said I had potential, but that I needed to swim year-round. In order to reach that potential, he felt I had to give up all other sports and focus on swimming. I agreed that I would do that. Coach Bradford brought in a private coach who knew all the latest breaststroke techniques. I went after it with passion, learning everything he could teach me, and worked hard. I swam three miles every night after school and more on the weekends. In my senior year, I finished fourth in the

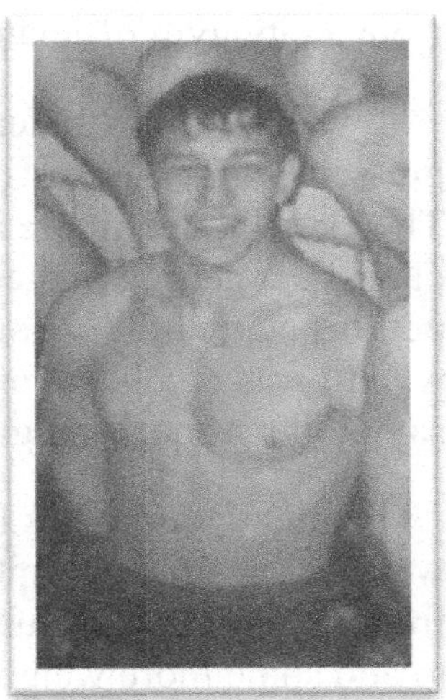

Figure 37 I was a winning part of the Andrean swim team.

northern Indiana competition, which allowed me to go to the Indiana state meet in Bloomington.

Even with my success in swimming, and seeing everything I put into it, Coach Doornbos, who was also the physical education teacher, never warmed up to me. Maybe it was because of the success I had in swimming that he didn't like me. In gym class we would have competitions doing sit-ups, push-ups, and pull-ups. I could do more of these than anyone in the school, even Coach Doornbos's footballers, and he didn't like that one bit.

Every year the school held what they called the Armageddon Games. When I was fifteen years old, and weighed a solid 150 pounds, I schemed my way into winning the weightlifting event. The lifts in the competition were press, clean and jerk, and bench press. Three judges from a city gym officiated the match.

I watched from under the bleachers as the event progressed and participants started with the lighter weights. They kept adding more and more weight and the participants kept getting bigger and bigger as the lighter competitors started falling away. My friends kept asking when I was going to start lifting. I kept putting them off saying it was not enough weight for me yet.

Finally, Doornbos's last champion lifted his heaviest weight. The crowd erupted into cheers. Then I walked out from my hiding place under the bleachers and told them to add some more weight. My first lift exceeded the champion. I pressed 230 pounds in front of a stunned crowd, winning the round.

As they set up the next round, I slipped back under the bleachers again. As the competition progressed, I won all three lifts that way, much to Doornbos's surprise and apparent dismay.

I might not have ever played football again, but I represented our school in a proud and positive way in both the pool and the Armageddon Games. I was proud that I was on top and counted it as another win for the school, and for me.

Part VII – Ladies' Man

This time of my life was certainly an adventure, and I was always up for one more. I was fifteen years old and my hormones were popping up their heads in more ways than one: pimples, body hair, interesting dreams, and more. It should come as no surprise that when David Gorski came down the stairs into Barbara Warus's basement with some news, I was stoked. Barb's finished basement was the perfect hang-out for a bunch of young high school kids. Her parents were happy to have us, probably to keep an eye out for their daughter. I'm sure they didn't imagine us guys having the conversations we did. Fortunately, Barb was upstairs getting snacks the day David told us about what happened when his brother Tony had taken him down to Gary's red-light district.

Not only our hormones, but our teenage perceptions of manliness, were fully engaged. Gary's red-light district was world famous, world famously dangerous, that is. A *Time* magazine article highlighted the fact that "Gary's main police station was one street away."

Locals called it "The Region." It was the ghetto of Gary, a strip about two blocks long around 13th and Adams Streets, mostly occupied by African Americans. Girls would hang out of the windows coming on to cars full of little fifteen and sixteen-year-old white boys cruising the street.

Dave was recounting all the explicit details of his first sexual encounter with all the bravado he could muster. Of course, we were all ears. He told us what happened and how exciting it was and then, not even taking a breath, he said it. Just what we were eager to hear, "Why don't you guys come, too?" We thought about it, for about a nanosecond, and, no surprise here, later that evening the five of us were cruising Adams Street. We took note of each of the beauties' whereabouts and which of the options we each found most appealing. Then we went home to plan our attack.

Our concerns about our personal safety were immediately satisfied because Dave's brother explained that the ladies of the evening would make sure that none of us would get mugged by the local boys. We were in the ladies' territory, and, with money in our pockets, they could ensure it landed in the right place. Five dollars was the price for companionship, and for a fifteen-year-old boy at that time, it was a significant bit of money. Nothing we could not each raise for what was, after all, a good cause.

With our change scraped together and safely stowed in our pockets, we headed out again, this time to engage, to party. Just as if we were going to any other social event, we were showered and shaved (even if we didn't need it) with clean clothes and, of course, aftershave, to give us the look and feel of men about town. I used my dad's Old Spice to make me smell more mature. All the preparations for our appearance gave us confidence. We were dudes going out and about the town. The ladies were ready, hanging out their windows just waiting for us to show up and fork over the fiver.

It was difficult to decide from all the options. The car slowed as we listened to what they had to say. Finally, one woman caught our attention. In a slow, suggestive voice, she said, "Hey, come on in boys. We'll show you a good time. Lots of pretty girls in here." We agreed that that establishment looked good, so we stopped in front of the window to talk to the lady. She took our attention as agreement to partake of her hospitality and she told us to drive around the back of the house, adding that we did not have to worry, nobody would bother us.

The back alley was dark. She opened the door spilling a lighted path out to us, while she waved us inside. We hopped out of the car and made our way over to her.

How jelly-legs Tom, nervous as hell, managed to walk to the house, let alone inside, I don't know. I was so excited for what was to come. This is a time in a young boy's life that he has thought about more than once. Probably closer to a million times. All I could think was that it was going to happen, right here, right now.

The woman, who I would call the mama san, looked different at a closer range and in stronger light. She was middle-aged and not so thin, and I remember thinking she looked nothing like the centerfolds that had come to life in my dreams. None the less, the excitement was not dampened.

She said she could take two at a time. What does she mean by that, we wondered? Joe and I were first. We followed her into the hallway where she stopped next to two ladies. One of them was around eighteen years old, I'd say, maybe less. And the other one was about forty years old, maybe more. Joe and I stood there looking at them, clutching our $5 in our sweaty palms. The younger one grabbed Joe and turned him down the hallway toward a door. I was left there with ... the interesting one. I was thinking, "Ha, my first experience is going to be with a black woman older than my mother." That didn't matter. I was committed. It had taken a lot of courage to get to this point, and I was not turning back.

From that back hallway of the small house, my lady led me through the same door where Joe and his woman had gone. I was relieved to see that Joe would be accommodated in another bedroom adjacent to ours, not with us. When the doors were shut, she immediately got to work. I was asked to leave just my shirt and socks on, and the interviewer prepared a ceramic pan of hot water and soap. That washing was the best part of the night. She told me, "It doesn't look like this is your first time, honey," though I imagine they said that to everyone. They make you feel like a dude.

After the glorious wash, the interviewer climbed up on the bed, reclined, and raised her skirt. I will never forget that sight. There are just not enough words to describe it. I, of course, recognized the Catholic missionary position, being the good little Catholic boy that I was. As things progressed, she told me to slow down, that it was not a race. I was a good listener. In following her instructions and taking my time, the night was ruined.

It was bad enough that I was paired with the oldest lady in the business. In our restraint, Joe had already finished, and he and his girlfriend came out of their room into ours. As he walked by, he said, “Good job, Tom!” He might as well have swatted me on the butt. With that disturbance and the mama san poking her head in saying, “Time’s up, Honey,” I couldn't finish my interview, no matter how much I wanted.

Back in Barb’s basement with all the guys, we had a big chat. We were all laughing, especially as Joe described what he saw when he came in my room. Of course, I was frustrated and humiliated, but also determined. I told them I did not want to leave it at that experience. I wanted to get the job done. We made plans to return so I could get across the finish line.

The next night we were back in Gary's famous red-light district. This time with a bit more discretion and time to cruise the streets. I decided I was going to choose the girl I wanted. Last time we’d been in the area, I had noticed a really pretty girl, about 25-years-old, and I wanted her. Luck would have it that I remembered where she had been, and we found her.

The guys let me out at the building where she was, and I told the mama san which girl I wanted. I was told that she was with a client. She would be with me soon if I did not mind waiting. It was worth the wait because when the door opened, she walked in wearing only a pair of shoes. She was beautiful, and now she was mine for the next two minutes. Maybe less. She brought a pan filled with the hot, soapy water and set it down on a low table. She said the same line, “It doesn't look like this is your first time, Honey." I thought with a smile, "Yeah, I am experienced."

That evening I finished my interview, and I was happy. "Now I'm a man!" I thought. When the boys stopped to pick me up, I strutted to the car, got in and said everything was A-OK, but there was enough semen in her room to man a battleship! They cracked up and we drove home chatting and laughing about our experiences. What I didn't know was that the last laugh would be on me.

It did not take more than a couple of days to find out I had brought back a little present from one of my interviewers. I knew it when I tried to pee. At first, I could not go, and it was painful. Finally, when it started to flow, blood came out. I was frightened to death. I knew there was a chance to get weird diseases. Of course, I didn't think it would happen to me. Plus, both times we had washed up thoroughly before hand, or, at least I had been washed up. It's not too difficult to guess we rode our horses bareback each time, is it? Not too bright. You know, we cannot think of everything in such exciting circumstances.

What does a guy in this situation do? I asked my friends. They didn't fess up to any like experiences or knowledge. I for sure could never tell my mother, so I just lived with it. It took a few weeks to get better and better every day, until it did actually go away. Boy, was I lucky or what?

It wasn't until much later, when I got in the Navy that I learned about various venereal diseases in our basic health training. In fact, that's when I knew that little Catholic boy, Tom Pado, had had gonorrhea.

DAMN THE PRESSURE, FULL SPEED AHEAD

After getting over my bout with the gonorrhea, I never got it again. So, I went about my life and my interest in the opposite sex. Even though I was on the varsity swim team as a freshman, my swimming skills did not matter much to my parents, if at all. It did, however, catch the eye of someone else.

With my sophisticated gift of gab and suave manly ways, I tended to attract girls. One of them, named Paula Melzer was the daughter of a single mother who lived in the Miller area on the beach in an amazing mansion home. One day I was there with her when a man visited. He was interested in dating Paula's mother. We struck up a conversation. He asked me if I played sports and I replied that I didn't play football, that I was a swimmer.

"Oh?" he said, "Are you any good?"

"I'm a freshman on the varsity team," I replied, "and I teach swimming at the CYO pool when I'm not practicing."

"Really?" he said. "Would you like to be a lifeguard on Lake Michigan? Do you have lifesaving certifications?"

"Yes, and yes, I have every lifesaving certification," I said.

"OK," he said, as he pulled out a business card and started writing on the back of it. "Go to this address and talk to this man and you'll have a job."

I did not walk to the municipal building the next day, I practically ran. I was going to earn some money. In addition, I saw the opportunity to be a part of the scene on Miller Beach. It was a place where all the rich kids went.

The kids that were always happy and upbeat. The kids that went to great schools and were all highly educated. It was a place I had never thought I would spend much time.

It was a given from the moment I walked in with that man's business card, that I had the job. He told me how I would get paid and issued me a shiny whistle, a red jacket, pants, and shorts each emblazoned with LIFE-GUARD loud and proud. The next day I reported to the Miller Beach bathhouse to begin this new adventure.

All summer long for the next three summers, I was part of the Lake Michigan Miller Beach lifeguard patrol team. We manned fifteen perches along the shore, rode along in the police boat with its flashing red lights or patrolled the weedy banks in a jeep. All together there were about seventeen of us, and we were the stars of the beach.

I would get a paycheck for $177 three times over each summer of my freshman, sophomore, and junior years of high school. Money was not going to be the biggest and best outcome of this job. No, not by a long shot.

All the lifeguards conspired to create our own sign language motioning each other to communicate and playing games, mostly to impress the chicks on the beach with the prestige that went along with the job. Everybody went to Miller Beach to swim during the summer and not only would there be lots of girls in bikinis, there would be lots of invitations to social events like the dance at Chapel of the Dunes.

Although I was now well aware of the opposite sex and had had experience of the "professional" sort, I had not really seriously dated anyone. I had not found anyone that I considered the girl for me. My expectations were not all that high when I joined the other lifeguards at the dance at Chapel of the Dunes. By that point of the summer we had already attended a few other dances and I expected it would be the average kind of dance, not much more.

Figure 38 The girl of my dreams, Cindy Robinson.

You can scoff at love at first sight, but when I saw her, I knew. She took my breath away when I caught sight of her across the room. She was about an inch taller than me, and just the most beautiful female I had ever seen. I strode right across the room, held out my hand and said, "Hi, I'm Tom Pado and I'm a lifeguard." We danced, and I fell in love with Cindy Robinson that night.

Figure 39 Prom really was a dream with Cindy.

Cindy was physically stunning, intellectually stunning, too. Her charisma and intellect shot straight to my heart. Every once in a while, during our time together, she would use her wit and make a comment that would make me clutch my chest and say, "Ouch. Damn. That hurt."

I fretted over how I was going to get a girl like her to like me. My ability to be social was the strength I would always fall back upon in these sorts of situations and I turned it on. I gave her my best bullshit, telling her what a great and talented guy I was. You know what? Somehow it worked. She became my girlfriend and we dated for about four years.

I loved every minute of the time I spent with Cindy. We got along so well, we never fought. With the clashes in my house on a nightly basis, this was a new and wonderful experience. I spent a lot of time with Cindy and her family, enjoying dinners and talking and just being a part of a normal family. It was one of the best times of my life. I had a surrogate family and the girl of my dreams.

One evening, Cindy and I went to a drive-in restaurant called Calvin's. They served the typical hamburgers, fries, and Cokes perched on a tray on the side of the car window. The guys would burn out as they left the drive-in in their cars. It was just like you saw in the 1970s TV show *Happy Days*, happy and free.

Figure 40 Cindy and me, young and happy.

We were eating our burgers, watching two cars racing toward the drive-in. One car hit the curb and flew up into the air, flipped over and landed upside down. Miraculously, the car was jammed on the Calvin's sign, so it wasn't completely flat on the ground yet, but it was slipping off its support.

I ran over and looked underneath. The driver was hanging upside down, still stuck to the seat because as uncommon as it was at the time, he was wearing a seat-belt. His head was about a foot from the concrete. If the car slipped, he would certainly have died. I hollered to my friends, all healthy as hell, "Somebody call the police, and somebody call an ambulance. The rest of you get over here and help me flip this car back over!"

Everybody came running. Joe Cerda was there, Tom Kerlin, and Allan Templin. We all got a good grip and flipped the car right over. I will always remember seeing that kid slop back down into the driver's seat, still alive. He was one lucky boy.

Not all our dates were as exciting as that. Even so, every one of them left me with a thrill in my heart.

By my sophomore year in high school, I debuted a beautiful 4-foot silver rocket that I had fashioned out of a tube with a copper rocket motor inside. It was complete with fins, nose cone, and a payload of spiders, waiting to be loaded with five pounds of sugar mixture.

Making the fuel was a challenge. By this time, my parents had forbidden me from making explosives with the family stove. In such a situation, with such potential for scientific discovery, my philosophy was to ask for forgiveness, rather than permission. And I usually got lucky. That day, however, when my dad was at work and my mom out shopping, my luck ran out.

I knew I had to hurry to get done before either of my parents got home. My plan was to heat a fuel mixture in one of my mom's pans and then pour it into a copper pipe fuselage. The stove got it hot enough to bring it to a syrupy molasses consistency. When I poured it into the pipe it cooled instantaneously, clogging the opening of the fuselage. I put the pan back on the stove and tried to push down the hardened fuel with a wooden spoon.

What escaped my attention was that some of the fuel had dribbled down the side of the pan when I poured it. I looked over to the pot just as the dribble was ignited by flame beneath the burner and acted like a fuse climbing back to the mother lode. There were several pounds of fuel there, and I knew what would happen. I had to act quickly.

I lifted the pan off the stove and lowered it to the floor to avoid scorching the ceiling. I couldn't place it on the linoleum because it would leave a mark that would convict me. So, I just held the pot a few inches above the kitchen floor. I was reasonably sure that the explosion would remain contained in the pan. When it lit, it created an intense amount of smoke that filled the house to the point that you couldn’t see your outstretched hand.

It alerted my five-year-old sister, who screamed in horror from the kitchen doorway. From her vantage point it looked like her older brother was on fire. Despite all my reassurances, Debbie was sure I, and the house, were burning. She ran outside screaming, alerting the whole neighborhood.

Meanwhile, I was dealing with only a ruined pan--everything else was fine. However, the smoke was a dead giveaway that I was doing something I shouldn't be doing. I ran upstairs and turned on an extractor fan. The smoke poured out of the house, giving total credence to the screaming little girl, and the neighbors were ready to call the fire department when I ran up to stop them.

The neighbors wanted to know what happened.

"Oh, er, I was just making rocket fuel on the stove and it caught fire. I contained the fire and everything's A-OK!" I said, with my best look of nonchalance, while panting from the running. Their eyes bugged out of their heads at "making rocket fuel on the stove." As far as neighbors go, mine weren't to be envied because they lived next to me and I saw every day as an adventure.

As I reflected a few days later on the incident, it made me mad. I realized that if my Dad had been there working with me and I was not hurrying to hide my activity, everything would have turned out better. This realization was part of the reason this incident concluded my rocket explorations.

Part VIII - The Edge of Adulthood

My earliest recognition of the gas stations at the end of our block was around the beginning of the 1950s. There were three gas stations all together. Two were regular gas stations, Standard Oil and Gulf. Each one had full-service gasoline pumps, and then a couple of bays to repair cars. Quite often you would see signs saying that there was a mechanic on duty. This meant you could get your oil changed, brakes repaired, and most any other kind of mechanical work.

Generally, when you pulled up to one of the pumps a man would come out of the station and fill your car with gas, clean your windows, put air in your tires, and check your oil. At the end he would take your money and run back into the station to put your money in the cash register and make change if necessary. This took a little bit of time.

There was another gas station called Martin's. It was the discount station. It was set up to sell the lowest price gasoline, oil, and cigarettes to its customers. Martin's did not have any repair bays.

There were usually two or three guys dressed in blue uniforms. I think they even had hats. They wore a change machine on their belt at their waist. When a customer pulled up to their pumps, they all immediately went to work to provide the fastest service around. One of the guys would be filling the gas tank, one would be checking the air pressure on the tires, and the third would be cleaning the windshield.

They would bring an oil-change machine over to the car, raise the hood, remove the oil reservoir cap and push a hose into the engine. The machine was about three feet tall and had a suction pump that sucked all the oil out through the oil filler pipe at the top of the engine. This meant that the oil change would go quickly, as no one had to get underneath the car, pull a plug, and drain the oil.

The oil that was put back into the engine was another of Martin's innovative business practices that was considered an advantage for their customers. They would take the oil removed from a car, send it away to be professionally filtered, and then have it returned. The reconditioned oil is what Martin's sold at their pump bays to replenish oil that had been removed. It was packaged in clear bottles, so you could see the reconditioned oil looked clean, and it was, without question, cheaper than oil you purchased elsewhere.

Everything about Martin's was to make stops there fast and cheap. Cigarettes, candy, soda pop, and other snacks were sold there for less than at the full-service stations. It was a speedy operation all the way around.

Martin's gas stations were strategically located near the roads leading to Lake Michigan and to the U.S. Steel Mill. This was before the Eisenhower interstate projects and Routes 12 and 20, which turned into Fifth Avenue in Gary, were main thoroughfares.

U.S. Steel was eight miles long, three miles wide, and employed 27,000 people. Every eight hours, as shifts changed, thousands of vehicles would fill these roads. The Martin's gas stations did a bustling business, especially since budget-minded millworkers were in a hurry to get to and from jobs and home.

My friends and I used to visit these gas stations. We would buy candy and Coca Cola, both being a quick nickel.

The Coke machines were unique at Martin's just like the quick oil-change machine. It was like a bathtub where cold water circulated around the bottles. You would put your nickel in the slot and then guide the bottle down a framework until the end where a mechanism would release it as long you put the neck in the right way. I liked maneuvering the bottles in the Coke machine at Martin's but what we really liked were the candy machines.

The candy options at each of the stations were different. So, with cheap candy and Cokes, Martin's was the place we stopped most often. The attendants were all out by the fueling pumps and didn't like us to hang around. They would yell at us to "get your shit and go."

They might not have liked us kids to hang around but that didn't seem to apply to other people, like my mom.

When my mom dyed her hair and started dressing in her stirrup pants and tight tops, she got a lot of attention from the guys at Martin's. It was the attention she was trying to get from my dad. She would pull her car up and all these men would run up to service it. From my perspective, when I was with her, it didn't look like a lot of services being done to the car.

My mother would get out, prance around the car, and these men would all be fussing over her. Quite often she would strike a pose and ask them, "How do I look today?" The answers would all be complimentary. I started to notice that there was one man who paid particular attention to her. He would always be left talking to her alone after all the others walked away. This went on for a couple of years.

After my grandfather died, I inherited his 1950 Buick. It was the same car we used when he and I went garbage picking from the alleyways in years past. Being a teenager that was always broke, Martin's was the gas station I most often frequented. Plus, it was the one at the end of our street and I was still always on the lookout for my mom.

One night, after dark, I was driving by and happened to notice my mom's car parked out behind the gas station. It was kind of a secluded spot and my curiosity got the better of me. I don't know if I wondered if Mom was in trouble or had a problem, but I definitely wanted to know why she was there in that spot. I turned in the alley and drove by. I could see my mother and this gas station guy named Poe in the backseat. He was the guy she was always left talking with previously. I guess you could say she was getting her oil changed.

I pulled up next to the car and I saw my mother's head pop up and she looked me straight in the eye. I will never forget the look on her face. It was a look of terror and is forever burned in my mind. My heart was pounding out of my chest. I thought to myself that I never liked those gas station guys. My next thought, immediately, was that I knew there was going to be trouble.

It wasn't much more than a few days after discovering my mom and Poe at the gas station that it became an issue between her and me. She became hard and stern toward me and finally she told me that I was never to tell my dad what I had seen.

After years of being the chit between them, I was tired of it. I'd had enough of her saying she was leaving dad and him telling me he was going to leave her. At no point did either of them seem to ever consider the position they were putting me in, and my sister. They didn't see that their instability created such fear for us.

For some reason I felt I had to tell my father and eventually, I did. I was correct, all hell broke loose. What my dad had suspected all along and sometimes verbalized to my mother during arguments at home, was found to be true.

After the dust settled on this incident, the fighting continued. Now the words were a little harder and a bit fiercer. I was glad to be able to escape to Barbara's house and did so more frequently.

By this time, I realized that what kept my parents together was economics. It was becoming more and more evident as the area that once housed lots of growing families was becoming more and more run-down. Homes were being burglarized, drugs were being sold on the corners, and gun shots could be heard on occasion. My mother was absolutely unwilling to sell the house and move, and the ghetto was creeping up on us. Eventually, our home was in the ghetto.

Their fighting continued and one day, I had had enough. I began screaming, "I hate this. I can't stand it anymore! I am tired of you guys always fighting!" I yelled back at them and they just looked at me. I think that was the first time they saw that their fighting was affecting me. I walked out the back door and sat on the steps sobbing. Alone. I had snapped, and I do not think they expected it. Nor do I think they cared too much about how it affected me or my sister, because the fighting never did stop. I just found myself staying away as much as possible.

High school was coming to an end for me. It seemed that Andrean High School's demanding entrance exam culled out the students who were not really Andrean material. In the beginning, as freshman, lots of students were admitted. At the end of each year, students were required to pass all their classes in order to pass on to the next grade. If students did not maintain their grades, they did not return when the new schoolyear began. That meant that every year the ranks of my class shrunk. I was amazed that I was not one of the students asked to leave. Somehow, like I had with the entrance exam, I managed to pass each year on to the following year. Perhaps Sister Isabel's influence had followed me through the years.

My senior year, I wasn't sure I would make it to graduation. My great friend Tom Kerlin helped me with my studies. He used his tape recorder to record the history stories that would be on the final exam, and I sat there and listened over and over until I knew them front to back.

I had one instructor for both Spanish and geometry and I puzzled him greatly because a bad student is a bad student and a good student is a good student, right? Not me. I was failing Spanish but was the top student in geometry. He could never figure it out, and you know what? I never tried to explain. I didn't know why either.

Figure 41 I made it. I graduated from Andrean High School, 1965

As exams were not my forte, I naturally avoided the PSAT and SAT university entrance exams. That meant no college for Tommy. I couldn't believe that there were three students with grades lower than mine. For a kid with the academic struggles I had since the first day stepping into a classroom, I rejoiced with my diploma in hand, even if I was graduating 409 out of a class of 412.

It was 1965. I had no money. I had no prospects for college, and I wasn't married. Where would a healthy 18-year-old find himself? That's right. Vietnam. The draft letter arrived before I graduated and with my testing abilities, I knew I would never pass the exam to get into the submarine service in the Navy, so I decided to become a Marine.

For the second time in my life, my parents' patchy wisdom would once again be life-changing for me. Just like their decision to enroll me into St. Luke's had been a turning point for me, the time they took to talk me out of the Marines and into the Navy was equally as important.

It wasn't quite as calm as that sounds, as you wouldn't expect it to be in my house. When I told my parents of my intention to be a Marine, my mom went nuts. My dad was standing there, and my mom got right up into his face and said, "Talk to your son. Tell him to go into the Navy." And, he did just as she told him to do.

Part of Dad's argument was well understood by me when he said, "Do you want to be a boy scout, live in a tent, and eat out of a can or do you want to have a warm bed and a home-cooked meal every night?" I knew exactly what he was saying. Another point he made was about the possibility of dying. I took his advice and not only joined the Navy; I was going to go after Submarine Service as well.

The next day when I went down to the Navy recruiter's office for the official test, my mind and body were strung up as taut as a guitar string, with even more than the usual tightness that exams evoked in me. This was serious. It was more than just some academic test. It was about what was going to happen to me in real life. I couldn't believe my luck when the whole test didn't seem so hard. I was thanking Lee Freel and my lucky stars, and I realized that even if I had struggled at the bottom of the class at Andrean High School, I had received a competent education, thanks to Sister Isabel's strict demands. It was a milestone for me. No, it was another win in the Tom Pado column and I was pleased.

The recruiter told me that I did so well I could have my pick of any training I desired. With my confidence built up, I chose a tough classification, intercommunications. I felt on top of the world and couldn't see how it could get any better. I planned to reap the benefits of all the struggles I had in school as well as the time spent talking and working in Lee's basement.

The date was set, and I boarded a train, waving goodbye to my Cindy. We wrote letters twice a day, and her words got me through the 10-week basic training. In those days and weeks, something new started to grow in me. I painstakingly followed the rules even if it was a challenge and I had no idea why the rules were necessary. I prepared meticulously for the inspections that all of us recruits faced every day. I would hammer at the folds of my packed clothes until the edges were perfectly square. The resulting approbation from the commanders fueled my confidence, and I did everything to my best, with earnestness. I graduated Boot Camp with the top award of "Outstanding Recruit" and more self-confidence than I'd ever known before in my life. I was feeling what it really felt like to be top dog in the pack. Another win for Pado.

I came home, and Cindy and I dated for another year or so. Then, she graduated from high school, and I knew we wouldn't be dating anymore. I was in the Navy. I had no hair, no money, and I was going nowhere fast. She was headed to college. I knew when she got to university and the boys there saw her and got to know her, she would be gone. And that's the way it went. Cindy went off to school, graduated, and got married, and I went off on a submarine to the bottom of the ocean.

Implications for My Future

The screaming between my parents weighed heavily on me. Even though I felt I had no immediate association to it, I also felt somehow strangely responsible for it. In a naïve way my young mind held on to the thought that if I was good enough at something to make them proud of me, they would rally together over the son they had created together. Enough, anyway, to find love between them and stop the screaming. That never happened.

The constancy and inevitability of the daily screaming bouts were like cords that bound me and constricted me, driving me out of the house. It drove me to immerse myself in my interests and give them everything I had both mentally and physically. It drove me to excel so I could prove to them that I, their son, was worthy of their love, their attention, and that they, together, would build a home and environment to nurture the potential in me. That never happened, either.

I knew that I was worthy of love. Cindy had loved me. I had friends like Ronnie Kazmerski, Tom Kerlin, Allan Templin, Lee Freel, and Barbara Warus, who showed me I had good attributes and a good heart.

I also knew that, despite my academic struggles, that I was intelligent. I had so many thoughts and ideas spinning in my head that I was in a constant state of seeking. I absorbed information and sought out answers to questions I had, in a variety of ways. Some were traditional, like books. Others were completely experimental.

What I didn't realize is that because of this, I got a full education. I mean, it's not just the three Rs. It's also music, sports, and hobbies. Music gets your mind in order. Team sports gives you experience in working with a group that has a common goal led by a manager. Finally, personal enrichment projects allow you to explore your passions that, in turn, broadens your knowledge and perspective. It's all important.

I wasn't afraid to try anything and often that got me into trouble. Providence must have been watching out for me because no one got hurt. Well, not hurt too badly. The accidental mustard gas concoction had potential to blister skin and lungs and physically hurt people. My exploding rocket did leave scars on Jim Grosdanis.

Looking back, I realize there was good reason for my mother's concern. I was dangerous as a youth, not in the way of drugs, gangs, or crime, but in my quest for approval and to satisfy my own curiosity. Even as an adult I know that this is my nature. I seek answers to my questions without really knowing I had a question, or unsure of where my exploration will lead.

My innate ability to get along with people, to bring my ideas to life, and to follow every opportunity going at it with great enthusiasm had resulted in many personal achievements, many wins. Yet something was not quite right. At the end of this magical time, I left it all behind, including those people who had filled the empty places in my heart. I literally took off to find out what the world was all about and what my place in it would be. There had to be more out there and something that would make me feel complete and satisfied.

Section Three - Rough Seas in the Navy

Part I – Finding the Man in Me

I had passed the Navy recruitment test easily. Once I passed it, I understood that my struggling to make even the bottom of my class at Andrean High School meant I still received a competent education there. That knowledge gave me confidence to face the ten weeks of basic training, commonly referred to as Boot Camp.

Boot camp is not easy but with my newfound confidence and support from Cindy, I believed I sailed through it. Cindy was the best girlfriend a guy at boot camp could have. We wrote to each other twice every day and you can bet I looked forward to mail call and those letters. Her words kept me moving forward on many days. During this time some of the guys got a "Dear John" letter and it was a really tough time for them. I was lucky that I never got one and learned to appreciate that.

Boot camp was the transition from my being a boy to becoming a man. One thing that was abundantly clear very early on was the fact that you were here alone, on your own, without any sort of personal support from home. The Navy taught us everything: how to shave, how to wash and store our clothing, how to make a bed, and, of course, everything we needed to start our life as a sailor. One of the biggest perks, to me, was that they drilled us into physical shape. I lost thirty pounds in that ten weeks. I gained more and more self-confidence and was in the best physical shape of my life. I felt great.

Figure 42 I lost my hair and was handed a mop. Welcome to the Navy.

You might guess that being in the military was a challenge for someone like me who followed my own set of rules. Believe it or not, I did painstakingly follow the rules, even though some days it was excruciating. I knew that I had an opportunity here and I was going to go after it with the same enthusiasm because I knew it could result in something good for me.

Recruits went through inspections every day. All our military-issued clothing was packed and inspected daily, and each inspection became the yardstick of our ability and merit as sailors. I was able to pack my clothes, so the edges of the folds were square, which was something really unique that the officers had never seen before. My uniforms always had that just-ironed look and it impressed my commanders. Their approval made me try harder and I attacked it all with my trademark gusto.

I always wanted to know why we were doing something or learning something in school. That curiosity followed me into the Navy, a place where asking why wasn't met with much enthusiasm. I learned pretty quickly that I was better off trying to figure out the why by myself rather than ask the question. What I learned was that there was a reason for every action we took.

For instance, we had to march in step following a certain path to the galley for every meal. We would thread our way in and out of buildings, paths, and other places.

On the floor under the galley door was a kick plate that was about eight inches wide and slightly raised. It was always polished to a bright sheen. No one, and I mean no one, was allowed to accidently kick that shiny surface. We really caught it if we did.

As a side note, there was always a sentry posted at that location. He had been selected, obviously, for his size and demeanor. His wrath was something to behold for impressionable new recruits. He would holler out loud, "Pick that foot up. Don't you dare step on the plate!" We were half asleep, and it would scare us to death when he hollered out at us.

It took a while, to finally figure out why stumbling on, or scuffing, that plate in the doorway was so offensive. When I realized that every doorway represented a submarine hatchway, I realized that we had to pass through those hatchways quickly without tripping over them. That meant we had to automatically raise our foot higher than we might normally, to go through it.

The Navy was very clever about how they taught us. They made training as real as possible. During a real GQ (general quarters), a large portion of the crew would be sleeping. That meant the sailors would have to go from a dead sleep to double timing it through the ship, and yes, the biggest obstacle was the hatchway. You guessed it, you had to lift your foot high to prevent tripping. That's when the memory of that great big quartermaster all spit-shined, official looking and hollering out, "Pick that foot up!" would come to mind.

If anyone tripped, it would mean he, and all the sailors behind him were going to be late getting to their GQ station, and that could mean death for the whole crew. Yes, just stumbling on that hatchway could mean the sinking of the ship, something like trying to get out of a burning theater when everyone piles up at the door. Running through the hatchways were vital to our survival, and the Navy wanted to be sure we were prepared to survive.

Figure 43 First liberty after boot camp. Be aware girls.

I started explaining the reasons for things we were doing and learning to other recruits. It wasn't long before that was noticed, and I was assigned the position of Educational Petty Officer. My job was to explain to the other new recruits the reasoning behind learning what we felt was meaningless, benign crap. It was the same thing I had been doing in front of the commanding officers. Now I had a title. At the same time, I was still oblivious to knowing I was being watched as a candidate for the Outstanding Recruit award.

At the end of Boot Camp came graduation and that was a big deal. I got to wear my dress uniform for the first time, and I was proud. I might not be a tall man in stature but on that day, I felt ten feet tall. I had earned the respect of my commanders and was named the Outstanding Recruit. I was proud that my efforts were noticed and appreciated. It made me try even harder and overdo everything. I liked the Navy. I was on a roll and I saw no reason to stop. I was part of the most powerful military in the world. I knew I was going somewhere.

I was very proud of myself and what I had discovered about myself. I thought, finally, my parents would be proud of their son. I called home to share all the good news and tell them what I had done and what my next steps were going to be. They didn't hear much because Mom spent her time on the phone yelling at me. I don't remember all the reasons except I hadn't called more often. I figured the phone lines work both ways and I had no more money to pay for long-distance calls than they did. I do remember that they did not come to my Boot Camp graduation and I don't think they even heard me when I told them about the Outstanding Recruit award or that I was in the top of the class and going to more schools. I hung up and was glad the call was over.

After basic training and my success there, I spent almost a year in various Navy schools. I completed Electronics, Communication, Diving, and Submarine Schools. I first went to basic Electricity and Electronics School where I learned the inner workings of radios and amplifiers like push pull amplifiers and the magnetic amplifier, transformers, capacitors, resistors, diodes, and batteries.

Then I went to Interior Communications School. There they taught me everything inside a ship used for communications like intercom systems, sound powered telephones, and the engine order telegraph. That is the device they use to direct and control the speed of the ship in the engine room. In movies you have probably seen a big brass looking pedestal by the helm. This is used to enter commands like all ahead full, all ahead one third, or all back one third.

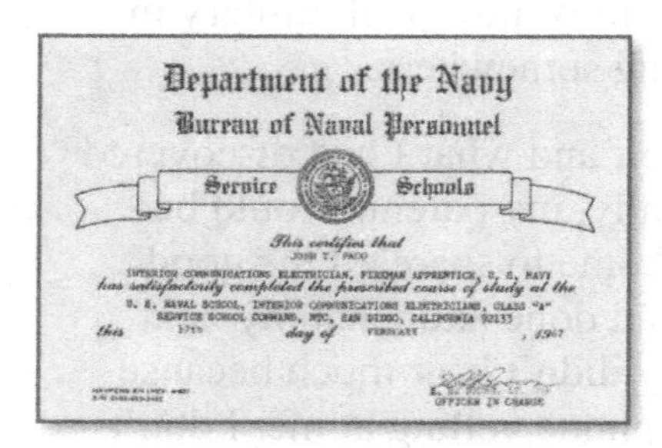

Department of the Navy
Bureau of Naval Personnel
Service Schools

This certifies that
JOHN T. PADO
INTERIOR COMMUNICATIONS ELECTRICIAN, FIREMAN APPRENTICE, U. S. NAVY
has satisfactorily completed the prescribed course of study at the
U. S. NAVAL SCHOOL, INTERIOR COMMUNICATIONS ELECTRICIANS, CLASS "A"
SERVICE SCHOOL COMMAND, NTC, SAN DIEGO, CALIFORNIA 92133
this 17th day of FEBRUARY, 1967

OFFICER IN CHARGE

Figure 44 Interior Communications School graduation

I also learned to repair a device called a Pith Sword. It was lowered through the bottom of the ship and told us how fast we were moving.

My favorite device, though, was the gyrocompass. I never knew how it worked and in the Navy school I found out. Their mechanisms were very cleverly designed.

They used a law of physics called precession. In general, a force applied to a spinning object is excreted ninety degrees from that force. I know you have seen and felt this over your lifetime. You have seen it on a spinning top, and you have probably felt it from the spin on the front tire of your bicycle. You try to turn the tire one way and it feels like it wants to go another way – that's precession.

In a gyro, they use this law combined with a weight system called Mercury or oil ballistics. This causes the gyro to indicate north. This principle and how it worked with the gyro always amazed me.

It might seem funny or odd that I also went to Motion Picture School. An IC (inter-communication) rated person, like me, was well suited to go to this school because the electronics we learned were similar to the electronics in a motion picture projector.

Believe me, there was another good reason to choose this particular school. As you might expect, I learned how to run a 16mm film movie projector and also how to repair it. Actually, there were two reasons to decide to invest my time in this school. The first reason was the financial bonus. I got paid one dollar for each movie I showed on the boat. It added up quickly when movies were one of a very few entertainments available when we were out to sea.

Best of all, I got to choose the movies we took to sea from the movie storage at the PX on shore. Generally, I selected about seventy different movies each time. I would poll my mates to see what kind of movies they wanted and that would start the selection process. That, in retrospect, was the second reason I took this school. I became an important part of the social order on the boat. I had a big responsibility to keep up morale with the entertainment. Although that was fun, I also took it very seriously. I would go to the PX and look through these little books that provided a synopsis of the movie and a record of which boat had checked it out. The most interesting part about that was the handwritten comments on the inside covers of the books. Phrases such as Lifer Movie, lots of skin (these were always picked), cowboy, sci-fi, etc. gave me some insight into how sailors on other boats liked, or did not like, each film. Some of the comments would make sense to anyone. Others liked Lifer movies, probably would not mean anything to someone in the general public. A Lifer in the military was someone who was making a career of the military, and the movies with those notes were especially appreciated by them because they were inspiring and patriotic. As you might expect, not everyone was intent on a long-term career in the military, so these comments were one way I used to find a variety of movies that would appeal to everyone.

The movies came in two or three 16mm reels in a case that was 20 inches by 20 inches by 6 inches deep. You can imagine how much space seventy of these movies would require and how heavy they would be.

Movies were important to the crew for a lot of different reasons. I watched the movie *Enemy Below*, which is about a WWII submarine while I was on a WWII submarine deep below the ocean's surface. While we watched the movie, we made the comment, "I'm sure glad there aren't any sea battles going on in this war." We were talking about the current Vietnam conflict. The movie really brought home how different a submariner's experience was between different wars. This particular movie was a slice of what life on a WWII sub must have been for my dad and cast him in a new light in my mind.

The next school I went to was Submarine School. I was so excited and knew it would be one of the most interesting learning experiences I would have to date. I wasn't disappointed. Submarine school changes depending on the time in history in which a submariner, or potential submariner, would attend. During the school the instruction would showcase a class of submarine that was relevant at that particular time. When I attended, we studied the Skipjack class of submarines. These were nuclear submarines.

We learned all the principles of how a submarine works from its sodium reactor to torpedoes. Then we got to go down to the lower base where all the submarines were moored and actually go on board one of them. I was excited and once again, my anticipation was well rewarded.

Figure 45 Submarine School graduation

What a sight to see. My recollection is that there were about ten piers that could each moor two subs at a time. It was awesome, in the truest sense of the word, to see that much firepower sitting in front of me. I distinctly remember my thoughts standing on the pier at the time. I was thinking that in front of me were submarines that were powerful enough to kill all life on earth. I know that is a scary thought and wasn't considered lightly by me then, or even now today. I realized the reason they were there was not to kill all life on earth but to act as a deterrent so that would not happen. Now, in hindsight, I think the military did the right thing. The Cold War had ended, and the thought of nuclear annihilation was much less likely. Thanks in part to submarines.

I realize that the first moments I laid eyes on the fleet of submarines and stepped on board had brought me full circle. The very thing that scared me so much as a child was nuclear war and bombs being dropped on my small world. Now I was going to be part of the deterrent inside one of these mighty ocean-going submarines. I would do my part to help relieve that fear for other people in America and around the world. I was proud to be an American and part of the United States Navy. Not just that, I was looking at the apex of mankind's knowledge and I knew I was going to be part of this mighty group, just like my dad. I will never forget that day and have had many days since when a situation, a sound, or a sight reminds me of those moments and my thoughts.

Figure 46 Navy diving equipment just like Lloyd Bridges

In Submarine School we also learned how a sub dives and surfaces and all the engineering that goes together to build a submarine. It was my favorite school. It touched my mind, my spirit, and my heart.

I wasn't done after submarine school. I took one more, the U. S. Navy diving school. Again, it was my past that projected my future. The swimming skills I learned at Goodfellow, the YMCA, and on the high school swim team, which had led to becoming a lifeguard on Lake Michigan, were noted and were the reason I was selected for the Diving School. I was the perfect candidate. The bonus was that every submarine crew included two divers and the divers were paid extra. We would do repairs on the outside of the submarine as well as other jobs in the ocean water. I loved diving because I loved diving. I didn't realize that this would be another element of my education that would lead me to great places in the future. For the moment, while I was in the Navy, it was fun, and I made a few more dollars to take to the bars.

I was assigned to the submarine, *U.S.S. Becuna.* Once on board, I applied all I had learned and absorbed everything I could about this submarine in particular. Just like the one in the Museum of Science and Industry, every submarine was a compact space dedicated to the form and function of science. People were still much of an afterthought and personal space was pretty much non-existent. Even our bunks were separated by less than twelve inches. I was happy to be on the bottom bunk because I could wiggle out and flip over from my back to my face and wiggle back in to change sleeping positions. If you were in a bunk that was two feet off the floor, flipping position was practically impossible.

Figure 47 The U.S.S. Becuna in New London Connecticut

I did learn that being on the bottom bunk has its drawbacks as well. More than once I would be the recipient of a wet night's sleep thanks to a mate who had over-imbibed and, in a drunken stupor, relieved himself in his bunk. All the bunks had a flash cover made out of vinyl. It was zipped up and he was lying on top of it, so his urine ran across the vinyl cover on his bunk and began to drip down on me. It was steady, and it didn't take long for me to figure out as I traced the drips back to their source.

There was a real reason for the vinyl cases and that was to keep our bedding dry in case of minor flooding on the sub. With this accommodation we could fix the flooding and still have dry bunks. This was my first experience with minor flooding on the sub. I don't think that's what the Navy's expectation was for minor flooding. The only good thing about an incident of this nature was that the culprit would be roused up and made to clean up the mess in his bed. In mine, too. It really is little pleasures on a submarine that are golden!

Let me tell you, there was nothing golden about my biggest problem after being shipped off to sea. I had sea sickness. I was mortified. I had worked hard to get here and now I was crawling on the floor puking my guts out. About the only thing I knew about sea sickness was the word. People got seasick and threw up.

Oh, it is so much, much more than that. This is how it went for me. As soon as we got out of port and the gentle up and down motion started, I started to feel bad and pretty soon I am throwing up. There is no mercy for seasick mates on a boat. If you were on duty, you were expected to be there throwing up or not.

I was told to go to the galley and get my new best friend; an empty No. 10 can. When it was really bad, and I wasn't alone, there we would be pushing our cans like dogs on all fours and vomiting. Let me tell you, it really made me excited about my choice to join the Navy. Out of the crew of sixty, there would be four or five of us. Remarkably, no one ever made fun of us. In fact, it was kind of a point of pride that we did our jobs even while being seasick. I think it showed how tough we could be, and we earned the respect of our mates.

The first year at sea was terrible. Year two was more manageable, or I got used to being sick. The more I had to deal with it and the more we went to sea, the better I could handle it. After a while I knew the first six hours or so would be difficult and then I had strategies to help me get through my time at sea and I could manage the voyage without getting sick.

I learned to seek fresh air and places where the rocking of the boat was less noticeable. The best remedy was to get up on deck by the Conning Tower while we were running above water and focus on the horizon. Watching the horizon calmed the sickness. When we had to go back inside to dive, we had to find other methods to control the queasiness.

As a result, I learned what happens in your head to cause the sickness. Your eyes and mind see the bulkheads, which are the walls in a boat, and you tell yourself to stand up straight. It is all good until equilibrium starts to wobble with the motion and then confuses the mind. Any type of pitch yaw, rolling, or movement was not good for me. There I would be on the floor with my can. My eyes and my brain were experiencing the same situation in different ways and it was not a good thing.

I learned how to use the fulcrum as my guide. The tipping point is in the rear of the boat, and the center of the back is the particular spot where there is the least amount of motion. I spent as much time in that area as I could if I started to get sick. Likewise, if we were at sea, I did everything in my power to stay out of the forward torpedo room. It was too much of a pitch and roll and I would be clutching the floor.

I also learned that after we would dive, if I would go get something to eat after the sub leveled and calmed, it was better. Getting something in my belly helped me to feel a little more solid. Not that it worked ALL the time. Hey, I was willing to try just about anything. After a while I realized that being underwater was better. There was no rocking and rolling and that helped me get back to normal. Maybe the calmness below the waves is another reason I liked submarines.

Sometimes it would just get so bad I would just think, "Just kill me. I don't care." One particular bout of sea sickness was so bad that the doctor finally conceded and gave me a shot of something. That did it. I could eat, sleep, and work without a problem. That was only one time and I never found out what was in that syringe. I guess it kind of gave me hope, though, because after that I knew if it got really bad, there was a fix.

Years later I learned that my dad got seasick, too. When he was sick, all he could keep down was saltines and milk. I am glad that I figured out a way not to have to resort to that. Food is important to me and a regular diet of milk and saltines is not high on my favorite menu items.

The fact remains that I never completely overcame it. And my civilian life at sea was still beleaguered with the malady. I still get seasick at times, particularly if I have been away from the sea for an extended period. Most of the time I am good, but then stick me in the cockpit of a sailboat and I am not okay. At least I learned how to mitigate the problem and, just like in the Navy, no one ever gives me grief for it. I like to think it is because I hide it well, or that people are impressed with my fortitude. Although it might just be because I was the boss and they either were afraid to say much (unlikely) or they were just thankful that it wasn't them.

The topics in each of the Navy schools fascinated me and learning was easy. When I got on the *Becuna*, I applied what I had learned and went after more learning with my usual enthusiasm. Having a few extra duties such as diving, I became a third-class petty officer. I started to be assigned other sailors and then headed a team in a project or task.

We participated in many exercises and war games. We also visited ports in a variety of locales including Charleston, Florida, Puerto Rico, Spain, Scotland, Rocklin Maine, St. Thomas and off the coast of Africa. Our second primary activity was making repairs. Because I was a diver, I would be a member of the teams working outside the submarine in addition to projects inside the sub. Other times we would pull into the harbor and do planned maintenance.

The *U.S.S. Becuna* was an older submarine and required a tremendous amount of maintenance and repairs. That meant we had lots of problems to solve and I got lots of experience in finding solutions. Now I see how all the experiences I was accumulating in my life were cogs on the gears that would drive my future.

Part II – My Achilles Heel Gets the Better of Me

It is a lonely life on a submarine with sixty-plus other guys, if you know what I mean. There is an old Navy joke about submariners that sixty guys go down in a submarine and thirty couples come back up. I took it as a ribbing, and you could see it was their defense against knowing that submariners were considered a "cut above" other sailors.

We came back good friends for a reason. It was because we had been vetted over the first year for our demeanor preceding being assigned to a sub. None of us had any space to get away from each other for any amount of time. The ability to be cool and keep your cool was important. If you couldn't cut it, you were gone.

We all missed female companionship. When we got back to port, any port, we all were off in search of drinks, music, and, of course, girls.

I always knew girls were my Achilles heel and it was nowhere more pronounced than the time I spent in the Navy. I figure it was likely because of the acceptance they provided. In fact, my weakness for them sent me to the brig. I couldn't help it. There must be some truth to the saying about "a man in a uniform" and being a submariner, I discovered that I could have girls around me a lot. Never really shy, I did feel awkward around girls. I compensated with the manly bravery juice known around the world as alcohol.

One girl in particular caught my fancy. Her name was Ellen and she was a student nurse at the hospital in New London, Connecticut where we were stationed at the time. We met in a bar we all called Fiddlers. She was with a group of girls and when the music would come on, my mates and I would ask girls to dance. I loved to dance. She was attractive, and she said yes. Boy could that girl dance. Together, we would make up little dance routines and moves. We were really good dance partners.

Figure 48 Ellen Garvey, me, and her sisters

Ellen was taller than me, had long red hair, and she always wore a smile on her face. It didn't take long for her to become my girlfriend. She had something like eleven brothers and sisters and even after we were a couple for a while, she still would not take me home to her family. Having a girlfriend usually meant having access to a family to go to for meals and fun times. Finally, I asked her why she never took me home to her family. She said that her sisters always took her boyfriends and she liked me too much to want that to happen in this instance.

As it happened, Thanksgiving came rolling around and she decided to bring me home for the holiday. Although her sisters were fun and attentive, her fears were never realized. I guess I liked Ellen more, too. We dated for a long time.

As a new couple, I wanted to spend more time with her. I saw the Navy as an impediment to that. Going off to sea for months at a time and then having to be on duty when we arrived back at port made it difficult. I had a solution for my dilemma. I skipped out, or went AWOL, just before Christmas in my third year of service.

At first, Ellen and I took off for New York City. I did not have much money, so we stayed in a cheap hotel, took a ride in a horse-drawn carriage in Central Park, and then promptly got stranded in a long line of vehicles on a bridge in a snowstorm. My best friend, David Graversen, was with us for the weekend and he had to be back at work the next day after the snowstorm. A police officer had just knocked on the window of the car to tell us we would run out of gas if we kept the motor running be-cause we were not go-ing anywhere for a long time. He sug-gested we lock it up and make the trek through the storm to a shelter on land at the end of the bridge. We sat in the car for a long time and then I made the decision we were just going to go for it. I maneuvered the car around the other cars in the traffic jam, drove on sidewalks and other places we prob-ably should not have been. I managed to get us off the bridge and back to base.

Figure 49 Me, Ellen Garvey, and David Graversen at Thanksgiving gathering.

Although we got back and David went to work, I did not. I was spending my time with Ellen. We spent a good bit of our time in the bars where we would meet my ship-mates. They would tell me that my absence was noticed and asked when I thought I would be coming back. I told them I intended to return when I ran out of money. That took eighteen days. It was a glorious time for me, and I didn't have a care in the world.

That wonderful time lasted right up until the moment I called home to the family at Christmas. My mother started off screaming at me. At first, I was taken aback, because even though I knew she was a screamer, I didn't have any idea what there was for her to be screaming at me. Then words like FBI and the state police peppered what I could understand, and I knew. There had been calls and visits to my parents' home in Gary. I was a fugitive and the Navy, with all its resources, was looking for me. Even at that point I looked over at the sweet face of my dear Ellen and thought to myself that it was all worth it. I knew I had to go back. I was not really deserting the military, just taking a bit of a holiday.

By the time I made my way back to the *Becuna*, I was in big trouble. I was court martialed and tried right there on the boat. I was confined to the ship until my sentence was determined, which did not take more than a few days. I was sentenced to thirty days in the brig, the military prison. I was removed from the *Becuna* and sent to the nearest military prison.

After a prisoner has been in jail a couple of days, the guards come to get you and take you to a "talk with the warden." It was humiliating. They put chains around my waist and attached handcuffs which are used to hold my wrists. It is at times like these that you realize certain things, even beyond the humiliation. It is difficult to walk with your hands cuffed to your waist. And there are no smiles, no handshakes, and the warden is all business. It was all very serious business.

As it turns out, my case had been investigated and friends I had seen during my time AWOL were questioned. We had had a lot of fun and during one particularly raucous party, a friend had snapped some photos of me being wild, and in retrospect, silly. In one photo I was lying on the floor with my legs and arms extended upward. I was doing the "dead bug" imitation. The warden did not find the photos in the least bit funny and asked, very seriously, why I was behaving in this manner. I told him I was humiliated, that this is not who I am, I was just having what I thought was fun. I admitted that this entire episode was not me and I would never be in this situation again. I knew I had done wrong.

Prison was a deterrent for me because it was where I met men who truly were criminals. I lived with two other inmates for a month, twenty-four hours a day. Like most of the rest of the men in the prison, they were true deserters and hard-core criminals who were very interested in the drug life. One of my cell mates was Tyrone.

In the brig, there was nothing to do except sit at the picnic tables and talk. Most of the inmates wanted to talk all the time about getting high, which was not my idea of fun. Tyrone was different in that along with talking about getting high, he was full of stories. Tyrone never intended to get caught and he never intended to return to the military. He had spent time in civilian jails, too. He said he didn't much mind them because you had TV, an open space, and could spend as much time in your cell as you wanted. The best part was that they fed him, clothed him, housed him, and he didn't have any bills to pay. In my mind that sounded like a place to drive me crazy. I would be trying to figure out how to build an aircraft carrier. He was very laid back about it all. He had great stories that were very different than anything I had ever experienced so they captured my attention.

Tyrone told me all about living the heroin drug life he led outside the Navy. His stories were about things I had no understanding of and, to be honest, they were shocking and captivating. Not that I would want that life. Just that some of what you hear and see in the movies is, in fact, reality for some people. It was from his stories I formulated a trick to play on the guards.

You might think that thirty days is not that long, just do the stint and then go back to the boat. After a couple of weeks, I was bored and, as is my nature, I decided to have some fun.

I picked the Sunday visit from my girlfriend to begin my ruse. I did that so they would think my visitor was acting as a mule, bringing drugs to me inside the jail. The timing was perfect. I slipped a guy some talcum powder disguised to look like a packet of heroin and made sure one of the other cell mates saw it when I passed it. Of course, my phony drug deal was reported and forced a contraband inspection. They called us all out of our cells and made us stand at attention in the hall while they went through every cell. Mattresses were tossed on the floor, pillows and other linens patted down, they even checked to see if there were any bricks loose in the walls. Then they took each of us into a private interrogation room one-by-one.

Inside the room were four people. Two were checking my body and two were checking my clothes, which were now on a bench. I was standing there naked with these two guys looking in places no one has ever looked. They used words like, bend over, spread this, lift them, and open wide. In the end, I got my wish. I wasn't bored that day.

Believe it or not, Ellen visited me during my stay in jail. She'd come in with a smile and her shapely self in a pretty dress. The other guys would tell me they knew when she had visited me, and I wondered why until I finally asked how they knew. "We could smell her," they'd say. I didn't realize they got close enough to smell me, and her scent on me.

The thirty days in the brig were neither the best that I had in the Navy, nor my proudest, either. There were lots of rules to follow in the Navy. In prison it was worse. I mean, I even had to ask permission to go pee. Because of my going AWOL all of the accomplishments and promotions I had achieved over my previous three years of service were taken away. It was a lesson learned for sure. One I knew I did not want to repeat.

In the end, Ellen and I broke up, which is pretty much the way it goes for a lot of men in the military. We would be gone off to sea for long periods and that made for a big challenge. The other challenge was that many of the girls were looking to get married. I could not even take care of myself, let alone be able to take on the responsibility of a wife and marriage. She was a nice girl; funny, pretty, and kind to me. I knew, though, that it was not a good idea to marry her.

About a month after I got out of the brig, two FBI agents came to the *Becuna* to see me. They wanted to talk to me about my time in jail. I immediately thought it had to be about the phony heroin alert I had caused. I felt I had done nothing to deserve any more punishment, so I went with them back to their offices. I was sure I would not be spending much time with them and would be walking out a free man after the interview.

They put me in a room just like you see in the movies. All the walls were made from pegboard painted white, except for one that featured a huge, wall-size mirror. We all know that the mirror was, of course, a two-way window and someone was out there watching us. There was a table in the middle of the room with chairs on opposite sides. They put me in one of the chairs and left me there. I sat there for, I think, about five minutes. It did not seem very long before one of the agents came back in. He carried one of those old tape recorders that you used to see in the cop movies. The kind that you had to push two buttons at once to record something. I know because that is just what he did. He pushed the two buttons and then stated my name and the topic of the interview. It wasn't about my heroin incident.

The topic was Tyrone, my former cellmate. Tyrone was from one of the boroughs of New York City and he knew about the tawdrier underbelly of the city. I told the FBI agents all I knew about Tyrone from our conversations in jail. He was awaiting his court-martial when I met him. I knew he was a real deserter from the military, I think the Marines, because the jail only held Navy personnel, which included the Marines. He had been out on the run for almost two years. In that time, he had grown out his hair and he had a magnificent afro, which was popular at the time. He knew he was going to be dishonorably discharged. He also knew that the civilian police would be at the prison gates when he was released, and he would be charged with forging government checks and selling heroin.

While I was in jail with Tyrone, we had plenty of time to talk. I didn't have many stories that he would be interested in hearing. He had lots of stories I was interested in hearing. He told me how he and his girlfriend would follow the mailman around apartment complexes. On the first of each month, the federal checks would be delivered in brown window envelopes. On the fifteenth of each month, the state checks were delivered in white window envelopes. They would steal the checks out of the mail-boxes. Once they got them in their hands, they would take them to a local supermarket where they knew one of the cashiers. The cashier would cash the checks, take her cut, and give them the rest of the money. They would then use the money to buy heroin, which they used and sold to other addicts.

Tyrone also told me about heroin parties, just in case I ever went to one. He obviously surmised that I would not be familiar with that kind of a situation. He was right about that, and even though I was thinking there was no chance I would find myself at a heroin party, I was a rapt audience.

He said that when you get to the party there is usually a big punch bowl in the center of a table. Everyone that comes in was supposed to put their heroin into the bowl. Then somebody pours about a half-gallon of hot water into the bowl of heroin. Then everybody gets their "works' out. He explained that "works" is what the paraphernalia used to inject the heroin is called. Tyrone said there was a trick to this party scenario. The trick is to not take a big injection first up, because it would take a long while for it to wear off. If you do, then when you wake up in the morning and you are craving more heroin, you go back to the bowl and it will probably be empty. The reason you take a small bit the first time, is so when you go back for seconds, earlier than the next morning, there is still some left and you can then take a lot more. I thanked him for the information and told him I would put it away for a future rainy day. I doubt he ever expected that I would have such a rainy day where I was going.

Tyrone told me that he would never have gotten caught if it had not been for his girlfriend's mother. The mother knew that Tyrone was married to another woman while he was seeing her daughter and doing heroin with her. The mother eventually got fed up with him and turned him in. She told the authorities who he was and where he could be found. Tyrone was shocked that her mother would do that because her daughter was involved. One day there was a knock on the door and there stood two FBI agents. They arrested him on the spot.

Mostly everyone in the jail were real deserters. They had been gone from the military for long periods of time, even years like Tyrone. Most of the talk was about drugs and the crazy things they got into while they were on the run. These people did not intend to ever come back to the service, especially the Marines, because they did not want to go to the fields of Vietnam.

I did not consider myself a real deserter. I had only been gone for a couple of weeks and then I came back on my own. Even though I knew I would be in big trouble, returning was the right thing for me to do.

Now here I was being interrogated by the FBI. I told the agent that after hearing everybody's stories, it started to get boring and I did not have such spectacular stories to tell. Instead, I devised a way to kill time and have some fun, too. I explained the phony heroin episode, ending that I figured that was what they wanted to talk about with me. After I was finished explaining the scheme, the agent had a big laugh. He thanked me and told me not to worry, because they were only interested in Tyrone.

I think I made his day. I am sure he does not often hear stories like mine, more innocent and mischievous than criminal. His body language was very positive on the way out. He shook my hand and thanked me again. Then he said I wouldn't be hearing from them again. I was good to go.

There was no way I was going to call my parents with the news of my most recent adventures. Dad would understand what it meant. Mom would just yell at me. It wasn't worth my time or the cost of the call to subject myself to the reason I was eager to leave home. Fact was that I was thinking less and less about family back home and concentrating on learning and forging my own path.

Part III – My Covert Ops

We had pulled into the Philadelphia Naval Shipyard alongside another submarine. Both were ready to undergo a shipyard overhaul, which was a complete disassembly of our sub. This is done every five or six years. With our competitive nature, we had a goal on top of the goal of completing the overhaul and that was to get it done better and faster so that we could beat the other sub out of harbor.

The maintenance meant a complete disassembly of every part of the sub to check it for damage, wear, and for upgrades. Then we had to reassemble everything, so it was in top notch, sea-worthy condition ready for war. That would take about six months. Having another sub doing the same right across the harbor meant we were pushing ourselves and the task at hand as hard as possible. We just knew we were the better crew, and we'd prove it by completing the maintenance and heading out to sea before the other sub.

As was my habit when I entered any new environment, I took the time to scope it out. A shipyard is comprised of many different buildings and each houses a different shop for different purposes. Each one is numbered and referred to by those numbers. For example, shop 26 is the welding shop, shop 51 is the electrical shop, and shop 56 the pipe shop.

The workers in the shops, we referred to them as yard birds, were mostly comprised of former members of the Navy. They mostly still wore the same kind of dungarees issued to sailors, work shirts, and hard hats with their shop number emblazoned on it. Not all the work could be done in the shops, so they would pack their tools in heavy leather totes and come to the sub with them slung across one shoulder. The bags were sturdy, the tools were heavy, and the yard birds were strong and capable men. They understood what we were doing and how we wanted work done because they had been in our place at one time.

The parts for each submarine were kept within the shops in caged sections. As time passed, I became the go-to guy when parts or supplies were needed because I knew each shop, where it was located, and what was in it. I knew where to go to get whatever we needed.

Sometimes, nah, most times, if we needed something and it was in a gated cage (that wasn't necessarily designated for our boat), I would still manage to get it. I won't say exactly how. We always got what we needed when we needed it. I made sure of that.

At least I did until one time when we were getting down to the final stages. One of the last pieces to be reassembled was the rescue buoy mechanism. We had the buoy. We had the bale and the cable. We were missing the bronze alloy release pin that made the entire apparatus work. The pin was a particular and distinct piece manufactured from a special alloy that was strong enough to keep the buoy in place on the topside of the sub despite the pull of its positive buoyancy to float to the surface as well as withstand the corrosive effects of sea air and salt water. It was built strong enough to save the crew in a disaster. The released messenger buoy would mark our position should our submarine be forced down to the bottom of the ocean and the crew trapped.

Figure 50 You can see where the messenger buoy would deploy from the top of the submarine. It is the under the oval plate next to the hatch in front of the conn tower.

That messenger buoy was not just the marker for our rescue. It was the mechanism by which the rescue bell could be attached. The bell, when attached, could rescue about ten of the crew members at a time by locating and attaching to the hatch so it could be safely opened under the water. With about seventy men aboard the sub, it would do about seven runs to get us all out to safety. The pin was a critical safety part and no sub could ever leave the harbor without it.

The pin for our ship should have been in our shed inside the cage that held a variety of things for our sub. It wasn't. It wasn't out in the shop being crack checked or repaired, either. We spread out along the pier checking shops one by one to find the pin.

Failing at finding it, we inquired about getting a new one. The formula for the alloy is detailed and complex and takes time to manufacture. It would take weeks to get the material in for the shop to machine it into a new pin. Weeks. That meant we would watch the other sub pull out well before we would be able to leave the harbor.

The search team gathered in the galley to communicate and review what we had found, which was nothing. When the information about getting a new one made was reported, groans filled the room. Because we all knew our storage shed was left open for our convenience, we also knew it would be convenient for members of the other crew to also have access to it.

In fact, some of our yard birds told us they had heard the other crew laughing and talking about how they had taken our pin out of the storage shed so they could beat us out. That's when our suspicions began to gel. Whether they threw our pin into the harbor water or took and used ours because theirs was missing or damaged, the important point of fact was obvious – they had one – and we didn't.

We knew they had a pin, and had installed it, because the buoys were in place on the topside of the boat. One can't be installed without the other. Plus, we knew their torpedoes with nuclear warheads had been loaded, too, because both the hatches, bow and stern, were under guard. They always had two guards, not just one when nukes were on board. They weren't just guards; they were armed guards.

Being typical submariners, the grumbling turned into accusations and the determination was made that we should just go get the pin they installed because it was obvious, they had absconded with ours. Heck, it might just have been OUR PIN that was INSTALLED on their sub. We were riled up and I piped up, "I'll go get it!" After all, I was the guy to go to when parts were needed. I was the guy that got us what we needed to beat those losers out of the yard.

We hatched a plan. Well, it wasn't so much a plan as just the idea of trading out a yard bird for his shirt, hard hat, and bag of tools. It just so happened that the yard bird from the pipe shop was on board and his tools were perfect for the job to be done. He was happy to get some of the mess supplies for a quick rental fee for his duds and tools. I put on his shirt, placed his hardhat with the big 3-8 low over my eyes, and threw his tool bag over my shoulder.

Now, I am not a tall guy, short, you might say, but I was strong. As strong as I was, I will tell you that bag was heavy. The weight of the bag kind of took me by surprise. Once I jimmied it around a bit, I could walk like it wasn't a load. All together it probably weighed about fifteen or twenty pounds full of tools.

By this time night had fallen, but there was no real comfort in that. My experience is that naval yards are always well lit, and even at night the lights make everything bright as daylight. It is not only for security purposes. It is also because some jobs required round the clock attention. There were always people going from shop to ship and back to the shop. Of course, there are a few shadows, and I was counting on them. In hindsight, that was as stupid a thought as any I'd ever had.

I scoped out the route I would take. We were parallel to the other submarine in the harbor. I just had to traverse a big U getting from the hatch I would ascend through on our sub to the hatch on their boat closest to where the pin would have been installed in the bow of the sub. Across the boat, down the gangplank, onto the pier, across their gangplank, onto their boat, down the hatch. Bob's your uncle. No problem.

Except there were those guards. By this time, the pistols on their hips had transformed, in my mind, to grenade launchers and canons. HUGE weapons that I knew would be aimed right at me. And, mixed in with all the sailors and yard birds walking around the harbor were the occasional yard security and officers, too. How many of them would see right through my "disguise" or recognize me from the sub and call me out, sounding the alarm that something was up?

I had said I'd do it and well, I am a man of my word, even if some would consider my promises foolish. Arrogance is a great antiseptic for stupidity. I had heard that once and never forgot it. It seemed to apply to this situation.

I poked my head up out of the hatch and my eyes surveyed the path I would follow. Not much going on, not many people around, it should be okay. I climbed up the ladder, which we kept at about a 45-degree angle. That made it easier to carry heavy loads like the bag of tools on my shoulder. I very nonchalantly grabbed a pole to help pull myself up onto the deck of the sub and started walking.

I considered whistling as I crossed the pier and walked onto those thievin' SOB's boat, thinking it would make me appear like I belonged. I decided against it. It would call too much attention to me, and besides that, I had never learned to whistle, and it was a dumb thought. I walked in silence.

I say silence, although I could swear that the jelly I felt in my legs was sloshing and sounding like waves on the beach. It isn't until you are trying to be invisible that you think about how you walk and look. Do people actually swing their arms when they walk? Do I look like I'm stiff? Am I strutting too much or sauntering? Do I look like I belong in these clothes, walking toward that sub? Like I have a reason to be there – besides stealing a part? All these thoughts were buzzing through my head as I walked out of the shadows into plain sight for God and everyone else to see.

As sailors we are trained to salute the flag when boarding a Navy boat and I had to consciously stop my hand from flying up as I stepped onto their sub. The guard would have immediately noticed it if a yard bird saluted, and he turned to face me as I boarded. Whew, I saved myself there. He looked me straight in the eye.

I think I froze mid-step. Then he looked away, turning the HUGE canon on his hip away from me. I carried on toward the hatch. I turned to put my foot on the ladder, which I expected to be at a 45-degree angle like the one on our boat. I shifted my weight down and fell through the hole. Their ladder was straight up and down, and I never even touched it. Instead, my stocky body and the heavy tool bag fell about four feet onto the hull of the sub – and knocked the air out of me as it reached up and smacked my head. I just lay there.

The racket must have been awful, or at least it was to me. I peered up through the hatch, trying to catch my breath and waiting for the guard's head, or worse, his weapon to come into view. I laid there for what seemed a week. In reality it was probably only a couple of minutes. Not hearing any steps coming toward me or seeing what I dreaded most in the circle view of the sky, I flipped over and shimmied my way between the pipes and superstructure of the boat. The sub was constructed just like ours, so I knew it like I knew the back of my hand… except for that ladder angle. Damn them. Anyway, I knew exactly where that pin would be and how to get to it. I continued crawling, toting the tool bag as quietly as possible.

There it was. Damn, it was completely installed. By that I mean the pin was in place, the air had been bled out and the hydraulic fluid had filled the system. Once that has been done, the entire mechanism was spray painted with a special thick epoxy to keep it sealed and in place. I could get the pin, but it was going to take brute force.

I rifled through the tool bag for tools. I found a wrench and a hammer and decided that would do the job. With the wrench I wore a slit into the epoxy at the end of the pin by wobbling the thing back and forth and back and forth. That went pretty quickly and pretty quietly. It was really making a mess. Once I got through that I knew what I had to do next and it wasn't going to be quiet – or quick.

I centered the wrench on the end of the pin where I knew it wouldn't slip and drew back the hammer. Pow! And I listened. No steps. Nothing. I drew back the hammer again and slammed into the wrench again. And I listened. No steps. No guard. Nothing. The noise alerted no one. I can only believe it blended in with the usual non-stop work of the shipyard.

I had anticipated a tap-tap-tap on the shoulder as I walked across the yard, as I walked across the gangplank, and then again as I was trying to dislodge the pin. It never came.

That was it, I then went back at it full force, again and again. Pow! Pow! Pow! The pin was lodged tight but starting to move. I stopped to listen. Nothing. Pow! Pow! Pow! After what seemed an age, it gave away completely, and the glycerin oozed out as the pin slid into my hands. I was golden! I had the pin! Woo-hoo! Yippee.

I slipped my precious cargo into the bag along with the wrench and hammer, leaving the mess for them. It wouldn't matter whether I tried to clean it up or not, the pin would be missing, and they would know it. The pin weighed about ten pounds, which added to the load of the bag. Funny thing, though, now that I had it in hand, the bag didn't seem to be that heavy. Must have been the adrenalin.

I reversed my path crawling along the hull of the boat until I came to the hatchway. This time I knew to climb straight up and did so with what I can only imagine was the grace of a deer.

It was all my jelly legs could do to not run and skip across the gangplank, around the pier, across our gang-plank and to the safety down the hatch on our boat. Drawing in all the discipline I had, I slowed my heart, and took the path one step at a time. When I got down the hatch and at the bottom of the ladder, I was met by the crew whooping and hollering.

They couldn't believe, first, that I would attempt it, and second, that I had been successful. We held it up and paraded it around like it was the Stanley Cup. Man, what a feeling. We celebrated and cheered. We were going to beat them out even though they had tried to underhandedly win the race. I had stopped them. I felt good. No, I felt GOOD. I was THE MAN.

Figure 51 I was a submariner ready to celebrate.

As we all dropped into our bunks, I was the one replaying the episode in my head. I knew that the beat of every hammer stroke sounded like the boom of a marching band's bass drum, echoing through the entire boat. I felt lucky, relieved, exuberant, cocky, and said a small prayer of thanksgiving.

In the morning we were all going about our duties when a long, black limousine pulled up beside the pier. I immediately knew who that would probably be, and I wasn't wrong. Stepping out of the back was a red-faced captain, the captain of what I considered the offending sub. He marched up and told the COB (chief of the boat) that he needed to see our Captain straight away. The COB snapped with a "Yes, sir!" and turned to go alert my Captain. The COB returned with him and the two met face-to-face.

We all held our breath. No one more than me. In fact, I started rolling up my sleeves knowing the next moment someone would be cuffing my wrists. There was lots of yelling and accusations. And, in the end, the pin was turned over to the other captain. He took it, returned to his limo and drove away.

We had lost the pin and would have to wait the weeks to fabricate a new one, while we would watch the other sub leave the harbor and pull out to sea. We had lost the competition. And, I figured, I would be made to atone for my deeds.

No one ever tapped me on the shoulder and asked that I follow him. In fact, I was never even reprimanded for my actions. My only supposition is that my Captain knew what had happened and knew it was me who had done it. He must have understood my motivation, just like other submariners before me. He was the captain of the sub and we had lost. I felt bad about that. Our maneuver told him that his crew was ready for war if called to duty.

After all the dust cleared, I was approached for the second time during my service in the Navy. This time it was by one of the officers in my submarine. Just like when I was in diving school, the officer said I would make a great member of an Underwater Demolition Team, the precursor to today's Navy SEALs. I was a good swimmer and I was gutsy. It would have meant two more years in the Navy. It wasn't the first time I had been the subject of recruiting for it. Even though it was an elite group, I was not sure that I wanted to stay and make that my future.

Part IV - Sub à la Pado

I could still feel the crush of the officer's handshake welcoming me to submarine service. I felt it was such an honor to be in the sub service, just like my dad. Although

I was happy to be there, after a while, my fingers were itching for something to do and my mind began to conjure up other projects I could do now to keep me busy and out of trouble. Heaven knew I couldn't afford another episode or court martial.

While walking through the passageways of the boat, I remembered back to some of my childhood inventions at the workbench in the basement of my parent's house in Gary, Indiana.

Just like my world had grown larger, my sights were set on something bigger than accidental chemistry experiments and mustard gas or injuring my friends while launching rockets into the skies back in Indiana.

I had been through submarine school and had a couple of years filled with sea-going learning about the submarine and I was a certified diver. It made sense that after some thought, I settled on the idea of building my own mini submarine. I would build a wet sub that would be capable of moving scuba divers under the sea like the famous underwater explorer Jacques Cousteau and we could get around on a sea-worthy scooter just like Lloyd Bridges had on TV. I loved scuba diving and felt confident I could be just like Lloyd, doing all sorts of things and having all sorts of adventures in the sea.

I began designing my sub while I was on board in my spare time. I knew I could buy some things, like a trolling motor. I started talking to people about parts of the project, never really sharing the entire thing. I was looking for their input and maybe, just maybe, some leads into the things I knew I would need. When I talked about how, if we were to construct a sub, we would need something for a hull. One guy mentioned that outside the base there were these jet airplane fuel tanks at a huge junkyard, along with all sorts of scrap and parts. Why couldn't we use one of the fuel tanks? He said he thought we would find the fuel tanks were about twenty feet long. Well, that set off fireworks and you knew what I was thinking, and where I would be going.

All my experiences and learning had taught me what I needed for the project and I knew how to get it, too. Grandpa's lessons in scrounging as a child were combined with lesson in comshaw in the Navy. The yard birds had materials, skills, and equipment in their shops that I did not have and undoubtedly could not afford. The practice of comshaw was common enough in the shipyard. It was the trading of items commandeered from the submarine's galley like tuna, sugar, and coffee, to get a project pushed through in a hurry before we went to sea.

Although comshaw was not generally used for personal projects, I wondered if I could use the underground currency to kickstart my own submarine building project, and maybe, company. After all, it is not often that you can get the help of the world's largest nuclear submarine base to build your own sub.

I told my friend and diving buddy, George Hallock, what I was thinking. He had many of the same kinds of skills as me, diving and mechanics, and when I explained my thinking, he was excited and decided that he'd like to be a part of this venture. My relationships with people were important to me personally. I have learned that good relationships were also important to others, too. When we had fun and people were happy, they were happy to participate in things with me. George became my helper and we would have great fun building the sub.

In my head I was thinking something like a biplane without the wings. With the estimate of the jet parts of about twenty feet, I drew a sketch and used actual measurements so that George and I, along with our scuba gear, would fit perfectly.

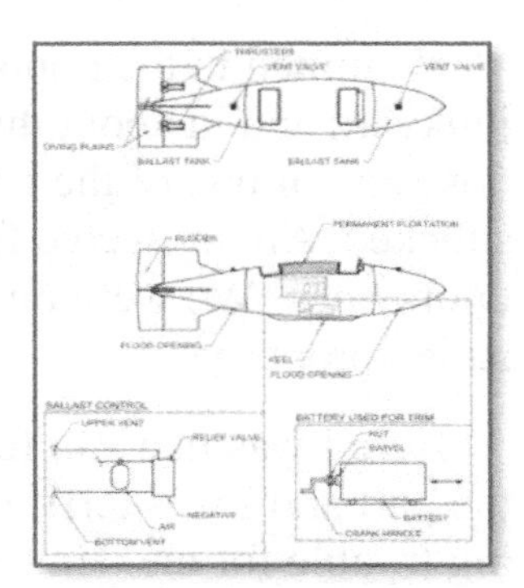

Figure 52 Schematic of the original sub design

My planning continued and I had a good idea of what I needed, including two trolling motors, not just one. I had another bit of an obstacle. I had no transportation. No wheels and I knew what I needed was big so not just any kind of wheels would do.

The buddy who had suggested the junkyard had a VW van and I asked him to take me there sometime. He told me to get in and off we went, even though it was Sunday and the junkyard was closed.

When we got there, it was obvious that the place was over full. There were belly tanks sitting out in front of the entrance. They were each about twenty feet long and I knew any one of them was just what was needed to make it work. I also knew that the junkyard wasn't going to part with it for peanuts and I barely had shells in my pocket.

My buddy said, "Don't worry, I can get it."

"How much?" I asked.

"Five bucks," he replied.

"OK. That I can get you. Let me know when you get it," I said and turned to leave.

He turned in the opposite direction back toward the junkyard and in about three minutes he was stuffing the nose end of one of the belly tanks in the van. I was shocked. About twelve feet hung out the back with the doors open. We were on the move with what I considered stolen property.

Here I was in a van full of civilians that had pinched the part and I was terrified. If I was caught, it would spell big trouble for me. How could we not get caught? I mean it was hanging out the back for all the world to see. I wasn't liking it at all. I was nervous but who was I going to tell?

When we stopped and unloaded, I handed him the five dollars. The next day I took a ride to the junkyard. I went in and inquired about buying a belly tank.

I asked, "How much would it cost?"

The salesman said, "Thirty-five dollars." Then he gave me a sales pitch saying they were fuel tanks from a fighter jet and made from high-quality aluminum.

He wasn't telling me anything I didn't know. That wasn't the point. I asked him if he delivered.

He said, "No."

"For that price," I said, "I figured you must deliver. I can only afford twenty bucks if I have to come pick it up."

He paused for a moment and finally said, "OK, you have a deal."

I paid him the twenty dollars, got a receipt, and walked out the door. I never went back. I felt I had done the right thing. I had a receipt for the tank in my hand and had made things right.

Up until that point I had no idea where we were moving my latest scored piece. I had been sharing with the boat chief about my project and he thought it was a neat idea. He was a lifer who was living off base in government housing. It was a place where there were no fences, so it would be easy to get parts, even big parts, in and out of the yard. So that's where we went with the belly tank from the jet. I showed up at his door, explaining my urgent dilemma, and he agreed to let me use his backyard. I promised I wouldn't bother him, and I made sure we didn't. George and I cleaned up after every work session and kept the whole area neat and tidy. I occasionally left cases of beer by his back door as "rent."

Now I had a base of operations to construct my sub. I had hauled in a twenty-foot belly tank from a U.S. Navy fighter jet as the first piece of the puzzle. It was exciting, just as it was when I was a kid in Gary, to be back facing the challenges of inventing. It was even more exciting because I knew I had everything I needed to complete my project – from the knowledge of how to do it, to the materials, and the assistance and expertise of skilled people to help.

When we needed some specialized work, we would have to get the sub to the base where there was a shop, people, and skills to choose from.

In order to transport and smuggle the sub into the base for the welding work, we had to cut the belly tank into three sections. Otherwise, it was much too large to get it past the guards. They would have stopped us immediately asking questions we didn't want to answer.

Each section was small enough to fit into the back of a minivan. What we needed was a bulkhead welded inside the hull to form a ballast tank. The last section we brought onto the base was the rear section, which needed the most welding for stern planes and a rudder. I had my ideas well thought-out in my head and a few rudimentary sketches on crumpled paper in my pocket.

It was a bright sunny Saturday afternoon when we walked into the No. 26 shop with the tail section and a pillowcase full of coffee, sugar, and canned tuna. We had more than enough underground currency to get help with the welding.

The shop was a welder's dream. It was full of welding machines and material needed to repair nuclear submarines. And I was seeing it all as standing ready for my command, feeling amazed that I get to use it all.

The boys in the shop greeted us with big smiles. The first thing they did was get the coffee, tuna, and sugar away from us and stowed away in their coffee room. Then the crew leader told a few of the workers to get the tail section and led us all to a big workbench. It was a very cool work area. The bench had big fluorescent lights hanging over it and a side table jutted out for mechanical drawings. It was perfect. We all stood around the table to discuss what was needed.

I explained that it was a frog man underwater delivery system. We did not lie. We just did not tell them that it was our underwater delivery system. Using the scratches on the paper in my pocket, we drew out a rough sketch on some paper and when we were done, they fine-tuned it into something the welders could use.

The boss asked if we wanted some coffee and showed us were to sit while they did the job. He told us it could take a while. As we waited, they would occasionally call us over to answer questions or explain details.

When it was done, about four hours later, it was immaculate – and perfect. We thanked the crew and headed to the door with our prize with smiles all around. Little did we know what was coming.

The tail piece at this point looked like the bottom of a rocket. More so, it looked like the type of objects we towed behind a U.S. submarine. These objects were usually outfitted with sonar equipment. Adding more to its official Navy appearance, the tank was still Navy gray, as that was the color of the fighter jet and the fins were matching aluminum as well. It looked very military.

We were outside toting the piece back to the van. It was cumbersome being about seven feet long and four feet high. There was no way we could hide something like that. Then, guess who drives by? It was a base security truck. We see the truck and look at each other. My heart was in my throat. When he slowed down and leaned out the window to say, "I have somewhere quick to go, but I'll be back to help you," I thought I would throw up. I certainly did not answer. I didn't need to because he sped off.

I thought, "Shit, now what do we do?" We could run, or we could try to get to the van, load it, and take off before he got back. It would not be good if he caught up with us later, though. We decided to just sit down and wait for him to return and take our chances. We did not have to wait long when we saw him coming around the corner of the building. His gray pickup truck stopped in front of us and he jumped out. The extra hands did make it easier to get it into the bed of his truck and we slid into the front seat with him. He asked what pier we were on and where to take us. I told him No. 8 and he hit the gas.

The drive was nerve-racking because I had no idea what I was going to do when we got to the pier where the *Becuna* was moored. He asked a few questions about what it was he had in the bed of the truck. I blurted out that it was classified. I am thinking that was a mistake, however, it worked. He said, “Sorry, no problem.”

George leaned into me and nudged me with his elbow. “Quick thinking, Tom!” Lots of things were going through my head. Congratulating myself wasn’t one of them. I was pondering what if one of the officers was at the sub when we got there? The chances of getting caught at the sub were high and that is all we needed. After two years of hard work, I did not want to lose it now.

When we got to the pier, I was all eyes and delighted to not spot one officer. There were a few sailors on the sub deck watching as we drove down the dock next to the *Becuna*. The base guard hopped out and helped us unload it. We thanked him, he shook our hands, returned to the truck, and drove off. Our shipmates gathered round and started to interrogate me. “What the hell is that, Pado?”

“Oh, just some stuff we are making,” I replied.

“Is that part of that sub you guys are building?” hollered one of the crowd.

“I’ll explain the whole story as soon as we get this thing out of here and I can get back,” I said as George and I scurried away with the piece.

While I toted the piece up the dock, George ran up the hill to get the van. I waited at the end of the dock, on my last raw nerve, for George to arrive. It felt like it took him forever. When he finally pulled up in front of me, we loaded the van and drove off. Unbelievably, getting off the base was without incident. It had been a close, razor's edge call and I did not want to repeat it. I felt relieved that we were close to being finished with the building phase. Just a few more steps and we would be able to test drive our new submarine.

When we got back to the *Becuna* we spilled the beans. It was pretty evident from what they had seen that I was telling the truth and we all had a pretty good laugh about being helped back by the security patrol.

I was pretty much a loner in the Navy. I did most things by myself. I made it a point not to wear a badge announcing what I was doing. I was always happy in my own head to be building something rather than showing it off to everyone. It goes back to my feelings that I was not as good as everyone else. I thought they'd figure I was nuts, so I did what I liked to do. It was part of my ethos, part of the chip I carried on my shoulder that shouted, "You ain't telling me that (I can't do it)."

You might have thought that the yellow we painted the finished sub would have been a statement thumbing my nose at naysayers and showing off. No, it was not. I chose to paint the submarine yellow for a practical reason. Yellow is the best color to see things under water because of the turbidity of the water. You can see yellow stand out from the background easier than any other color. I didn't want to take any chances in losing my masterpiece, my underwater motorized baby.

The day finally arrived. It was a warm July afternoon when George and I prepared to launch the submarine at the swampy retention pond, which was the site of a massive dirt excavation from the interstate highway boom in the early 1960s.

Our first speedbump was the simple fact that we had no trailer to get it to the launch site. Some guys down the street from the chief's house did, and in those days, a case of beer opened lots of doors and paved many paths, including getting our yellow submarine to the pond for launching.

Once we arrived, there were a few things we had to do to prepare for launch. Because we were eager, getting the battery in and installing the scuba tank seemed to take forever, although I know it was just a few minutes.

It was such an amazing feeling to put the sub to water and to have it take off and work just like I had planned. We were in the freshwater pond for over an hour; diving and driving. I was excited. I was also proud because I had had an idea and achieved all that it took to make it a working sub. It had taken a lot, and I had done it.

Now, years later, I am still impressed with the achievement. Not just because it was a project "on the side" but because it really took all kinds of shit to make it happen. I had to creatively procure parts, explain my ideas, teach a friend how to do many things, find transportation, get parts made, and everything else, and I did it all with a few pennies and nickels. I didn't even have dimes. We made a working treasure out of trash, something from used stuff, from junk. It still shows me what is possible when you combine good ideas with effort. It shows me what is possible when you take action on what you believe is right and worthy.

Even though that is a lesson that I can voice today, it was a lesson that became lodged deep inside. It was a lesson I would use later in life, without consciously calling it to mind.

On that day, our conscious thoughts were on the task at hand. We were using our treasure to explore the depth of the freshwater pond. To our surprise, once we had gotten into the water, we discovered people had been dumping a lot of things into the pond. We were dodging 55-gallon drums, a big old barbecue grill, a washing machine, and car parts. The neatest thing we found in the pond was an old Ford car. It was still sitting upright. We stopped the sub, got out, and looked around the car, wondering if there were any dead bodies inside or maybe something valuable. We found nothing like that. We did find a bunch of old fish and one nice-sized crawfish with her tail full of eggs. She was on the front seat and we startled her. Immediately she assumed the defensive stance with claws raised and ready to bite whoever was going to take up the challenge. She was protecting her babies, just as we would.

We moved on to let her settle back to her family and continued looking around the car. We managed to open the glove box and trunk. We didn't find anything there either. The car was simply a great home for the sea life. We left it like it was and went on our merry way. As we moved through the water, the fish would dart every which way while we were cruising, sometimes running into the sub. It really made them crazy.

By this time, dusk was falling, and we wanted to go back and celebrate our success with our mates. We left the 20-foot, 1,400-pound yellow submersible in the lake. We took the scuba bottle out and removed some of the electrics, just in case someone found it and tried to surface it. However, we felt it was safe at the bottom of the pond where few people would come driving by. There was a good chance when we returned tomorrow, it would be right where we left it. In fact, it turned out that we did not return until the following Saturday.

We had left the sub at the bottom of the pond for a whole week. As we arrived, we saw fresh tire tracks in the sand and my pulse jumped a bit thinking someone might have found our prized possession. We followed the tracks and at the end of the trail sat a new Oldsmobile with a red base sticker, indicating the owner was a Navy officer. In my mind that meant he was most likely an Annapolis graduate and submarine officer as well.

I looked up the water's edge and there he stood, looking out toward a dog running at him. The dog approached, and the officer bent down to retrieve a stick from the dog's mouth. As he did, he turned to throw it and looked right at us. We were stepping out of a van hitched to an empty boat trailer and I immediately knew he was wondering why two guys were coming to an empty retention pond with an empty boat trailer.

We opened the van and pulled out our scuba gear as he walked over and struck up a conversation. Obviously, his foremost interest and first question was what were we doing? I figured it was time to have some fun. I told him we were going to pull a yellow submarine out of this swamp. He was not amused. Instead he asked how it got there.

I told him how I had found some old parts just lying around and built it over the last couple of years. I explained we had tested it for the first time just last week. Then I said that after diving for a while it had gotten late and so we decided to just leave the vessel in the water, figuring it would be a good way to do a leak test, too.

He was still not laughing, nor do I think he was believing what I was saying neither. However, it was apparent he was not going to leave until he had sorted out the truth. I am sure he thought there was no way in hell that there was a sub in the swamp.

Figure 53 The Pado Submarine

He saw that we were in the Navy so pressed further, asking what boat we were on. When I told him that we were on the *USS Becuna,* he replied that he knew my captain very well. His tone and stance said clearly that if we did not bring a yellow something out of the swamp, George and I would be headed to the psychiatrist or to the doctor for drug screening. After all, it was 1969, a year filled with marijuana, LSD, and plenty of youngsters who thought, “we all live in a yellow submarine.”

We finished getting our gear ready and told him it would take a little while to get to the sub and get it up. He told us he would wait. Feeling his eyes boring holes into our backs, we entered the swamp, fully kitted out in scuba gear. With visibility of about thirty feet, it wasn’t long before we could see the yellow color in the distance. The sub was right where we had left it, watertight. It looked amazing sitting on the bottom of the pond with all the fish taking up residence around it. I immediately saw us as the divers in an aquarium, with the sub and fish swimming around. I liked this image.

We installed the scuba bottle, the fuse, and tested the thrusters. There had been no flooding, no leaks. Everything worked. George and I looked at each other and flashed thumbs up. We drove up toward the officer. I was eager to see his reaction. We blew the ballast tank and we surfaced the yellow mini sub perfectly about fifty yards away from the navy officer. We drove it right up in front of him. And what did he say? Yep, he swore like a sailor.

"Son of a bitch, mother f----r, where did you get that?" he said.

It was like he had forgotten everything I had just told him. I repeated the whole story. This time he believed me. This time I got some respect. I felt I had gotten the stamp of approval from a submarine officer, and that was very important to me. I may have been the lowest rank sailor in the Navy, but I was captain of my own submarine.

I often wonder, on the days following that first surfacing, when that officer was back at sea in his nuclear submarine with everything running smoothly, did he chime into the chitchat with, "You won't believe what I saw this weekend!"

My thoughts were not just about the sub we had crafted. Time was drawing near to the end of my Naval career. I had decided that I didn't want to stay and become a lifer. I didn't know what I would do after I got out, either.

When I left the Navy as a seaman apprentice, it was the same rank that I had when I first entered the Navy. I looked back and thought I had learned quite a bit about a lot of things, including myself. I built up my self-esteem. I learned I was not as dumb as I always thought I was. I was now confident that I could learn anything. I also learned I could build anything that I wanted. Sister Isabel would have been so proud of me, I just knew it in my heart.

I transported the yellow submarine back home to Gary. I hadn't told my parents about the submarine, so when I arrived with it, they were surprised. Dad was impressed. Mom kind of sniffed and said, "More junk. Where are you going to put that thing?" After which she turned and walked back into the house. In that moment I realized that I was living my own life.

When I arrived back home to Gary myself, I was much wiser and filled with knowledge that would serve me well over the coming years. More importantly, I received an honorable discharge which opened the doors for new opportunity to go to college on the G.I. Bill. It was time to start new adventures.

Implications for My Future

It's not uncommon to hear former soldiers and sailors say that the military "made me into a man," because it does do that. It was a true turning point in my personal maturity.

Beyond maturity, which also comes with time and experience, I learned from my experience in the Navy that there is a difference between being left to grow up on your own as a boy and being alone to forge your own path in life. There really are repercussions and benefits to making your own decisions, and you have to live with the consequences.

I was humbled by my mistakes. Going AWOL was not one of the best decisions I made. By going AWOL, I was exposed to the way of life many young people took with drugs and crime. It made me even more determined to avoid that trap in life. It also made me see the importance of thoughtful consideration rather than jumping at every impulse.

Just as being humbled by mistakes was an important lesson, I was proud of seeing what I, alone, could achieve. Perhaps it is because of my industrious nature, curiosity, or persistence, that I built the mini-sub. I learned that despite my feelings of inadequacy in so many areas of life, the areas where I did have strengths could shine bright.

I had discovered that in addition to telling stories and being funny, I genuinely liked people around me. Not all the time, because my mind was involved with ideas, but enough to understand that people liked to be around me. I always had someone who would want to go along with me in whatever direction I was headed. It might be to a bar to drink and dance, or to build a sub.

My loner tendencies gave me the opportunity to think about my own ideas and take the time to develop them. Doing that is what helped me achieve the title of Education Petty Officer. I figured out why we were doing what we were doing and then shared that knowledge with others to help them understand. Even though stripped of that achievement officially, I still had it in my heart and soul.

I knew why I had earned it, and I knew why I had lost it on my record.

Just like when I was a boy, I had little fear about outcomes or results, so taking action seemed a natural state for me. I learned what sets me apart from others. I like to take action, especially when it is based on my own ideas. Other people only do what they are told to do, like those who became the lifers, and they like it that way. That's fine because we need these career sailors in our great Navy. Still others have ideas, but never implement them or take action to create something based on their ideas.

Although I still wanted recognition and approval, in the end, I was less concerned about "fitting in" for myself personally. I didn't want to "fit in" with the military and that way of life. I wanted to live a life of my own making and on my own terms.

I loved the structure and everything I learned in the Navy. I wanted to take that learning and my ideas in my own direction. Not that I knew exactly what that direction was going to be. It didn't matter, because at that point I had confidence that whatever I could think of or envision, I could create.

Getting out of the Navy was a relief. I appreciated what I had gotten while I was there. What I didn't like was the day-to-day living. It was a long, hard grind. The work I did was hard, physical labor and the beds at night were uncomfortable. The pay was a pittance. The four years had taken me away from Cindy and even though I tried to replace her, nothing – or no one – stuck to my heart like she did.

I felt proud when the chief and others told me that I was an ideal submariner. I loved submarines and all the machines I had learned to operate and repair. I was immersed in the science of them as deeply as I was in the sea while inside them. Every day I was amazed by them and how they worked. The immensity of their weight, their purpose, their speed, everything was larger than anything I could have ever imagined in life.

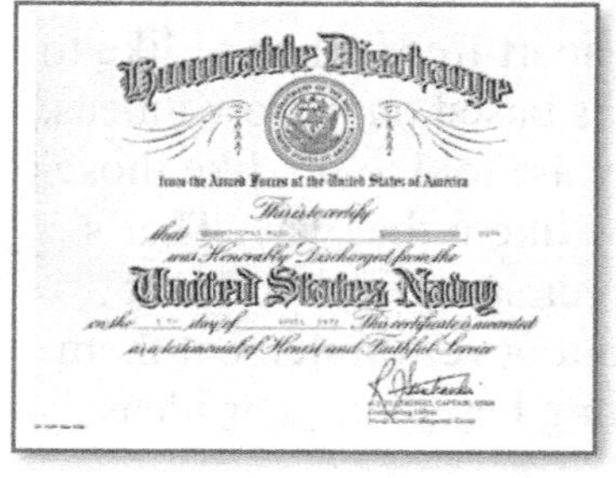
Honorable Discharge
from the Armed Forces of the United States of America
This is to certify
that
was Honorably Discharged from the
United States Navy
on the day of This certificate is awarded
as a testimonial of Honest and Faithful Service

Figure 54 I was proud to serve... but eager to go home.

As much as I loved the environment, I knew the Navy was controlling me and where I was going. They told me where to go, when to go, and what to do while I was there. They cut my hair, made me dress a certain way, and told me when I could go out for some fun. I wasn't making any money, and, in my mind, I didn't see any future for me there. They had a plan for me, and it didn't comport with any plan I had for myself. There was a hankering for freedom that was burbling in my belly. I craved making my own decisions, creating my own future, being the master of my own world. I craved freedom.

I didn't realize at the time, but the only place I would ever feel free was running a company of my own. I am not ambitious in the sense of seeking positions and titles. Titles mean very little to me, so I was never out to necessarily become a vice president or president or C-anything of a company. I knew in my heart that I could have any position I wanted or title that came with it. The Navy helped me to see a pattern I seemed to live out in every situation I encountered. People obviously saw things in me that I could not see myself. I rose up. I was handed responsibilities. I was offered challenges. I was given tasks, projects, and opportunities that others could not handle, and I always seemed to rise to the occasion and perform well.

Section Four - Going Home and Starting Life

Part I – Back to Gary

After my discharge from the Navy, you know where I was headed. Yep, back to good ol' Gary, Indiana. It was not accomplished with a smile on my face. It was what I considered my only option at the time. Back into the house with my parents. I had managed to avoid combat in the Vietnam War and still serve my country honorably, but I was back in the midst of the battles between my parents. The battles were fewer and not so fierce between them. While the conflicts had deescalated at home, the neighborhood was getting more and more dangerous. My dad had put seven locks on the door. When I saw that, the first thing I thought was, *"What if there was a fire?"* It would take a while to get the locks undone, and if anyone wanted to break in, all they had to do was break a window. The atmosphere was tenable. I still realized that there was still no loving banter. I realized my parents were just existing together in the same house.

Straight away I took a job working in the parts department for the Summerfield trucking company in Gary. Employees got a GM discount to purchase a truck and I took advantage of it. I bought a V-6 GMC half-ton pickup truck. It was tan. It was beautiful, and it was mine! I immediately borrowed a trailer and drove back to Connecticut to get the yellow submarine. It was coming home, too.

During the ride home, the submarine drew a crowd everywhere it went. Gas stations, restaurant parking lots, and even in the rest stops along the highways. There was a lot of energy around it and it was a grand time telling people about how it was built and what it was. In my head I kept thinking, "*This is so cool.*" I was getting recognition for my creation, just like I had always craved as a kid. It WAS cool, in oh, so many ways. You can believe that was a trip accomplished with a big smile, even though my face was turned toward Gary once again.

One thing I had learned in my time away was that the people with the big jobs, even in the Navy, were the people who went to college. I knew you had to do that if you wanted what I wanted. I needed money. I needed money to have things and buy things and do things. I wanted to travel, especially to Australia, because of the stories my dad had told of that place. I wondered if maybe I could get there in the Navy. I wanted to enjoy the food and culture and that was restricted in the service. I wanted freedom and time. Money was the answer. I knew I could not get anything like what I wanted by staying in the Navy.

To get what I wanted, I always knew I needed to go to school. With my grades, and lack of money in my pocket, I never saw it as an option. That is until someone told me about two things. The first was that with my honorable discharge, I qualified for college under the GI Bill. The second was that after I turned twenty-one years old, my grades no longer mattered. I did not even have to take SATs or ACTs or any other test to enroll in classes. What a new world that opened to me and I was determined to take full advantage.

I wanted to learn more about physics. Physics fascinated me. I did not have enough money to go to school full-time and I really, really did not want to live with my parents any longer. School was the first step out of my parent's house. I signed up for one class at Indiana University Northwest in Gary. Yep, that class was physics and I excelled in it.

I met a guy. Isn't that how many stories begin? Well, I did meet a guy named Ron Kurth who was a member of a local diving club called the Aquatics. The club was sponsored by the Burns Funeral Home. That might seem an odd arrangement to some though it didn't take me long to figure out it was for a good purpose. The purpose of the diving club was to recover dead bodies from the lakes and rivers of northern Indiana. At first, I thought, "No, nope, that's not for me," and refused to participate.

Figure 55 I was happy to dive with the club in Gary.

A bit later the club was going on a sport dive. They invited me along and I went. It was a great day. We spearfished, swam, and dove all day long. I had found like-minded friends finally and it felt good. So good, that I started spending more and more time with them. Eventually, one of them said, "If you're not doing anything, come by the funeral home and hang out with us. We have a dorm upstairs where all the ambulance drivers hang out while they wait for calls to make ambulance runs."

I figured, why not? When I arrived, it was a nice place. The funeral home was opulent with red carpets and fine furniture. It was quiet and, yes, peaceful.

There were four apartments upstairs. One was for the ambulance drivers and the three others were for the staff, the embalmers, and their families. Not all the apartments were occupied when I took the tour.

There was a six-car garage where the business's vehicles were housed. Next to that were two morgues. One was for Christians and the other was used for those of the Jewish faith. That surprised me at the time. I did not know that different religions had different ways to attend to followers after death and during the funeral rites.

Figure 56 Burns Funeral Home

Upstairs in the dorm for the ambulance drivers there was a color TV and, who would have guessed, several girls that hung around. Not only had I found like-minded friends, there were girls, too. You do not have to guess the rest. I found a home. What I did not know was I really did find a home because eventually I would be a live-in resident of the funeral home.

One day I asked the guys what they did down in the morgue. They told me to wait until the boss leaves and they would take me down and show me.

We waited and a few hours later, went downstairs to the morgue. When we walked inside there was a cadaver lying on the table. It was all open because a pathologist had just done an autopsy. That made it the perfect time to see a cadaver. Other people might have been bothered by the sight, but not me. I was absolutely amazed at what people looked like inside their body. The lungs looked very different than I had imagined, more like a sponge than a balloon. The liver was also much larger than I expected. All in all, I got a biology course on human anatomy with a real human body.

Shortly after I began hanging out at the funeral home with my diving friends, laws changed, and the home could no longer run an ambulance service. With the ambulance service eliminated, they still needed someone to pick up the dead bodies and bring them back to the funeral home. They were looking for an employee to do this. One of the job requirements was that the person had to live at the funeral home because many calls came in at night and they wanted someone right there to provide the service. With all the ambulance drivers gone, the dorm was empty. Perfect for a young, single guy like me.

Part II – Funeral Home Life

Since my visit to the morgue, I had developed an interest in what they were doing and none of it bothered me. They decided I was a good candidate for their live-in, nighttime body pickup technician, for lack of any other title. I took the job. Since it was a night-time job, I kept my day job at Summerfield to save money for college.

The dorm made a great apartment, especially with no rent, no electric bill, and no phone bill. And, oh yeah, the color TV stayed, too. The biggest perk, though, was that I no longer lived at home with my parents. I was free from the battleground. Even though the battles had become less frequent, and less fierce, it was not a place from which a young man could really start dating. Plus, after being away so long, who wants to live with their parents anyway, even if they were nice? Not me.

At the time I started working at the funeral home, Gary was changing. The steel mill was downsizing, reducing the labor force from 27,000 employees to about 5,000. With 80 percent of the workers being laid off, the area was seeing a dramatic economic change. The mix of families in the neighborhoods was changing and it showed up at the door of the home.

Even with that, when I was offered a full-time job by Mr. Burns, I accepted and left the parts counter at Summerfield's. Being on staff at the funeral home came with a variety of responsibilities. I drove cars and hearses in funeral processions, I set up for services, ran errands, and whatever else I was asked to do.

The home had a generous parking lot that was well lit. The local kids would congregate and play there. The owner, Eddie, was constantly sending us out to chase them away. It did not work too well, because the kids returned day after day.

One warm summer night, I decided to take another approach. It was a quiet night at the home with no showings, so I stood at an open window and watched the swarm of kids, probably ranging in age from ten to fourteen. It was a diverse group made up of a mixture of salt and pepper races, and some in-between.

The group grew closer and we started a conversation. Of course, the first thing they wanted to know was why I was not chasing them away. There was an easy answer, and I shared it with them. "No, I'm not chasing you away," I said. "I understand your situation."

That did not create much of a connection apparently because one of the kids hollered out, “You got any water? We’re thirsty.”

I thought *here is my chance.* I said, “Just a minute. I’ll be back.” I went into our waiting room that had coffee, soda pop, and bags of chips. I got a big pitcher and filled it with ice and cola. I picked up some paper cups and took them to the window. I scanned the crowd to find the one I judged to be the leader of the pack and handed the pitcher and cups to him. He shared it with the kids and returned it to me empty. From that point on, I had a great relationship with the kids.

That relationship paid off and grew. After making $150 per month in the Navy, when I got a $150 paycheck for one week, I was flush with money and was eager for the opportunities that a nice long day off offers. I had a (bad) habit of leaving my wallet tossed on the dash of the truck, and that day, I had left the bank and gone back to the home to plan my day. Not too long later while I was in the office, three of the kids came in with one of them carrying my wallet. Every single dollar was still in it as it was handed to me. I realized my mistake and gave them $5 as a reward, a fee for my learning, and mostly, my gratitude.

They were blown away. They said, “Thank you,” as they ran out the door all excited and chattering. Before they got out the door, I heard one of them say, “That’s $1.87 for each of us.”

Over the following weeks, I grew friendships with the boys. One day I was taking a girlfriend to the beach, so I asked them if they would like to come along. They were excited about the idea. I told them to go ask their parent’s permission, adding that we would probably not be home until after dark. Every one of them came back with positive answers. Off we went.

No trip to the beach is complete without drinks and snacks and that meant we had to stop at the market. I left them in the truck. When I returned with my purchases, they were all quiet and smirking at each other. My eyebrows were raised. I looked a little closer. No one seemed to be hurt or running.

When we got to the beach, I discovered there was something extra in the bed of my pickup besides a passel of boys. Guess what it was … only the best thing for a hot day at the beach … a nice, big watermelon. When I asked where that had come from, no one had any idea. We enjoyed every juicy bit of that watermelon, no questions asked.

Even though the beach was just a short drive away, none of the boys had ever been there. I could not believe that. It was another world to them, and they had a great time. I dropped off a bunch of happy kids at the end of that day … and I was a happy guy going home, too.

As time went on, we never had a problem with the kids when we had a showing or funeral. I would tell them one was scheduled, and they would respectfully take their activities elsewhere.

It got around time for my birthday and by this age I did not say much or expect much. I do not know how they found out. They had all chipped in and presented me with two gifts. One was a shoehorn tie rack and the other was the busiest tie you could ever have. They knew I wore a tie at work, and I have to admit that these two presents meant the world to me. The next day I wore that loud tie to work. Eddie came in, took one look at me, shook his head and said, "Christ, Pado, are we running a circus here?"

Figure 57 Eddie Burns

Eddie Burns reminded me of W.C. Fields with his big black suit and big cigar. He had a dry sense of humor that I loved. If any of us came in to work and no showings were scheduled, we would try to get away with not wearing a tie. The scene would be repeated time after time.

Eddie would take a look at me and say, "Christ, Pado, you're off today, right?"

Of course, he would know I was scheduled to work. I would reply, "No, Eddie."

"Well, you don't have a tie on," he'd say.

I knew that he expected us to look good and represent his business well when people would come in to arrange services for a loved one who had passed or pay a bill. Eddie was a good businessman. That was just one of the lessons I learned from him.

I spent a lot of time sitting in the lobby watching kids play in the parking lot. I never chased them away because I knew we had a relationship and would watch out for each other – and for Eddie's business.

I was only allowed to pick up corpses from the morgue. I would take them back to the funeral facility and watch the embalming process. I learned so much during this year about the human body and related it to diving. I came to understand how tissue, including organs and muscles, could react to the differing pressures. It was a hands-on course in diving anatomy.

On my nights off, I would go to my favorite watering hole called The Red Barn in Miller. Even though Cindy was gone from Miller, there was much drinking and dancing left there for me. I even ran into some of the people I had known from my lifeguard days. One girl asked what I was doing now that I was home from the Navy. I told her I was taking physics classes part-time at IU's annex in Gary and working at Burns Funeral Home. A dip and a spin and, whoosh, that girl was gone. I mean vaporized! She was just the first that disappeared once I mentioned my job at the funeral home, so I learned quickly to mete out my answers to questions of that sort.

Most of the girls would stay away once I told them. Then one night when I gave my answer, the girl of the moment grabbed my arm and said, "Gee, what's it like working there?" Of course, my first thought was I think she is curious and asking me to take her there. This one might stick around. Over my time as an employee at Burns, there were a few girls who were interested. Not many, but a few. I called them the Funeral Enthusiasts to my diving club friends. They understood.

Having found an interested soul, I asked the girl if she would like to go and have a look now since no one is there at night. That was it. We got into my truck and off we went to show her what she, and everyone else, was missing. She was excited. Just as I would every time thereafter, I gave her a tour of the home. It was beautifully decorated, and if there were any bodies in house, I shared a quick peek at them, too. I showed girls cremated remains in little cans that were waiting to be buried with their loved ones when they died.

I have to say that everyone who worked there were extremely professional. They respected the dead. What they said and how they worked showed this respect always. I did, too, even with these midnight tours, because it was the right thing to do.

At the end of the tour, we would end up back in my apartment. It was exciting for them, and for me, too. A few times I would take them home in the family car at four or five in the morning. One time I was taking a girl back to her home in Aetna. As luck would have it, I got stopped by the police. All the police around town knew the cars from Burns Funeral Home. It was not normal to see a big gray limo out and about at four in the morning. The police officer approached my window, shined his flashlight at me and asked me what was up with Eddie's car. I told him I worked for Burns and lived at the funeral home. I was just taking a female visitor back to her home. He flashed the light beam into the back to see the girl way in the back. Lucky for me, he grinned. He said, "Be careful driving," and let me go on my way.

You can learn a lot of things working and living in a funeral home. For instance, one time I was driving along with a body in the back on my way to the home. The vehicle had a window between the area where the body was placed and me as the driver. I usually left it open. I was driving along on Seventh Avenue and hit a bump. A sound came out of the back and startled me. It was the body gurgling. The jolt when I hit the bump allowed some gas and liquid to escape from its mouth. The noise and smell were both alarming. Most people would have been scared. I knew what it was and that it was a normal process in the body of a dead person. They were not alive, and it did not bother me. Once again in my life, I felt I was doing something that many other people could not. Patterns were emerging, and I was beginning to see and accept them.

Another thing I learned during my time at Burns still sticks with me. A lot of people die at two o'clock in the morning. I had just picked up a body from Mercy Hospital when someone referred to it as the two o'clock rush, explaining that it was common. I have often tried to find out why people die on the two o'clock hour. Other than a reference to people with diabetes, I have learned nothing definitive for an answer. I have since been told that the real reason for the increase in deaths at two in the morning is because if someone died near the end of a shift change, the staff would leave them until the new shift came on duty. I guess they did not want to handle the paperwork.

All in all, I found the funeral home a very interesting place. That was not only when I was first introduced to the place, but as I spent more time there. I was impressed by the people, their professionalism, and the thoughtful way in which they did their work. I was also fascinated by what I learned about people and their bodies, and the world's cultures there. Even with all that, and the fact that I was free to live on my own, I knew it was not what I wanted to do for a career.

Part III – Seeking Opportunity

After hanging out with the diving club friends for a while, I was eager to show them how my homemade sub worked. It was October and the beaches were virtually deserted. By this point, the sub had been painted a bright and sporty lime green and was a sight to behold on its way through the middle of Miller, Indiana. I hauled it to the Lake Street boat ramp to launch it with a group from the club. Tony Garbus and I would pilot it once launched. I never suspected what would happen.

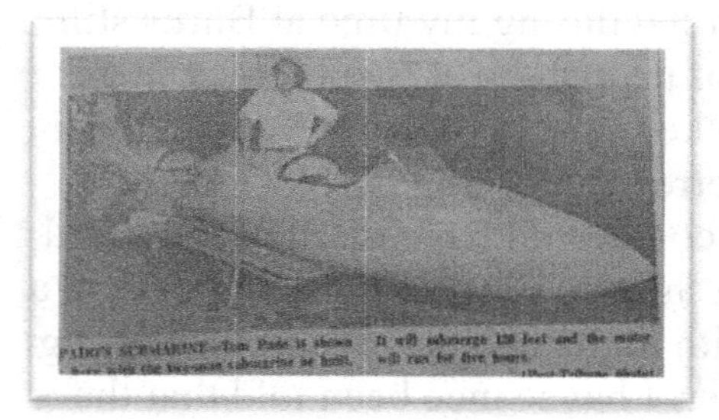

Figure 58 The U.S.S. Banana comes to Indiana

We launched it, and Tony and I dove and coursed around the shore for about an hour seeing nothing except sand. We finally surfaced and sought the shoreline. We got our bearings and headed to shore. We were shocked when we got there because the beach was filled with cars.

There were so many cars that had flooded the shoreline, filled with people who had come to see what was going on. Apparently, a local radio station had caught word of something happening and announced a sighting of a lime green submarine heading to the lake through Miller. The response was remarkable and when Tony and I emerged from the water with the sub, we were instant celebrities.

Two weeks later the Gary Post-Tribune sent a journalist out to write an article about me and the sub. I was proud of the accomplishment. It was a brief brush with celebrity that gave me a taste of what could be, and a yearning began to grow inside me. Not necessarily for celebrity, although I did enjoy that. No, I was yearning for more knowledge. I wanted to know, and do, more.

Figure 59 The Pado sub makes a splash in Gary (Gary Post-Tribune)

To this day, I see potential in objects. My ability to reuse and recycle what others see as useless junk is, according to some, legendary. For example, when I look at a Toyota Prius, I imagine turning it into an underwater craft

Figure 60 The Pado sub, the USS Banana being launched for a group outing.

that moves fast. All my life I have tinkered with things turning them into something, primarily because I never had any money, and I wanted something I couldn't afford. This ability, some might call it a quirk, has been a personal tool of mine that has made me comfortable in my old age. I have found great business and financial success building something I want out of things others see as useless junk. We will come back to that later.

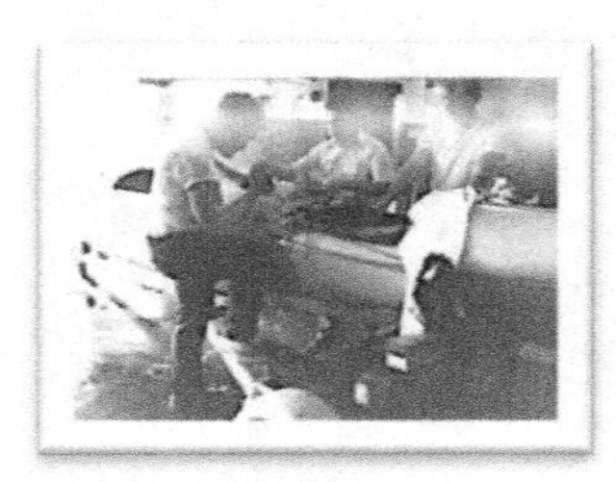

Figure 61 Tinkering with the sub

During the time I was hanging out with the diving club and working at the funeral home, I had a good friend named Nick Tarullo. He was a guy with a dry sense of humor and a killer intellect. We had gone to high school together and after I got out of the Navy we reconnected. We had several interests in common, and over time hung around together tinkering with the sub and diving together.

Nick's wife, Alice, was the person who provided a lead for the next step in my path. She learned about a school in Florida that she said was perfect for Nick and me. It was the Florida Institute of Technology, or FIT, and she said it offered all the classes that would be of interest to guys like us.

Nick and I took the bait. We got in my truck and drove down to FIT to check out the school. We agreed with Alice that it was perfect for us and we both filled out applications to attend. Nick was so smart that he was offered a scholastic scholarship that provided a full ride. I was not that lucky. I had no SATs to give the school. My application was completed with my Navy records and the grades for the few classes I had taken at Indiana University. I was accepted. The difference was that I had to pay for all my tuition. With the help of the GI Bill, a loan, and a few extra jobs, I was able to scrape together enough money to attend.

Now I see that the scraping and scrounging was important learning for me as I transitioned from a former Navy submariner into a serious college student. One part of it was letting go and selling my beloved submarine to the Aquatics diving club. I was sad to see it go. It was easier to let go when I knew it would be used. Because of my naval experience, I was able to get a job as assistant to the diving instructor. And, who knows why, or how it happened, I got the position of dorm director of a co-ed dorm. Go ahead, laugh. We all know it was like putting the fox in charge of the henhouse. I was giving it my all to go, because I knew college was important and I would make it memorable.

Implications for My Future

For a guy who had no idea what would happen once he left the Navy, I had landed somewhere I had never even considered would be part of my story – a funeral home of all places. Just like so many other parts of my life, this one seemed to fit right into place and what I got from the experience was of great benefit to me.

First, I learned about the anatomy of the human body and that fascinated me. I never imagined what the inside of people was really all about: muscles, organs, tendons, and how all the parts and pieces fit together and worked together. I even got to see what disease and injury does to a body. That gave me a new understanding, and respect, for the one place we have from which to live our entire lives – our body.

Eddie Burns taught me the value of having guidelines and standards for a business. He wanted all his employees to behave a certain way and look a certain way. He was determined to run his operation in a professional manner that represented the values of his business. Today we call it branding, back then it was just the way he ran his business.

While he was one to chase away the boys congregating on the blacktop, I figured out that by treating not only customers with kindness and respect, treating these young people that way made it possible for everyone to get what they wanted and needed. Building relationships in a slightly different way, that social aspect of who I am was once again a powerful tool in my pocket.

Between Eddie and the blacktop boys, it was once again reinforced that treating people, of all levels, colors, nationalities, and genders with kindness, respect, and honesty was the way to really create bonds and authentic relationships that would benefit all. My ability to look at the whole picture, find the problem, and fix it with a more common-sense approach was taking root. I realized that just saying, "Don't do that. Go away," was not the best way to handle a problem. Instead, it is better to recognize the real problem and fix it at its base.

Many of the things I did were just because they were fun. They were distractions from setting my sail in a direction and making time toward a goal. Fun can be fun, but sometimes it can get boring when it has no real depth to it. Real fun to me is thinking and learning and building something from nothing. That was part of what was missing during this period. There wasn't much of any challenge to keep my attention and I squandered my attention all over the place.

Therefore, the final lesson I learned from this chapter in my life was about distractions and focus. It was interesting to be part of the dive club. It was interesting and unique to be not just an employee at the funeral home. I was a resident. I had a few coins to spend and a bit of a niche fascination with some of the females I met. It wasn't enough. I wanted more. I wanted something else and this just wasn't it. So, I had to leave behind the interesting distractions, and get focused on what it was I wanted. I wasn't quite sure what that would turn out to be. I had some goals to reach and the only way I would reach them would be to set my attention and focus ahead.

Section Five - Higher Learning and Institutions

Part I - Florida

Leaving Gary and my part-time studies in Physics at Indiana University to enroll full-time at the Florida Institute of Technology (now called Florida Tech) was both exciting and unnerving for me. It was the best opportunity I saw for the future.

I told my parents I was leaving town to go to school in Florida. Apparently, Mom had been worried that I was going to be a funeral director because she expressed relief that I might go to school and find a 'real' career. I admit I had been without much direction. Her tone and words made me feel like she felt I would never amount to anything. The old feelings I had when I left home reared up, but this time, I had more wins in my pocket.

First of all, I knew that I needed college, most of all for the authority of that piece of paper. I also knew I craved the demands of substantive discourse about those topics in science I loved. I had a lot of questions to get answered, and other, new, things to learn.

And though I craved higher education in the sciences, I wasn't so sure I could cut the other academics and demands of the tougher courses. My strengths were in boats and their technology and FIT's specialty was oceanographic technology. I enrolled in the program to be a ship captain. The rest of it set my teeth on edge.

I had chosen the nautical degree because I thought I could pass it easily. What I did not know is that the first year we all took the same courses as every other program. You know, the general requirements of English, math, physics, chemistry, etc. When I studied, I found out that I could earn good grades. That year I did great. So, at the end of the year I went and asked if I could change my major to the course I really wanted. Oceanographic Technology. I was told my grades were good so I could change programs. I was overjoyed.

Oceanographic Technology was a double degree major. You learn Oceanography to understand how to work like a scientist and then you take engineering to learn how to build what you need in underwater operations. The purpose of the degree was to be able to talk to scientists about what they wanted to build to go underwater for their projects.

For example, if they wanted to study an animal at the bottom of the sea, our job would be to build them something to go down to study the creature. It opened up the underwater world to the scientist because we could create a wide variety of options for them. We took the information about what they needed and then built machines to meet that purpose. Everything was on the table from building a submersible, ROV, or autonomous robot.

This was the exact course made for me. It was if I had spent my entire life up to this point in training for this degree. All the stuff I was doing as a kid and then pursued as a young man. Everything played a part; from bug collecting, chemistry, rockets and mustard gas, electronics with Lee and the intercom, the Navy with electronic and engineering courses about submarines. My experiences living on a real submarine and fixing it and building my own mini sub. My physics classes at IU were a start and learning about human bodies at the funeral home. I could not have been more prepared to attack this program. This degree was meant for me!

Once I saw that I was on par with all the other kids, I changed my course of study and major to oceanographic technology, which what I was really interested in pursuing. It was much like when I was set loose in the library to pursue knowledge on my own with the limited skills I had learned from Sister Isabel. I was feeling my confidence grow every day.

In the Navy, I had read about Charles Darwin and the Beagle. He was the first famous oceanographer, and my role model. From his book I learned about the methods he used to capture samples of microscopic sea creatures. I followed his lead and did the same. This was perfect training to become an oceanographer, even more so an oceanographic technician. That was a role suited for an engineer, someone like me. Included in that course of study was enough science to understand oceanographers. In addition, I knew I could also learn about and then build machines that could dive to the bottom of the ocean to do research on deep sea creatures.

During my time at FIT I was beginning to routinely envision and design mini submersibles in my mind. I might have considered them for the study of ocean life, but that wasn't the realm of work in the ocean I was really interested in pursuing. My future would find other purposes for these machines.

DAMN THE PRESSURE, FULL SPEED AHEAD

The last big project at FIT was a capstone project designed for a team of students to apply all their accumulated knowledge to build a machine utilizing science and engineering. The idea was to create a project that would be a resume-builder for graduates as they went out into the real world. Pressure mounted as students understood the importance that the effectiveness of the machine would determine their final grade. Whatever the project, it had to work in the way it was intended.

I was chomping to get started. It was time for me to show everything I had learned from the Navy and my time at FIT. Groups were emerging and so were the ideas I had in my head.

During one of our evening soirees, I brought up the topic of our senior projects with three of my close friends, Laurilee Thompson, Don Pattersen, and Mike Senko. None of the three of them had any idea what they were going to do. I had already been looking around the school grounds to see what was on offer as far as parts I could use for my idea. It didn't take much more than my describing what I was planning for them to join me on Team Pado. They already knew me well and whether it was my idea for the project or my determination to build a submersible that convinced them did not matter to me. I was excited because I knew that their knowledge, skills, and resources would complement mine on the project.

I had a plan to build an underwater scooter. Yes, I was thinking back to my childhood watching Lloyd Bridges on *Sea Hunt.* Not only was it about the coolest piece of his equipment, I saw it had a useful purpose and would be an effective and practical tool for a business or industry.

That practical application was part of the criteria for the project.

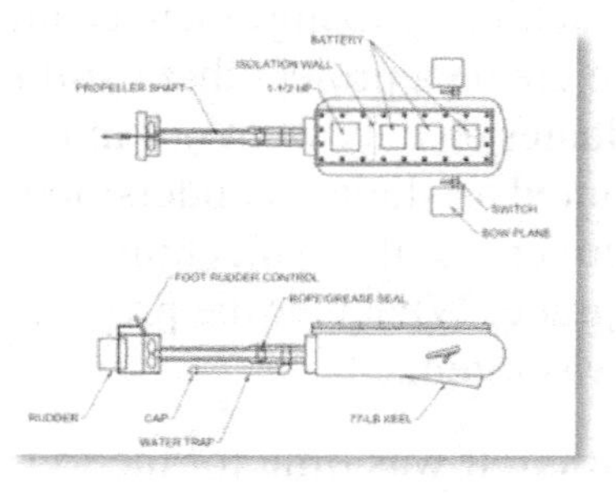

Figure 62 FIT scooter drawing

You see, Laurilee Thompson was, at the time, my girlfriend in addition to being one of the team members. I didn't know it initially, but her dad owned a fleet of shrimp boats and a manufacturing company to build these shrimp boats and other boats. This gave me the perfect segue between the underwater scooter project and practical application. This new piece of equipment would give the shrimp fisherman the ability to watch their catching field while trawling. Presenting my proposal to the team, they quickly agreed it was a perfect project.

We had to source and provide all the materials, supplies, and whatever was needed to build the machine on our own. I was, as usual, broke. That didn't stop me because I was also resourceful. I had heard of a failed submarine project that had been built by one of the professors named Mr. Woodberry. It was an old wet sub laid to rest in the storage yard.

When I went to see it, I found it had a propeller shaft, three giant batteries, and an engine source. It also had a great many bits and parts I would not need. When Mr. Woodberry and I talked, I discovered that he already knew I had built a similar wet sub while I was in the Navy. I implied I could make his submarine work, which I am not certain he believed. In any event, he agreed to let me take it. After looking at his design, I almost immediately saw why his submarine had failed. I really did know how to make it work. It would take some modifications. I knew exactly what I needed to do. Professor Woodberry's failed experiment would become the centerpiece for our project.

As soon as I got physical control of Woodberry's submarine, I ripped out all the usable parts and began working on the design for the underwater craft. The scavenged parts from the professor's project dictated a much larger machine than I had anticipated. I redrew the plans, so the operator would lie on top of the scooter, using his feet for rudder control.

True to my scavenging nature, I was able to find additional parts in FIT's storage. I took a bookcase and some lumber to fashion a cavity for the internal machinery. Styrofoam from old beer coolers was added for buoyancy.

The one thing I did not have was the equipment and resins to use to create the fiberglass shell covering. Fiberglass is used, and important, because it withstands the pressure of the water, preventing the shell of the submersible from being crushed. We had to have it. As I was lamenting this fact to the team, Laurilee arched up and said, "Hey, my dad builds boats up in Titusville, Florida. If I tell him what we need, I'm sure he will give it to his best daughter." What a great girlfriend!

We went up to where her dad had his business building boats. Boy, did I get a shock. We arrived at a huge factory that built a variety of boats. My jaw dropped.

I never expected that Laurilee came from a family with a huge, successful business. In the 1970s at an oceanography school, everyone dressed like hippies. Nothing fancy and no brand names at all. I couldn't ever look at any of the students and say what kind of family they came from and we were not interested in knowing. We never talked about anything like that. So, after I got my wits about me, I met Laurilee's dad. He was a great guy, just like the rest of her family. We got to meet them all. Just like when any college student goes home, her mom had to feed her, and the rest of us, too. We had a great meal and the wonderful hospitality of a caring family.

The surprises kept coming because I had no idea that Laurilee was also proficient at using the resins. She was exceptionally smart and a very hard worker, experienced in the materials as well as the techniques to layer the gel and make it smooth and sleek. Now I see the danger in what could have happened without her knowledge. It was invaluable. For example, I never knew that if you mixed the resins in incorrect proportions, they would catch fire. Thank the Lord that she did. It was an unexpected bonus to find such a girlfriend and co-worker.

After Laurilee applied the fiberglass covering and it dried, the team spent hours sanding down the fiberglass to form the best shape for the submersible. The right shape emerged, but it was looking rough. Other classmates and some of the professors began making bets that it was not going to work. I was confident in the project and worked hard to keep my teammates equally as optimistic. That was one of the most difficult tasks during the project and I really did not like being the butt of the jokes.

Despite the nay-sayers and doubters, we pushed onward. We fashioned a nose cone for hydrodynamics. I was thinking about the rockets I built in my youth and was amazed at how much I had learned since then. I knew how to figure the dimensions and how to find the center of gravity and the center of buoyancy so I could determine how it would float yet sink when needed.

The front, which held the batteries, was the float. The back end was heavy metal. Finding the metacentric height and engineering the size and shape of a keel and where to place it was the trick to getting the balance right. I settled out at 77 pounds exactly, balancing the positive and negative buoyancy and the fore and aft trim all went into the computations. When I finished the calculations, I knew I was right, without a doubt.

The day came when we were finally ready to start testing the underwater scooter. There was a crowd assembled. They had all come to see our machine fail. I knew they would be disappointed. Not wanting to be arrogant, I did not make much of a show about it.

Figure 63 Me on my scooter. What a thrill!

When it went into the water, it was perfect. Absolutely perfect. When I surfaced, there were shouts of "ME NEXT!" After seeing how well it worked, they all wanted to try it. I took most of them for a spin, pulling up to nine swimmers at a time. They were not laughing any more. No, they were loving it.

When we tested it with actual divers in a nearby waterway, we found it could pull four fully kitted divers behind it. They were coupled hand to ankle plus the driver. It could go much faster than one could swim allowing divers to save their energy for later. It was the best underwater experience I had had at FIT.

FIT Students Build Undersea Scooter To Study Shrimp

Figure 64 FIT final project in the news

I was exceedingly proud of my grade on the underwater scooter project. I received an "A" for a six-hour course on it and best of all, graduated with honors. Who would have ever thought the kid who could not read or write until he was well into school would be able to achieve such accomplishments? Perhaps, maybe, Sister Isabel? To this day, when I look back at the rudimentary plans to build the scooter at FIT and all the calculations I made in order for it to function, I am amazed – and proud of myself.

I also saw the value of the fact that we had a team that got along together. We were a great team. We partied together, worked hard together, and some of us even loved each other. We had everything to make the project perfect: the team, the parts, and the plan.

As it turned out, I was right about it all. Like I said, I never thought I would get an "A." We all got an "A" on the project and in the course. We all wore big smiles when Mr. Woodberry told us it was the best project he had ever evaluated. He commended us saying it was a good team effort, it was well-planned, and it worked beyond anyone's expectations. It was not an easy project by any means and getting those comments and the most important grade for our degree was exactly what we were all looking to achieve. It was a great point on my resume, I know, because it helped me get into the Smithsonian Institute.

After the project was completed, evaluated and over, Mr. Woodberry came to me and asked me to bring the sub up to the pool because Mr. Ed Link was coming to look at the school. Mr. Woodberry knew it was a great project to show off because Mr. Link was an inventor himself.

He was the inventor of the Link Trainer. It was the precursor to simulators in the training of airplane pilots. It taught pilots how to fly while they were still on the ground. His company went on to build moon simulators for use in the space program. Mr. Link was also the head of the Smithsonian Institute's facility in Fort Pierce, Florida, which is where I eventually went to work.

Originally, Mr. Woodberry did not want our team to be there next to our project when Mr. Link came to see it. I told him that if the team could not be there, we were not going to bring the sub to the pool. It took some negotiating. I convinced him so I eventually got my way. We were there when Mr. Link came through. It was amazing to meet this famous man. This meeting had nothing to do with my future with the Smithsonian Institute. I was just thrilled to be able to meet someone who had done such incredible things.

Part II – Captain Fireplug

In case you have forgotten, my physical stature is considered short and squat. While that has been both a blessing and a bane, my classmates took it further saying I reminded them of a fire hydrant. When news about the underwater scooter project began circulating, something else became news.

Because of my position as a dorm director and team leader of this complex scooter project, I had been pegged as a boss, a leader. The school newspaper cartoonist created Captain Fireplug and started publishing a cartoon strip called *The Adventures of Captain Fireplug.* Captain Fireplug was a hero, righting the wrongs committed by evil villains like the Foul-Mouth Swimmer. The comedy was flat unless you knew the underlying politics. I still felt the drawings were cool. I recognized myself right away and so did my classmates. I felt it was positive and I loved it.

Figure 65 Graduation from FIT in 1974. My sister, Debbie came.

My graduation was pretty low-key. My sister, Debbie, who was living in Florida, came to the ceremony. My parents said it was too expensive to come. I was accustomed to them not coming to my events, so it made little difference to me. I was proud of myself.

After graduating from FIT, I enrolled in Florida Atlantic University's (FAU) master's program. By this time in my education – formal or my own learning – the curriculum was old hat to me. I found that class after class was rehashing what I already knew. It was new to other students, but not to me. I quit after one year.

My time at FAU was important. While I was there, I took a trip up the coast to buy some SCUBA equipment and fell in love. I have come to realize that our lives are marked by small moments. These moments are the treasures we hold into old age. We review the chapters of our life and begin to see patterns and the serendipity that shapes what we become.

I mark my life by many events. My failure of third grade and the lack of attention from my parents left me with a 'chip' on my shoulder. I carried it almost like a badge and let it be a recurring theme throughout my life. It left me feeling insecure and lacking confidence. No matter how hard I worked, when I accomplished something significant, I was always amazed at myself.

For instance, when I achieved the long-held dream of becoming a submariner, I was shocked that I made it through all the requirements and had the right temperament. Then for a kid who was constantly in remedial reading, going to college seemed a dream too far dared. My hard work in the Navy and my insatiable curiosity paved the way to those hallowed halls – and the honors I achieved there.

All that to show that step by step, event by event, lives are changed. And another one was coming my direction at this point in my life.

Part III – The Smithsonian Institute

On the dock, just 25 miles away from where I was living, I discovered the *Johnson Sea Link.* It was a lock out submersible with a large plexiglass sphere for the pilots and a rear compartment for two lock out divers. It was sitting on the aft deck of the *RV Johnson* held in place by the crane that was used to raise and lower it in and out of the ocean.

I knew immediately that it was a research vessel. It was a special design that combs the depths of the oceans to discover new animals and sea life. Just as immediately as I sighted the submersible, I knew what I wanted to do next in life and I knew I would do whatever I had to do to achieve my next dream.

What I had stumbled upon was a Smithsonian Institute research facility. Of course, I immediately looked up what the facility was working on and I knew I had to work there. The skills I had were a perfect match for their sub crew. Even the director told me that when I interviewed with him. However, there were no openings. There was no room for me. Other applicants might have walked away hearing that, but I was not just another applicant. No, I had a mission set in my head. I did not get huffy and storm out. I was polite and keen. The director was impressed enough to ask me to check back in two weeks' time.

What I did next changed the course of my life. When I returned, I asked if there was anything, anything at all, that I could do around the facility. And I meant ANYTHING. At first, I was told no. Two weeks later, I returned again. There were still no openings. I was determined. I came back in another two weeks. Yes, I was that determined, that much of an eager beaver that would not give up or take no as a final answer. My style of being visible without being a pain paid off.

After a couple of months of consistent touches and inquiries, the director told me he would hire me for three dollars an hour. My job was digging a foundation for the new facility. I leapt at the offer and promptly began digging as my day job. My days as a graduate student in school were over, I was working. I wasn't doing exactly what I wanted to do; however, I had a plan.

On the grounds of the facility was a shed where they stored the equipment for the manual labor crew. Housed in the back of that shed was the submersible. The very same one I had seen the crane arm holding in place on that ship months earlier. The one that would be dangling from the crane arm over the open ocean in the days to come.

You would know that every lunch break found me and my bologna sandwich climbing inside the submersible to study its controls and construction. No one ever chased me away from it or, for that matter, ever said anything.

In a short time, I knew how everything on the control panel worked. Everything, that is, except for this glass jar beside the panel. Hanging out of it was a green funnel. I puzzled over that contraption for a long time. Finally, I asked a member of the sub crew what it was.

"That's a human range extender," said the crewman.

"A what? A human range extender. I've never heard of that. What is it for?" I asked.

“When you’ve got to pee,” the crewman answered.

“Oh,” I replied, wanting to slap my forehead.

Then my curiosity got the better of me and I asked how then do you take a poop? He obliged in explaining that they had plastic mittens to wear. You put them on and poop in your hand. Then you pull the plastic mitten backwards over your hand holding the warm poop in it. After it was turned inside out, you tie a knot in the end and discard it. Now you know. Being a submariner or underwater explorer is neither for the faint of heart, or the modest. And it is a challenge for someone with short arms.

For eight months I labored digging on the foundation for the Smithsonian Institute facility. To survive on my three-dollar-an-hour job, I lived with two other guys and traveled three hours a day. I did not care. I was chasing a dream.

To what extent was I willing to go for that dream? I found out that the crew gathered after work at a fabric-free entertainment club to party. I made a point to go in there and party, too. Eventually, the crew began to talk to me. They knew I wanted to be part of the team and they brought me in little by little. Relationships formed and before long I became a regular part of the group, hanging out with the sub crew. I felt I was getting closer.

Just like in the Navy, I became the ‘go-to’ guy. I would perform some of the jobs they did not want to do or that kept them later at work, so they could go out carousing. I would do the paint touch-ups on the subs. I would sand or drill, or whatever they needed to have done to build their trust.

DAMN THE PRESSURE, FULL SPEED AHEAD

Word came around that the SCORE project was coming up. SCORE stood for Scientific Cooperative Operational Research Expedition. The project was a month-long underwater habitat living project in the Bahamas. The purpose was to enable the study of a vertical wall of the coral reef down to depths of two-hundred-fifty feet. It was carried out by the Commerce Department's National Oceanic and Atmospheric Administration, the Harbor Branch Foundation, Inc. of Fort Pierce, Florida, and the Perry Foundation, Inc. of Riviera Beach, Florida.

The coral reef was of no particular interest to me. I was interested in what they were doing and using to accommodate the research. They were using saturation diving, deep air excursions, and submersible lock-out techniques with the *Johnson-Sea-Link.* Besides the submersible, there were underwater laboratories and a variety of underwater safety stations along with the surface vessels and facilities on land.

I desperately wanted to be a part of the crew. I can recall sitting on the shore watching them sail out to sea on a long ship with the submarine sitting on the deck. The ship had a crew of a seaman, an engine man, a navigator, and the captain and I was not any of those men. I was devastated and slumped my way back to work.

Then the unimaginable happened. I got a phone call from the ship. I listened carefully to hear that the navigator had had a heart attack. Thankfully he did not die. His situation resulted in them calling me to ask if I wanted to replace the navigator on their research vessel. After a second to digest what I had just heard, I simply cried out, "Hang up. I'm coming!"

The logistics of getting out to the ship were not going to hamper me and my chance. I employed the help of a friend. Bernie pulled aerial banners with a small plane over the coast. I asked him to fly me to the Palm Beach airport in his plane. There I jumped a flight to Freeport where the crew picked me up.

When I arrived, I discovered my friends had a pool going on how fast I would catch up with them. I made it as quickly as I could, and I did not care about their fun. I was part of the crew, just as I had dreamed about every day for almost a year.

As the replacement navigator, I knew what to do from my experience in the Navy, and I carried it off beautifully. The ship was the *Research Vessel Johnson*, or commonly known as the *RV Johnson*. It was a converted Coast Guard cutter. If I remember correctly, it was a little more than one hundred feet long. Modifications had been made on the hull to be able to carry the weight of the submarine and launching crane on the stern of the vessel.

Being navigator meant my duties were to pilot courses and give ETAs (estimated times of arrival). This was easy. All you needed was a ruler, a compass, and a chronometer. A chronometer is a timepiece that is so precise and accurate that it can be used to determine longitude based on celestial navigation.

Other duties I had on the ship were to helm, or steer, the ship and then other general seaman duties since the ship had a very small crew of four. Quite often we would double up on other tasks, in other words, help each other. When things got slow, I could always be found on the back deck helping the sub crew. It was a perfect set up for me. Everyone had to be a jack-of-all-trades and I loved it.

I was on the ship a couple of months when I started hearing some rumors. Finally, one day when we came into port, the rumors got real. There was a second submersible being built. I saw some of the parts, the big aluminum frame and pressure housings that had been farmed out to other companies for manufacture, arriving. This time, the build team was also the crew that would take it to sea and operate it there. I went to see the crew and discovered they were short one man. I, again in the right place at the right time, was chosen to fill the open position.

My excitement was bone deep. I went home and told my friends and we celebrated into the wee hours of the morning. There is nothing like working hard, seeing an opportunity and then grabbing it with both hands. Nothing. I had proven I was sharp and eager, and I made it onto the crew for the second submarine. I was not going to let anyone, including myself, down. I would perform, no, outperform, my highest expectations.

Figure 66 Diving operations with the Johnson Sea Link.

Our crew worked together to get it built and I pulled my weight without a stumble. I proved my ability and worth, because once the *Johnson-Sea-Link II* was built, I was given the honor of taking the first test dive to a thousand feet. It was the first dive of this magnificent machine, peering deep into the wonders of the ocean to places few people had ever been. I was so excited and enthralled with the adventure that I did not even think about the danger inherent to the task.

When the big day came, it was another bright sunny Florida day. John Fike and I got into the sub, shut the hatch and headed to the bottom of the sea off of Fort Pierce. On the way down, the water was very clear. We bounced around a little on the surface. As we flooded the ballast tanks it got calm and quiet. The machine, not my heart! We reported our status to our mothership every hundred feet we descended. At about three hundred feet down, the water began turning from light blue to dark blue. This change was due to the diminishing sunlight. We turned on our own lights, which were very powerful and lit up everything around us. It seemed odd. We did not see any fish yet.

We continued to descend and shortly we needed to engage the scrubber. The scrubber is a device that removes the carbon dioxide out of the air in the sub. It is common practice to let the carbon dioxide build up then run the scrubber for about twenty minutes. It is a noisy operation. Noise doesn't matter because it was a critical necessity if you want to stay alive. We carried on without reporting.

During the entirety of the dive we operated the sonar system. Sonar is similar to radar. The difference is that it is underwater and uses soundwaves instead of radio waves. It is very effective, as I would find out shortly.

When we got to the seabed it was kind of underwhelming. The floor just looked like an expanse of a gray mud. We maneuvered around looking for anything of interest while testing out the thrusters going in all directions: right, left, forward, aft, and full blast forward. The thrusters generated a lot of noise that we could hear inside the sub. There were eight of them and we could use them to push the submarine in all directions. We finally settled down on the gray seabed.

Suddenly, we pick something up on the sonar. It was about eight feet long and it was heading our way. It was exciting and my mind went back to the suspense on the first, and best, submarine movie I ever saw, *20,000 Leagues Under the Sea* and the scene when the Nautilus was attacked by the giant squid. What would we see when it got to us?

Diving in one of the research submersibles was different than diving in a submarine during my Navy days. I was deeper in the *Johnson Sea Link II* than I had ever been in a submarine and the only thing between me and the water was a thin acrylic bubble. I could see everything surrounding the sub and it was incredible.

John, who was the pilot, had had lots of underwater experience, and he guessed that it was probably a shark. Sharks living this deep under the water have six gills because they need an extra one to adapt to the low oxygen content of the water at these depths. When the animal swam across our field of vision, it was indeed a gray, six-gilled shark, just like John said. It swam by, to me, in slow motion. It was the only exciting thing we saw that day. I will never forget it.

After the shark was gone, John said we were going to turn out the lights. We did and boy, it was dark. I mean black. It was the middle of the day, so the sun was high in the sky and gave the impression of twilight deep in the water. However, since our eyes had been exposed to such bright lights on the submersible, when we turned them off, it was like being blindfolded. I was waiting for him to turn the lights back on. He didn't. We sat in the dark and he couldn't see me rolling my eyes.

Then a funny thing happened. My eyes began to adjust to the darkness, and just like at night on land, my vision adapted, and I could see again. In fact, I felt I could see a little farther than when we had our lights on, just not as much detail.

I remembered from college that after getting 1800 feet down in pure water, there is no light. Sunlight cannot penetrate deeper than that. Another point is that when you are using ambient light to see, a lot of the colors of the rainbow are not present. Red is the first color to go and that happens in the first ten feet or so. That's why without the lights on, everything took on a gray appearance. It is like a dark night with just a little bit of moon shine where things feel a little surreal.

As we finished the dive, we headed for the surface. There was a lot of noise with the high air pressure pushing water out of the ballast tanks. It's a welcome relief when you feel yourself coming off the bottom, especially when it is a first dive, a test, and you are heading for the surface. We adjusted our ascent to be at the same speed as the air bubbles escaping from the bottom of the ballast tank. You might not think air bubbles could be beautiful. Outside our window they were six to eight inches across and they were gorgeous. They almost looked like jellyfish with the top being a little flat and trailing out beneath. It was like a mirror shaking back and forth as the bubbles wobbled their way to the surface.

When we get to the surface, a diver jumps off the mothership, swims a line over to us and connects the tow line. This is all accomplished while the ship continues on its way forward. After the tow line is connected, we slowly make our way to the stern of the ship being pulled along as the diver stands atop the submersible. He is in position to hook us up to the launch and recovery crane as it swings around to catch us. Once the cable takes hold, there are a few sharp wiggles and then we start to rise up out of the ocean and onto the deck. We hit the deck with a thud and that is when divers always let out a long breath of air that you do not realize you have been holding the entire dive. It is a huge sigh of relief because you have made it back. The next big event is when we open the hatch and take another big breath of fresh, sea air. It was wonderful that day to be surrounded by smiles for a successful mission. I have to tell you, even without the big smiles, it is like that at the end of every dive.

The next two years were some of the best of my life. Dive after dive, I learned so much about the mechanics of moving underwater and what was under the sea. The machines, the ocean, the sea life, it was all amazing to me.

Calls to my parents were practically non-existent. It wasn't until sometime later that I told them of my association with the Smithsonian Institute. I talked only with my dad about the dives. I was out in the ocean, on islands and under the sea. I didn't see a reason to subject myself to their general attitude and I had come to realize that no matter what I did, I would never feel support from them and feel that they were proud of me. I guess it was mostly my mom. My dad was more supportive. He got quiet in his old age. I think it was his heart. It did not work too well. I just think they did not understand how hard I had to work to get this job and how important it was to me and my career. I had to set my own sail and be true to myself.

Implications for My Future

Just as I had believed, college was important to my future. It wasn't just the academics. I already had a lot of the academics from my own personal study and the Navy schools. No, college was truly important for the experiences I was afforded and the environment that existed.

Learning to assuage my own curiosity had always been a personal trait. My time at college and then at the Smithsonian reinforced my need to satisfy a thirst for knowledge. To this day I spend more time than most people I know just seeking out answers to questions, or information that can allow me to draw my own conclusions and generate my own answers.

In addition to learning, once again I see how important the simple act of taking action is in the big picture. You can think about things all you want. Until you actually do something with what you learn, nothing truly happens. That is where having an environment that makes action, experimentation, and creation safe and productive is key. School offered a place where whatever you can imagine, you can try to create. Yes, I had to use my own resourcefulness to gather the materials and supplies. That was easy because I could try to do – or build – whatever the design was that I had in mind.

Another part of that was taking the lead, officially. All my life I was the one that convinced others to do my bidding, or I did it myself. In the final project, and in some of the work at the Smithsonian, I had to be part of a team and, often, lead the team myself. There was no forging forward on my own.

None of what I did during these years was easy, but it was necessary. For future success, one must build a treasure of knowledge and skill and then have hands-on experiences. Going through that process not only proves to the individual their abilities and worth and gives them confidence. No, it shows the world what they can do, too.

And that is what I did. Through knowledge, hard work and calculated risk, I put my life on the line for something I helped build – and I got the biggest buzz ever. In the years to come, I looked for the earned buzz. The ones you have to work for, not the cheap high that drugs give you. No, I got high on living life with all its ups and downs.

I've heard this saying, "In pure water, fish do not grow." I would revise it to say, "In pure water, fish do not grow – or cannot live." In pure water, there is no food, no oxygen and you cannot sustain life. Staying in such a static environment does not enrich the mind, nor does it feed the soul. Life is to be lived and experienced. You have to take chances on whatever is put in front of you. You have to take risks to really live, grow, achieve, and excel.

The approach I take when I am assessing a plan to take a risk starts as a mindset. I do not make plans and then think about everywhere it could fail. I have found that those thoughts generally create such doubt that a person could elect not to make the move. Instead, I make my plan and then tell myself I can succeed. That allows me to take action and move forward. I believe you can't let fear be the governing principle of your life.

I believe that the person who has the most to lose, has the most to gain. To clarify, let me give you an example. Some people live very ordered lives. They plan everything. Nothing is spontaneous or left to chance. I think they would prefer to sit in a square white room and be fed square white food with no risk. I feel that when they die, there will be a plain white expanse on their headstone with nothing written on it.

On the other hand, there are people you can call to go and do something at any moment in time. If they are not otherwise engaged, chances are excellent that they will take off right then, eager to go off on an adventure.

They will face the risks to go and do. Because what will happen if they don't is what happens to a fish if you put it in pure water. It looks clear and clean. But the fish will die from lack of nourishment.

After my time in college and at the Smithsonian Institute, I was ready to put everything I had learned and done to another use. I was ready for more. That was good, and good timing, too. Because one day, the oil companies came calling.

Section Six - Going Pro

Part I – Oceaneering Comes Calling

A group from Oceaneering, Inc. arrived at our shop to talk about what we were doing, and to recruit. A new age was dawning for the oil industry and they were looking for people experienced with the type of technology they were beginning to utilize. Once again, I was in the right place at the right time. I accepted their offer for a job because it sounded like a new adventure based on those things that interested me – engineering and innovating machines to be used deep under water. I saw a way to sate my curiosity, increase my knowledge and expertise, and explore new territory for myself, and, apparently for them, too.

Figure 67 Oceaneering opened new doors for me and for the oil industry.

They had a new high-tech submersible with the latest human-type arm on it. It was called an anthropomorphic manipulator, a mechanical arm that could operate like a human's arm. It could do some amazing things from the front of a submarine. The arm operator was inside while the arm was outside doing all sorts of tasks necessary for underwater drilling and production.

Oceaneering, Inc. was a high-tech diving company with exclusive rights to this human-like manipulator. The arm was manufactured for them by General Electric. Together, the two companies cornered the market on what was to be the future of deep-water intervention work for oil drilling and production. It was a smart move for both of them.

At this stage, Oceaneering was a diving company. It was started by Lad Handelman and Mike Hughes. Handelman was an ex-abalone diver from Santa Barbara, California, and Hughes owned his own diving company. When they got into a conversation with Don Sites about the future of diving there were a few other small diving companies involved, but I do not know their names. The end result was Oceaneering, Inc. The name came from a combination of ocean and engineering, which is where their work converged. Diving companies originally were hardhat diving services. As the industry aged, there was much greater potential coming in engineering.

In the beginning, and still today, the oil industry rents equipment and contracts for services when they need something done. The service companies would include everything from helicopters and seismic services to boats and labor. The oil company would simply contract all the different elements of the projects they undertook. Because the oil wells were at sea, the diving companies were, at first, contracted laborers to assemble the wellheads and blow out preventers (BOPs) on the sea floor. For divers, it became increasingly risky as the depths increased and the work became more and more perilous.

In fact, it was getting more and more technical just to do the job. Mitigating the danger to the divers meant finding new ways to get to the depths required and move away from saturation diving systems. The financial outlay was enormous to pay for the equipment and supplies like the helium gas. It could cost a million dollars or more for a one-hour dive at one-thousand feet.

Figure 68 I was the first arm operator and crew chief of the first attempt at a work class ROV in the North Sea.

Because of the services they were being asked to provide, the diving companies found the need for ships as well as engineering staff and capabilities. They began to do "everything" and that was the point in which Oceaneering stepped up with the potential for Remote Operated Vehicles, ROVs.

The leaders at Oceaneering were keeping their eye on what was coming in the future for their industry. In this case, they got it correct and I later got to go along for the ride as their first Atmospheric Roving Manipulator System (ARMS) submarine pilot, holding the crew chief position. It was another first for me, and, not inconsequentially, for the oil industry.

The job paid $40,000 for six months' work. I leapt at it, not because it was a huge amount of money in 1977, but because I saw an opportunity to again be on the cutting edge of the technology I loved. Although I would have done it for free, I was glad to have enough money to live comfortably for once in my life. Because of my training and experience, I fit this new direction for the oil industry like a glove. I was a scientist and an engineer as well. I had practical hands-on experience in underwater robotics, and, of utmost importance, I knew what worked and what did not work.

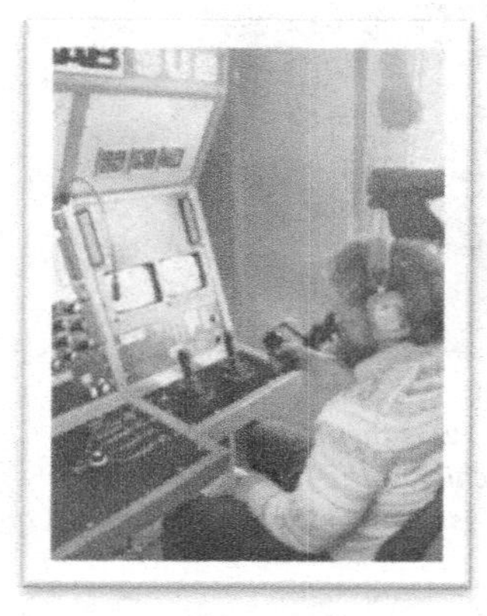

Figure 69 The start of a new era in underwater oil drilling.

I was sent to Aberdeen, Scotland to keep track of the building and development of the Drillship Pacnorce. This was the ship on which I was to install the ARMS diving system. It was a new, cutting edge Norwegian ship that was under construction. The construction of the ship fell behind by almost a year. While I was in a holding pattern waiting for that project to begin, I was sent to manage other jobs involving ROVs as the offshore supervisor. During this period of waiting for my primary role to begin, I learned a lot from the temporary assignments I was given. In the first project I was to oversee, there were a lot of problems. My team was sent to Norway to demonstrate the capabilities of the new submersible technology. A pipeline was being laid across the Norwegian Trench out to new oil fields. As a safety precaution, the company that owned the pipeline wanted to be sure they were prepared for any emergencies. The primary task of this demonstration project was to provide a way to effect repairs on a pipeline that might break apart on the sea floor in the Trench. That meant we were to explosively cut apart and then weld together pipe at 1,100 feet.

Figure 70 I am on the right in the picture below as we are getting the Tango 1 ready to dive in the Norwegian Trench.

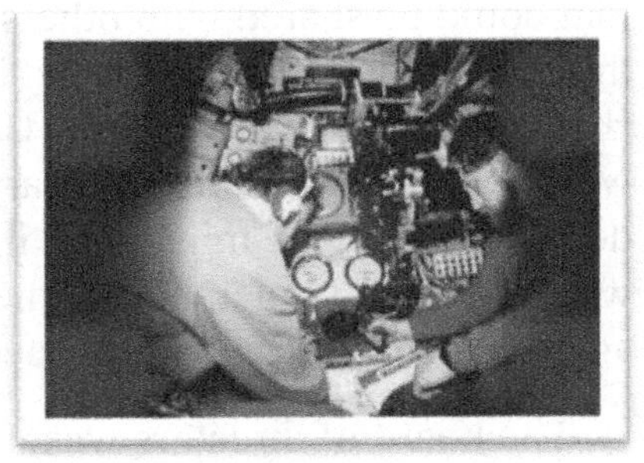

There were several companies competing for the job. Ours was the only one with a submersible using explosives. Our competitors were sending divers down using saturation diving, which meant there was a risk to lives. The time involved was excruciating, and in an emergency, time is a concern.

It was so early in the evolution of ROVs that not all the bugs had been worked out. We labored with minds and hands to make it work. In the end, a diver on another team died. We were able to show it was possible to repair the pipe if and when the need ever arose, without risking the life of a diver and in the fastest and most efficient manner available.

It was my responsibility to oversee the installation and use of the GE arm in its first use offshore. I was also tasked with documenting the manipulator system so that other teams could subsequently implement the new equipment on future projects.

During my time at Florida Institute of Technology I took several photography classes and learned how to create instructional documents. This fit right in with my lack of writing skills, and my understanding that engineers would rather see an image, read a short note, and carry on. It was definitely the quickest and easiest way to relay the information. I knew no one wanted to read pages of written-out instructions. Therefore, I wouldn't be giving them that!

As I tackled the first project, I took photos and diagrammed the sequence of events in all the processes, creating a show-and-tell manual. I knew everyone was hungry for information about this new high-tech equipment that could be shared with others. Once completed, I sent the manual on to headquarters. Unbeknownst to me, it arrived at the office at the same time the board of directors was meeting. An astute secretary walked it into the president suggesting he might find it useful for the meeting. I was told after a quick perusal he called her back in and asked her to make a copy for every member of the board.

The board of directors was impressed with the work I did because it justified the expense of the project from the reports I generated. I was demonstrating the work I could do for them and building a name for myself.

I was excited to hear about this development. I was much more than a documentation provider and systems analyst. I was eager to show what else I could do.

As I said, I was learning a great deal from these experiences. The second demonstration project wasn't as successful as far as getting a new customer. That being said, it was exceedingly beneficial for me as a designer and builder. It is always a great thing to build a cutting-edge piece of equipment. You have to repair them at some point. There had been no real thought given to that and when the equipment broke down, we had to take it to land, order parts from across the world and wait. And wait. And wait. Time is a costly expense to the oil industry and every day we were down, was at a high cost.

Figure 71 Me in a WASP ADS (Atmosphere Diving suit).

On this second project I supervised, my documentation was created with all pictures, no text. Instead of text, I decided I would supply the audio to go with the photographs in a slide show. My slide show, and my audio, was commandeered and I found myself in Texas at a big oil industry trade show called OTC, the Offshore Technology Conference. My presentation was the centerpiece of our exhibit and I talked oil executives through the whole thing and then handed them off to the salespeople. My star was quickly rising.

My next assignment was one that would make the record books and remain vivid in my own memory bank.

It was a clear day on August 3, 1978. There was not much wind. The temperature was in the mid 70s. It was a perfect day to go diving. I wasn't thinking of scuba diving. I had been down fifty or a hundred feet as a diver.

No, on this day I would be diving in one of the latest developments in underwater craft of its day, going to depths divers would never attempt. Being the ARMS submersible pilot and crew chief, I would be leading its test drive. After all the years of school and the Navy, I was about to dive in one of the most sophisticated submersibles ever built and I felt great.

Figure 72 ARMS bell we broke a depth record on its maiden dive.

The submersible was called ARMS, which is an acronym standing for Atmospheric Roving Manipulator System because that is exactly what it does. Its unique feature was the human-like arm attached to the exterior of the submersible. The sub was fitted with a Force feedback system that allowed the operator to feel whatever the arm grabbed in its grip. When the pilot grabbed something outside with the arm, he could feel the object on the inside of the sub. This allowed gentle or firm pressure to be applied to the object outside the sub. It was amazing, cutting edge technology built by the space division of General Electric.

Two months earlier, my team had come to install the ARMS submersible on the host ship. I was working with talented and knowledgeable men like Jim English and Scott Mallard. We were excited that the ARMS was installed on a drillship that was the latest of its kind as well. It was called the Ben Ocean Lancer and was contracted to Chevron. It was 507 feet long and weighed more than

17,200 tons and was manned by a crew of 110. It was anchored to the seabed not by anchors and chains, but by a dynamic positioning system. The dynamic positioning system made it possible to hold the drillship in place by multiple thrusters that were controlled by a computer that communicated with a satellite. This system kept the Ben Ocean Lancer in place directly over the well for three months without being permanently anchored to the seabed.

We had installed a system in the middle of the ship to protect the submersible from moving around from the giant waves in rough weather. It was called the Moon Pool. If you were on another ship passing by the Ben Ocean Lancer, you would never know the submersible was in the guts of this large vessel.

By this time, after my experiences with Smithsonian Institute research teams, I was more fully aware of the risks and dangers in test dives. While that was coolly stored in the back of my brain, my excitement took center stage. If successful, this would be a new badge for me to wear.

Once again John Fike was with me in this submersible for its maiden voyage. The test dive would be taking us down to a depth of 2,842 feet off the coast of Halifax, Nova Scotia. We were ready to get into the ten-ton submersible and take it into the cold water off Canada. A dive of this depth had never been done before in this type of equipment. There was a reporter and a film crew there to document the record-breaking dive. We climbed into the sub and were ready.

Plans for this dive had been ongoing for some time and while I had faith in what we had built, the unknown was still present. There were no guarantees that everything would go well with the sub at these depths. That morning I sat down before the dive and wrote a good-bye letter, telling my fiancé how much I loved her, and that even if I did not come back, I was still doing what I loved to do. Luckily for John and me, everything would go well. I respected the danger we faced and kept that letter. I still have it today.

I got married in Florida eight days after that dive on a much-needed vacation.

ARMS Makes Record Dive

Figure 73 ARMS dive sets record

The dive was serious business. It was a bit of a media show, too. The cameraman was filming outside looking into the sub as we were preparing to launch into the moon pool. The moon pool is a system where there is an opening cut out of the bowels of the ship that becomes, essentially, a gateway to the ocean. Being a protected area, it is a calm place in which to launch. By introducing bubbles into the water, it reduces the density of the water, allowing the submersible to descend through it easier and more smoothly. This allows us to continue our work even in terrible weather and the roughest of seas, which is a common problem in the North Sea.

A message came over the radio telling me to look busy for the camera shot as we went down through the moon pool. I moved around doing things; flicking levers and switches. One of the levers was the equalization valve. It allows you to get out of the sub when you surface. There is always a differential pressure strong enough that the hatch cannot be opened on the surface, which is the reason for the valve. Because I was nervous, I left the valve open by mistake.

As we started our descent, everything was going as planned, and then we noticed a leak. A leak is definitely one of those things you never want to see in a sub. The cold North Atlantic seawater was coming in fast. Troubleshooting – no, quickly thinking fast on your feet – is what keeps you alive in these situations. We ran through all the possibilities and found the equalization valve switch open. We got it closed and stop the stream of water. It was not a good way to start the dive. Thanks to our quick thinking we solved it and continued descending.

Going through the protocols of the test dive, we were caught out when we learned that our communications with the surface did not work and we had no control over our vertical descent. Both could be life threatening. In this instance, that meant threatening to OUR lives. We assumed the electrical wire in the umbilical was probably broken, which meant we could not speak to the surface to alert them to stop the bell from going deeper. We would have to wait until we got deep enough where our hydrophone could operate. Remember, this was its maiden dive. We really were testing everything in the ocean for the first time and getting some information that was both good and alarming.

The hydrophone was our backup communication system. It is essentially a microphone and speaker and when paired with another on the bottom of the boat, it sends a shrill, high-pitched sound that can be received and translated into a voice. Basically, it is a loudspeaker through the water. In order to use it, we had to be below the moon pool and under the ship about forty feet. That meant we just had to wait until we descended far enough.

After the dive was over and we debriefed to analyze what had happened, we discovered that the weight of the submersible had snapped the cable on the communication system. At this time, the bell was mechanically lowered on a cable. Remember, we were supposed to use the communication system to tell the people lowering us whether to go slower, faster, or to stop. Therefore, it was critical that the cable connecting us with the mother ship stay intact.

As a precaution, we would be brought up if the surface control station could not contact us for ten minutes. It would not have saved us in all situations like massive flooding, but it would have helped us in a lot of operational situations.

When we lost communication with the mother ship, we were pretty much at the mercy of the sea and circumstances until we reached the depth to use the hydrophone. Although it was only seconds, it seemed forever.

Once we were able to communicate and get our descent back under control, we could breathe again. These two events were nerve racking. Tragedies, especially underwater, happen when a series of events go wrong simultaneously. We could handle any one event and sometimes two and still maintain safety. Beyond that, things get dicey and get scary pretty fast. Sometimes we just have to have faith in all the preparations we did to get to this point. These situations test our capabilities and make us show not just our skills. No, we had to demonstrate our mettle, too.

The rest of the dive was interesting. We were on our way down to 2,842 feet for the next few hours with a couple of liters of icy cold water at our feet. In the past, the deepest I had ever been was a thousand feet beneath the surface. I was excited about this new opportunity, this new adventure.

I remember from the JSLII that at about three-hundred feet, it always started to get dark. The water was exceptionally blue. It took about two hours to get to the bottom of the ocean. We were stopping every couple hundred feet to make sure everything was OK. As we went further down, we started to see creatures that I had never seen before, not in books or on other dives. They were mostly jellyfish-looking creatures with brilliant colors. The sightseeing made the time go faster. We were engaged with the ocean life. This calmed my heart and mind after the flooding and communications troubles.

When we reached a depth of 2,400 feet, we heard an explosion. It was loud, like a gunshot in a can. I thought about Apollo 13. I swear I sucked the rubber cushion that I was sitting on right up my butt. John sucked up the other half on his side as well. I know our hearts were beating more than 100 beats a minute because I could hear mine pounding away. We needed to settle down quickly in order to figure out this new problem – whatever it was. The adrenaline was rushing through our systems full bore.

We sat silent for a moment and both of us were running through the possibilities of what could cause the explosion. John, being more experienced than I, said he thought it was the flotation made from syntactic foam. There were flotation blocks on the outside of the capsule.

Syntactic foam consists of marble-sized fiber balls covered with an epoxy compound to form a desired shape that could withstand very high pressure at depth. The blocks did just what the name implies. They provide extra buoyancy for the craft to get it back to the surface in the case of an emergency. That meant the fiber balls in the floatation blocks were a very important item for our survival.

Over the next hundred feet as we continued to descend, these fiber balls continued to explode. When we got to 2,700 feet, the explosions were so numerous that it sounded much like a machine gun. The sound was unnerving, as was the thought that we were losing this emergency contingency system. Our heart rates and breathing were racing once again. I truly understood what it meant when someone said their heart was in their throat because I was thinking about that good-bye letter I had written being delivered to my fiancé. Although it was only minutes, it seemed like hours before the explosions stopped.

Figure 74 The flotation balls on the ARMS I that just about pushed us over the edge.

Despite the possible loss of this emergency stopgap, we continued our descent. We made it the entire 2,842 feet to the ocean floor. At that point, we needed to see if there still was sufficient buoyancy in the sub to bring us back to the surface.

One of the unique features of this submersible was the anchoring system. Through a system of floats and weights, we could keep the sub in place with an anchor and then, when ready to ascend, the floats let the sub rise.

If, at any point, the sub is disconnected from the ship or the sea floor, the sub could maneuver on its own, except for depth. With the anchoring system, the bell would continue to rise. That was an emergency backup plan that allowed us to know we could save ourselves, and that was a good feeling to have in my back pocket, believe me. I loved the sea, but definitely did not want to be out lost somewhere in it.

I let out the anchoring system and the sub started to rise. The relief was immense. I was thinking I was surprised we did not shit our pants. Then I smiled because I realized that rubber cushion was up there.

After we confirmed that we could get the sub to rise again, we started to calm down so we could get back to work. We inspected the Blowout Preventer (BOP) and found it working properly.

At one point, we found ourselves in the midst of a school of cod. They were each about three feet long and there were hundreds of them swimming around us. It was like watching fish in an aquarium except this time, we were the ones in a glass container. One thing I have learned during my diving career is that even in the most extreme situations, the ocean life has a calming effect on me.

Every foot we rose on our ascent to the surface made us feel better. When we got back on the deck and opened that hatch, we let out the breath we were holding tight inside and sucked in the sweet, fresh sea air. There is nothing more delicious than that.

Figure 75 Not many people in the world hold this designation. I am proud to be one of them.

Getting to the depth and then getting back to the mother ship does not mean the test is complete. After inspecting the submersible, we determined that the explosions coming from the flotation blocks were due to the outer skin. After the blocks were molded in the manufacturing process, they were sanded. This sanding made the walls of the outer fiber balls thinner. They were not able to withstand the pressure, and therefore, exploded. Some things have to be learned the hard way and that is exactly what testing is all about. Although unnerving, this is what is expected when testing new equipment.

Our record dive was a huge success for Oceaneering and the start of new diving technology soon to be used for deep sea drilling. We went on to make more successful record dives with the ARMS system. The first paved the way. As the years went by, the men inside were replaced by robots. Being able to be one of the first, and last, in the era of manned submersibles was an experience I will not ever forget. It was exciting. It was fun. It was important for the development of what was to come. We were pioneers.

It was the edge of innovation at the time and it is incredible to see how the concept has evolved. That original ARMS submersible sits in a scrapyard in Indonesia forty years after that world-record maiden dive. I would love to have it sit in my backyard or in a museum. It is a piece of history in the evolution of deep-sea submersibles and deep-sea drilling for the oil companies.

Figure 76 The original ARMS bell sits abandoned in Indonesia.

The relationship with my parents took on a new element. During this time, I was making some money and when they learned of that, they called. It was only when they wanted me to send them money that I heard from them. For the most part I would send them some. There was still a place in my heart for them. They had their life and I had mine. My dad was interested in what I was doing. We talked and I could tell he was slowing down because his heart was getting worse. I don't think my mother ever understood what I talked about. It was too far out of her orbit. I think if I was honest with myself, I wish they would have understood the journey I had to get to this point in my life and how happy I was to make it this far. I myself couldn't believe what I had achieved.

In order to showcase the ARMS and its capabilities, Oceaneering made a film of that initial record-breaking dive starring my partner, John Fike, and me. The film showed how well the new GE ARMS worked.

Because we were featured throughout the film, John and I became the faces for the new technology. At the end, the camera shows me crawling out of the capsule and freezes on my smiling face. Because of that movie, I became an ambassador and was sent around the world to tell people about what we did. It was a whirlwind.

Figure 77 This dive marked a turning point in my career.

The company set up black-tie affairs and after dinner the movie would be shown. I was later introduced and answered questions from the audience. In making the rounds of the big gala events, I showed what we were innovating, I talked about it, and I explained it so everyone understood how it worked and what it could do.

The tour was a great success and I met people with influence from around the world. The company was happy with me and the way I explained the new technology. Those social skills I developed at a young age were being honed to a fine edge. I was at ease with important people and I was often told I had a great smile. The company decided they wanted me to be their high-tech marketing man.

That was great, and it also opened a new opportunity for me. Not only was I in front of important and influential change-makers, I was going to learn about the diving construction side of the business. Since I knew nothing about underwater construction, I was sent to work alongside the construction divers in the field. I would be engaged in an organized tutorial. I would see and learn about the process by going to sites in various stages of construction. I got a hands-on education about how various jobs should be completed. This was another endeavor that was not easy. I would be gone for several weeks or a month or more visiting various sites in a lot of different countries across the globe.

I had never heard of anyone getting the kind of experience in the oil fields that I was getting. I learned jacket installation, pipeline installation, underwater welding, and JIM suit operations. It was a checklist of skills that anyone in the oil industry would just about die to get. Oceaneering felt by combining my old school diving knowledge with my new high-tech education, I would be a great asset to their company. And in the end, it paid off for them. For me, as well. I was well-compensated for my work and I was building a wealth of knowledge.

At the end of this training period, I became available to any Oceaneering, Inc. sales office around the world. The Singapore office picked me up. It was the opportunity of a lifetime. A twenty-million-dollar contract had come up for bid just as I was stepping into the arena. It was the largest diving contract in the world at that time. I saw it as a prime opportunity to be a rainmaker in the organization and I took it very seriously, even though my style was considered a bit unorthodox.

As I had so often shown in the past, the adage, “Where there’s a will, there’s a way,” applied to me – in spades. I took on the challenge of sales as if it were a do or die mission. I tried to make it fun, though, too. I presented myself as a fun guy – in addition to being highly schooled and experienced in the high-tech and engineering side of the business. I very much enjoyed the social situations and I was constantly interested in meeting new people.

Maybe it came from the unmet needs as a child, but I tried to make strangers as comfortable as possible because I wanted them to become my friend regardless of the outcome of our business dealings. I was determined to build relationships by being everybody's friend. I had a lot of fun during this period of my career. I worked hard, too, to adapt to a new career path. I needed to switch from scientist and researcher to become a salesman.

I labored to make the most of it. In the process, I managed to piss off my boss, Jerry Smythe. He presented himself as you would expect a salesman would; nice looking, well dressed, and very organized. I always thought he had it all together. Me? I would also give away the T-shirts, take people out for meals, and generally approach selling in an orthodox manner. However, in contrast, I also had a completely unorthodox approach. I needed to stand out among other quite-famous competitors. I would add scientific and engineering explanations to my talks. I knew I had to work harder than everybody else, and I did.

I also had other tricks in my bag. As a sales dude, I would do everything to get prospects to come my way. When a client left our meeting in his office for a bathroom break or to attend to a pressing matter, I would leap up on his desk and place a small Oceaneering company sticker on the light above. Later, when my prospective client was staring toward the heavens during a contemplative moment, there would be my sticker, reminding him of me – and what we could offer him.

Once, on returning to one of my clients, Shell Brunei, the gentleman mentioned, with a chuckle, as he pointed to a two-inch sticker on the back of his lamp that he had noticed. With a big smile I said, "Gee, I don't have a clue how that got there." I felt that Shell engineer appreciated my effort. In fact, in retrospect, perhaps that childishness showed the client I was sincere, not manufactured, more uniquely human. I believe that people who have character, honesty, a genuine-ness about them are appreciated. It might appear to be unsophisticated. In reality, it is more sophisticated than pretending to be something you are not.

As with other companies, Oceaneering also gave out promotional trinkets. One of them was a diving bell trapped in a squeezable clear plastic bottle. The bell would descend to the bottom of the compartment when the bottle was squeezed. There were tiny anchors, cannons, and another diving bell you could snag. By releasing the pressure on the bottle, the sunken treasure would rise. The next task was to put what you snagged into the treasure chest suspended halfway up the water column. The object was to fill the treasure chest. It took some practice. Everyone said it was a lot of fun and very addictive. These came unassembled in a box, which is exactly how many of the reps would hand them out. Not me.

No, I would spend hours at night in a hotel room filling them up with just the right amount of water so that squeezing the compartment would make the bell go down with ease. Then I would present them to clients as a thinking man's toy. They did not have to do anything but enjoy the gift. I called it a decision-makers' helper. I told them, "When you're thinking about this contract, you can grab it to help you make your decision." It, of course, was covered in Oceaneering logos and stickers. It was classic bullshit heaped on my bullshit. It worked.

Another ploy I uncovered in Singapore, where I discovered there were no nudie magazines. Despite being a city rich with prostitutes, nudie magazines were considered culturally offensive. I would ask around to see if it was possible to get a few issues of *Playboy* on the black market. I was eventually directed to a shop in a remote district there called Holland Village. Once there, I waited for all the customers to clear out before asking the proprietor for any copies of *Playboy*. He ushered me into a back room that was filled with copies of the magazine from the 1960s and '70s. I picked out a few to earmark for some of my special clients that I knew would appreciate them. By the way, I had to pay a healthy premium for those old magazines. Not only were they rare, in Singapore, they were illegal.

On a subsequent trip to Borneo, I essentially smuggled some of the magazines into the country. It was a Muslim country and this type of material was highly illegal there. When I went to see my client, an Englishman with a stiff upper lip, I revealed my contraband. To my surprise, he opened his desk drawer and it was filled with a plethora of magazines, *Playboy* and others, too. He said, "Welcome to the club!"

Since I was a contributor to the "library," I was allowed borrowing rights as well. Those simple magazines were just another way I made an impression on my current and prospective customers. Some have become lifelong friends. Honestly, I do not believe many salesmen went the extra mile like I did to get the results I got.

One day, while I was waiting to go out to oil platforms with the Shell representative, John Girard, I was sitting in a restaurant with my camera. This camera had a special watertight case so I could do some underwater photography. A local gentleman sitting nearby asked me about the camera. When I told him what it was for, he got up and joined me at my table declaring that he was a reporter for the local newspaper, the Borneo Bulletin.

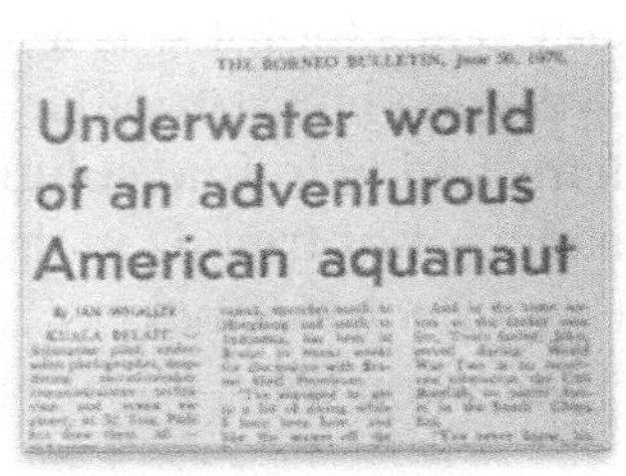

Underwater world of an adventurous American aquanaut

Figure78 Borneo Bulletin article I traded for pictures.

The Borneo Bulletin was the only local paper and he said he had about 30,000 readers across the island and most, if not all, of the Shell employees. He bargained with me to get some underwater photos of the oil platforms, offering to pay me seventy-five dollars per shot. I told him I didn't want money. I wanted an article. An article written about me. He readily agreed. The next issue had a full page spread about me and my photos. It was instant credibility in a foreign market.

At Shell, all 3,000 employees got a copy of the article. One of my competitors saw the article, crumpled it up and went to see the head honcho of Shell. He was angry, pushing the paper into the executive's face and saying that it wasn't fair. A good friend in the office told me the Shell boss told him, "You had just as much opportunity as the little fat guy and it's your fault you didn't take the opportunity to advertise a bit more. I don't feel sorry for you."

Being a party guy from Gary Indiana, it wasn't just my approach that was different from the typical stereotype of a salesman. Most salesmen, just like my boss, were usually sleek, suave, and well put together. Most were taller, and thinner, than me. I never put on airs. I knew exactly who I was and what I was capable of doing. I used my strengths to my advantage and tried to use my weaknesses in a positive way.

My bosses and the sales representatives competing against me were not aware of my most effective, and secret, sales tool. I was a listener. I would buddy up with everyone in a particular shop to understand their problems and help find solutions. I became well known and had a lot of friends in the oil industry. Some were influential decision makers, and others were just regular guys doing their jobs.

I was an asset to my employer, though my boss in Singapore, Jerry, did not like the way I got things done. I could feel the animosity. I just kept doing my thing in my own way, despite the fact that my own boss did not appreciate me. I was making sales, big sales.

One night at a cocktail party, I was drinking in the kitchen with my tie undone and chowing down on leftover hors d'oeuvres. In came my supervisor's wife. She stepped up and pulled me off to the side to have a few words. She asked me if I really wanted to be a salesman. I asked her what she meant. She replied, suggesting that I might really rather go back offshore and drive submarines and "stuff like that." I saw what was coming. I told her that I kind of liked sales and thought I was doing a good job at it. I knew my days were numbered. Later I heard my boss telling someone on the phone that he could not fire me until the current deal was done.

Knowing now that I was going to be fired, I embarked on what would be a risky strategy. I had no fear about the job. What I did fear was that by this time, I had a wife and a new baby. I was in a foreign country and knew if I lost my job, I would be deported. Back in the United States, I had no home and no savings. I had to forge ahead, placing my bets on the power of winning a huge contract.

Figure 79 The day I discovered my days at Oceaneering were numbered.

My personal life was in a tentative situation. My determination settled in because I felt I had had an ace up my sleeve with winning this big contract. Boy, was I ever wrong. That sale would have set us up nicely. This new development was throwing a wrench in that, so I decided to have some fun. I had nothing to lose.

I needed to make sure the C-level executives knew that I was the face responsible for securing the biggest contract in diving history. Granted, there were a lot of people behind the scenes that had input, however, I was the guy up front making sure they had the right information on how to form the contract. It was the information I gave that was key to addressing the critical elements of the deal. I was all over the Shell buildings, rarely seeing any of my competitors. This made Shell feel that my company was very interested in working with them.

Soon a call came from Shell giving me a heads up that a telex containing a statement of intent was coming in the morning. I knew morning, for Shell, was 7:30 a.m. I made a point of being in the office early to intercept their message. When the telex came in with their intention to close the deal, and since I knew I was getting fired, I decided to call the president of Oceaneering, Ed Wardwell, directly. I was the one who would announce the good news, not my boss.

President Wardwell was ecstatic. This was a contract the company desperately needed. Ed confided that he was seeing the bank that morning to increase the overdraft coverage. The company was in danger of going under and he was hoping one of the two big contracts would come through to save the company. It was this news that he could take to the bank to save the company. I hung up with him and called the senior vice president, Mike Hughes, who was a very good friend of mine. The news I shared made him very happy, too.

Three hours later when Jerry came in, he heard from his secretary that we had won the Shell contract. He immediately asked her to get President Wardwell on the phone. I heard him and yelled from my office, "Jerry, there's no need to do that. I called him at 7:30." It was now 10:30 and Jerry was livid. I guess you could say I stole his thunder, or you could say I took mine.

I had known exactly what I was doing. I did not care because my days in this job were numbered, whether we won the contract or not. The company had many offices around the world, so leaving Singapore did not really bother me. I figured I would just slot into another office. I thought that was the case. I was wrong. It didn't occur to me that Jerry would blackball me throughout the company. It was the one thing I did not expect, or plan for.

When Jerry let me go from my sales position, I really did figure the company would find another place for me. After all, I was the spearhead leading the company into the high-tech age and there were seven other Oceaneering offices around the world. There had to be room for me somewhere. I discovered that although top management was ready to dive deeper into the high-tech arena, those in middle management were not. What I had not grasped completely was that the middle management of the company was mostly comprised of other vice presidents who were ex-commercial and former Navy divers from the 1950s like Jerry.

The fact that I was the new breed of high-tech salesperson coming up the ranks did not sit well with them. The company was expanding into submersibles and underwater robots where none of them had any hands-on experience. I am sure they felt that if they hired me, knowing I worked in those areas, I might easily show them up and possibly even take their jobs. They had their own fraternity and I did not fit into it.

It became evident quickly enough. When Jerry fired me in Singapore, he called all his buddies in the other Oceaneering offices and told them not to hire me. That is exactly what happened. None of them would hire me. It did not matter that I had just secured the company's largest contract ever. I am certain he told them that this kid (me) would cut your throat. In reality, my fault was that I was the future of the company and those in middle management were struggling to keep up. They kept me out. Yes, Jerry had really played his part in screwing me over. As a side note, within a few years of my departure, most of them were gone, too.

I was lucky enough that others in the company found me a job even if it was not in management or in sales. Nope. I found myself several tiers down the corporate ladder. In fact, I discovered I would be working for an operations manager in the North Sea in Aberdeen Scotland. I figured I could do that. I had often started from the very bottom like I did at the Smithsonian digging the foundation.

When I arrived, I also discovered I was the only American there. I was a Yank working in an English fraternity now. It did not take me long to discover the man I worked for was not knowledgeable in his job. He knew the buzzwords and, I am sure, had walked by a submarine or two. It was evident to me though, that he did not have a deep understanding of the field. He was running submarines that were capable of diving to three thousand feet with two men inside them. His lack of knowledge was a safety issue, which is why, I later learned, I had been shipped off to Aberdeen. My job was to go out on all the jobs to see how the subs were functioning, make sure everyone was safe, and then come back to report to my boss.

It was in that reporting stage that the water started to churn with trouble. I returned from jobs with data and suggestions, and he would disagree. I saw his lack of knowledge about the submarines and safety become a difference of opinions. In most businesses, a difference of opinion is benign, sometimes even a challenge that results in positive changes. Not so in this situation. Here, the differences of opinions involved people's safety and the lives of the pilots.

In my heart I knew this man did not know what he was talking about and because of that, he was putting people's lives at risk. There was no convincing him of the errors in his thinking, and I could not condone that situation. I did what I never thought I would ever do. I resigned from Oceaneering, Inc.

The day I left Oceaneering was a very sad day. I really loved working there. I felt I was exactly the type of person they needed to show them the way into the high-tech future.

Implications for My Future

Of course, the opportunities to learn that always present themselves must be grabbed and grabbed with gusto! Not only was I helping design and build these innovative machines, I was getting to take them out into the depths, run them through their paces, and prove what I knew to be true.

My initial experiences with the brand-new ARMS submersibles allowed me to see the problems and, later, when I was building my own ROV submersibles, overcome those problems in a couple of ways. First, in the design process so my machines did not have those problems. Second, to create backup systems to improve safety so people would be safer running my ROVs. I learned from technicians and people on those sites doing the work, so I had first-hand knowledge of what did – and did not – work. The implication being that I had addressed every single thing that was wrong with the ROVs, and I could explain the problem and the solution.

I also jumped at the chance to put myself out there as the face of something that was new and wonderful. I was proclaiming the virtues of our work to the masses. There is nothing like doing it to develop skills and with my lack of self-confidence tucked deep in my pocket, I took center stage and, much to my own surprise, dazzled the audiences. I learned that the feeling I get from others quashes my concerns and fears. I might feel like I never really excelled. The feedback I got told me I was doing well.

Of everything I did during these days, I will always smile because the fun I had doing my job will always be the first thing I remember. I worked hard. It was not easy. I loved it. Maybe instead of just calling it fun, perhaps I should expand it to say that fun, to me, is learning, growing, building things, sharing excellence with others, and knowing in my heart that I am doing something worthwhile, important, and valuable. For me, it is the glee in living life to its fullest, personally and professionally, that is fun.

My time at Oceaneering, Inc. introduced me to the wild ride of life on the roller coaster of wheeling and dealing in the big time as well as the competitive nature of people. It is easy to get sucked into the negative backstabbing and underhanded dealing. My nature was to be honest and up-front with everyone – prospects, clients, coworkers, and competitors.

I think what made it easiest to maintain that position is that I believed in what I was doing and what I was selling. In my heart, I felt that we had a great product and I was truly solving the problems of my clients with that product. When you feel that way, it is also easy to want to do your best and get the best results you are capable of achieving.

Whether I was building a new submersible, diving to the bottom of the ocean, gaining knowledge in my field, making million-dollar sales, or making life-long friends, everything I did was rounding out my corners, my rough edges, and giving me the confidence to believe in what I knew and who I was. I could do things my own way and be successful. I learned that even when obstacles come into view, they are speed bumps, not walls or cliffs.

That perspective would be just the thing I needed to know later. Boy, was that ever the truth.

Part II – Landing in Florida, Again

About a month prior to my resignation, a representative from Perry Submarine Builders had come to Aberdeen to sell us more submarines. His name was John Newman and I think he was, at the time, the president of Perry Submarine Builders, a submarine manufacturing firm in Florida. In his patter to sell more subs to us, he mentioned in passing that if I ever wanted a job, he would give me one in Florida. I took it as truth.

I was a bit naïve. Thinking in the back of my head I would have a job waiting for me made quitting easier. Oceaneering was obligated to repatriate me and my family back to America. I felt I would have a soft landing in the sands of Florida with an opportunity at Perry Submarine Builders. I once again packed up my wife and young son and we looked toward Florida and a new job.

On arriving in Florida, the first thing I did was go knocking on the door of Perry Submarine Builders in Riviera Beach. I went to the front desk and asked to see Mr. Newman. I was sent up to his office where his secretary informed me that he was not in at the moment. She said he would be back soon. She asked if I wanted to wait. Of course, I would wait. I had to wait. I needed that job.

It was not too long before he came through the door. When he saw me, he had a surprised look on his face. It should have been a signal to me when he asked what I was doing there. I did not have a good feeling as he ushered me into his office. Brash, bold, and desperate, I told him I was there to take him up on his offer of a job. He said he knew I had come a long way and he felt bad about that. He was serious when he told me he did not have a marketing or sales job for me. I told him I was stuck in Florida with no income.

He made a call down to the manufacturing shop and found out they needed an electronics guy there. He told me that the best he could offer was a job for $6.50 an hour in the electronic shop. I had to catch my breath. I had to take it. The only luck I had that day was that a salesman in the office owned a duplex. He lived in one side and the other side was vacant. Even though the Florida sands did not afford the soft landing I expected, I had, at least, found a place for my family to live and at least a little bit of income to get us through the storm.

Here I was, once again at the bottom of the ladder working as an electronics technician. I was building the submarines I used to operate. It was a challenge to face that fact every morning. One day I was called up to the head office, which was literally the top floor of the building. I do not know if I would call it intuition as I was rising in the elevator, but I had a feeling something good was about to happen.

Previously, Oceaneering's competitor, Ocean Systems, had been trying to get into the high-tech deep diving drilling support business. Mr. Newman had done a deal with them several months before during which they put down a retainer of $80,000 on the submarine that I was currently building in the Perry Submarine Builders shop. Ocean Systems' strategy was to have a job in place for that submarine before they had to pay the full purchase price of one million dollars. The retainer was about to lapse, and Ocean Systems had not yet secured a job. They were about to lose their retainer or be forced to pay the entire one million dollars. Their strategy to secure the job before the full payment came due had not worked out.

When I arrived in Mr. Newman's office, another man named Don Disney, who was the salesman for Ocean Systems, was sitting there. The ex-Navy captain turned to look at me when I walked in. The two explained that they had a possible job for the summer if I was interested. I would be sent to the mouth of the Amazon River to work for Exxon. It became apparent that they needed someone to be the liaison between the submarine program and Exxon. They shared that they had been talking about the communication difficulties that were slowing the job down. As sub builders and divers, they didn't know how to speak "oil company." I was later told that it was in a discussion about that problem when a lightbulb went off over Mr. Newman's head. He told Don Disney that he just happened to have Oceaneering's best salesman and their world record holding diver on this type of equipment working right here in his company. That is when they called me up.

We sat and talked for a long time. They asked me many questions and I was able to answer them, in length, every time. I demonstrated that I had the knowledge of the equipment and processes, as well as the skill to sell them. Mr. Disney got more and more excited with each explanation I gave. He invited me to dinner that night where just the two of us could talk. We spent a good part of the night sharing old Navy stories over good food and good liquor. By the end of the meal, he was hinting that maybe Ocean Systems would want to hire me.

It was with great excitement I shared the events of the day with my wife. I could not believe the luck of Mr. Newman singling me out to talk with Ocean Systems. I now saw the possibility of my getting back into the upper levels of the submarine and oil industries.

At first, I thought briefly about letting my parents know I was back in the States. I knew that it wouldn't make much of difference. In fact, it would just be another sore point for my mother to scratch into an open wound and complain I didn't come to see them. I was feeling stressed enough, so I let it go.

Part III – Ocean Systems

Ocean Systems flew me out to Houston, Texas for about a week. During that time, we compiled a marketing presentation trying to solve the technical problems with the drilling at the mouth of the Amazon River for Exxon.

The most notable problem was working in the strong current there. At the end of the presentation, we had offered several alternatives. We had also noted that none of them were practical, technically. The fact was that there was nothing in the world at that time that could do the job. It was a bit of a letdown. What mattered was that it was an honest conclusion.

I returned to my job at Perry Submarine Builders full of hopes that Ocean Systems would come back and make me an offer for a job. It was not too long before my hopes were met. Ocean Systems offered me a job. It was not as a salesman. It was in marketing. They made me the contracts manager.

I moved my family (again!) to Texas and I went to work in my new office, writing contracts all day long. It did not take more than a few days to see that I was a fish out of water. As is my nature, I did the work to the best of my ability, and then I went around the office and made friends. I talked to everyone and told them the company was crazy for not making me a salesman. Most agreed with me and some even knew of my reputation from Oceaneering.

Eventually, I came to work one day and John Lowry, one of the top managers, called me into his office. He was famous for being the person who had written the Navy diving manual that every diver in the world uses. We had a chat and he was telling me that the $80,000 retainer period was coming to an end and he needed to find a job for that submarine – fast.

Figure 80 "Get out there and sell that damn sub!"

His plan to do that was centered on me. He made me international marketing manager. I would be the only person in the division and my sole job responsibility was to do whatever it took to find and get a deal under contract to make their plan work. I would leave Houston right away heading west, go around the world, and come back from the east, hopefully with the job under contract. No problem. I was ready to meet this new challenge.

I packed my bags, this time leaving my wife and son in Texas. My first trip took me back to familiar territory in Singapore. While I was there, I learned that Chevron Overseas had a job coming up in deep water off the northwest shelf of Australia. Houston management saw this as their last big chance. I was told to go see what I could do about getting in on the deal. I was excited about going to Australia because of the stories my dad had told me about the "land down under." I was even more excited about the job. It was in nice water, about one thousand feet deep with no currents, and it was for Chevron.

Chevron Overseas was the company I had been working with when we made the world record dive to 2,842 feet from the drillship Ben Ocean Lancer. I knew I would be amongst friends once again.

One of the major selling points was that I would go along and run the job. I would actually go offshore. It is important to note that Ocean Systems did not have an office at this time in Perth, and Oceaneering had been there for ten years or more. Another one of my sales points was that I knew Oceaneering was not going to pull their top crews and send them to this job in Australia. I knew it was more likely they would bring one experienced person and several green hands. It was a luxury to know Oceaneering, the company that was now my competitor.

In addition, I knew every crewman on their five submersibles and which ones were the cream of that crop. I also knew what it would take to sell the best crewmen on coming to work for me. One of the enticements I had in my pocket was the forty percent higher union wages being paid and the opportunity to work in the place known as one of the jewels in the crown of the oil industry – Perth Australia. It was indeed the greatest place in the world to work.

The Ocean Systems Vice President over Asia had come from Singapore and was there for the end of my sales pitch. As I finished, he leaned over and told the Chevron executives, “If you take the job, the fat boy’s coming with it.” They loved his comment and we all had a chuckle.

Afterward, on the way to the airport, I told the Vice President that I should stay in Australia until Chevron made a decision. That way I could answer their questions directly and show them how keen we were about getting their business. I could see he was agreeing with me and by the time we got to the airport, he got on the airplane and I got a cab back to the hotel. I believe that extra step went a long way with Chevron to show them how interested we were and how we attended to the details and their needs.

During the week I stayed in Perth, I got to see the truly remarkable place. Within days, I knew I would work for five dollars an hour to stay there. I felt if I got to come work on this job, I would like to make this my home for the rest of my life. I made that known to the people at Chevron. Not too long after that, I got the call. We had won the contract with Chevron. I had a feeling in the pit of my stomach. I knew, for some reason, that this moment would change my life.

I called Houston right away and they went nuts. I was so proud of this two-year contract with Chevron. First thing they told me to do was hightail it back to Houston. I jumped a plane as fast as I could. In the meantime, they sent my wife a basket of flowers, which I thought showed the style they had.

We had a little celebration when I arrived back in Houston. Then we got right to work because we had to finish the submarine in Florida. We hired the best people I knew in the business and installed the gear on the rig in Singapore. Apart from a few minor hiccups, we got the submarine fully functional on the rig and manned with a top-notch crew ready to go to work in Australia. All within the timeline established. We were off to a good start.

All of the rig personnel had a rotating schedule where we were on shore for two weeks and offshore for two weeks. Ocean Systems liked what I had done with Chevron so for the two weeks I was on shore my job was to sell more of these systems. Over the two years, I won five out of the only six jobs that came up for bid. We had two submarine jobs and three ROV jobs. One of the ROV jobs was the first ever drilling support job in the world using an ROV. Things were good.

I was on the road all the time and loving it. What made it work so well was that I was by myself on the other side of the world, running my own show with no fraternity of any kind looking over my shoulder. I could be as unorthodox as I wanted to be, and I took full advantage of that. I loved it.

Unknowingly, I was helping to pioneer the ROV business for Oceaneering. At that time, they wanted to enter the ROV business and decided to buy Ocean Systems to do it.

Part IV – Nagging Thoughts

What do you do when you find yourself at the peak of your game? A place where you know your industry, you've experienced every major job, and operated all the biggest – and best – equipment in the world? When you have been at the front end of all the innovation and changes and could see where the industry was going, and more, what needed to happen to get there?

I was making people tens of millions of dollars with my efforts. It made me ask, "Why can't I do that for myself?" The nagging thoughts in the back of my mind were getting stronger and stronger about branching out on my own. The only answer was to become an entrepreneur. It was the logical next step and answered the questions that had been floating in my head. That was the answer for me. I knew I had everything I needed, except the crucial ingredient: money.

What flipped the switch for me was a TV interview I heard with an Australian politician. He asked why Australians can't be more entrepreneurial like Americans. He explained the government was putting together funding in various departments to help entrepreneurs.

Australia has had a reputation for using their assets to develop their country. They have a country the size of the United States with a much smaller population. It is full of resources and is a lovely place to live, I think one of the best places in the world to live.

Over the years, when the country was facing a shortage or dilemma of some sort, they looked to find the solution from outside the country. For instance, after WWII the country was facing a housing shortage. They looked to the Italians, some of the best home builders in the world. They enticed Italians to come to Australia to build homes and many of them stayed. Later, as another example, they were looking to expand the farming industry. They basically gave land away. If someone got a parcel of land, farmed it for five years, the land became their own.

When I got to Australia, the buzz around the world was high-tech. The politicians began using rhetoric to encourage the development of high-tech industries and making that a big deal around the country. There I was in Australia sitting all by myself, so I figured I would raise my hand.

I knew this was my answer. I had a possible path to funding. I could build my own company using ideas for

ROVs that had been developing in my head over the last several years. Before I could sell anything, I had to have something tangible to show and explain what I could do with it. I took steps to have lunch with a man who could make the drawings I needed to apply for patents on the machines in my mind. He agreed that he could do that, so I sketched out my ideas on the back of a pub placemat. I had a direction and a focus and soon I would have technical drawings of what I was going to build.

When I received the completed drawings, they were perfect. He even offered me the names of several local patent attorneys. I took the drawings and ideas to the attorney, Kevin Lord, and I was on my way.

However, I was still an employee of Ocean Systems. And I had drawings in hand for new equipment in their industry. I knew I had to make it right with them, even though I wanted to build these new ROVs in my own company. I had to tie up all the loose ends. I proceeded to contact the office in Houston and offered them my thoughts and ideas on the ROV I was trying to patent. I got a telex back stating they did not want the idea and that they now had enough knowledge and know-how in Houston to build an ROV. They let me, and my ideas, go. I was now free.

Eventually, Oceaneering did buy Ocean Systems because Ocean Systems was then the world leader in drilling support technology using ROVs. They also got the three top men I was working with; Kevin McEvoy, Dick Frisby, and Kevin Kerins. They took Oceaneering to the future to where in 2013 they had a market capitalization of $9 billion.

Implications for My Future

Even when things did not pan out and I found myself in a bit of a pickle, my gut and heart told me to persevere. It is during those tough times that patience and calm help hone the skills that are truly some of the most critical for life. I knew that staying honest and humble, even when I knew I was right and others were not making the best decisions, would be the course of action that would serve me best.

My passion still burned bright for the industry and the work even when moving forward seemed questionable. Sticking to what I knew and loved was not easy. In some instances when people are pushed out and times appear to be desperate, they often pursue any port in the storm. They jump into other industries to keep food on the table and a roof over their heads. They leave what they love. I knew that wouldn't work for me. I knew it wouldn't be best in the long run. I opted to start over. Funny thing I learned is that after you achieve a certain level, there really is no starting over. You can't begin from the bottom in another industry. Because at that point, you know too much and have had experiences that will quickly elevate you back up into the level you lost. That is, of course, if you continue to share and work earnestly to do your best and the best for the organization.

When I had the freedom to run as a lone wolf to accomplish a goal, I found I thrived. I liked seeing a challenge and overcoming it by making my own rules and finding success in my own way. I know this independence comes from being on my own as a child and succeeding. It also came from never feeling someone was there behind me no matter what. I couldn't quit. I just had to work with what I had. Being who I am without pretense allows me to shift my energy into achievement.

Again, naturally, I talk a lot, build relationships, and make friends. The person I am and what I say or do might not be everyone's cup of tea. However, I have found that in the end, my authenticity has proven to be one of the greatest assets I possess. If I say I will do something, I do it. If I say I know something, I know it. Likewise, if I have to speak truths about not knowing something, I will. I will also make it a point to find out the answer. Once people get to know me, they know my word is my bond and my actions will support that.

That reliability, in play along with my desire to be straight up honest and do things the right way, has always been the best course of action in my adventures and ventures. When I had ideas that were in line with the future of the industry, I had to first offer them to my employer. It was the right thing to do. It could have ended differently. They could have embraced my ideas and saw the worth of what I was offering them. There were other things, the emotional and psychological elements, at play. In the end, those were costly elements for the players and the company – but not for me.

Authenticity, honesty, and a straightforward ethical compass is as much a part of my ethos as being a talker and making friends wherever I go. Now that the years have passed and I see the history of my life and achievements, I see those basic rudiments were always the foundation of my achievements. They were the personal gyroscope of my life keeping me level and allowing me to move forward.

I have also discovered that staying true to those basic tenets meant that I was moving forward, even when I felt I had fallen back a step or two – or fifteen. One thing builds upon another and eventually we all will get to the place we were meant to be. We do, that is, if we play the game honestly and forthrightly and keep looking to the future with passion and commitment.

Section Seven - My Own Business?

Part I - What Does Owning a Business Mean?

From Day One of branching out on my own, I had one primary objective: to design and build the world's best ROVs and equipment to support the deep-water drilling rigs for oil companies. That was all of it. I wanted to be the go-to guy for the big oil industry. Simple, right? I had the knowledge, the contacts, and the reputation ready to make it happen. Sure, as long as all I had to worry about was the actual designing and manufacturing of the machines.

When you go out on your own to do these things there is something else you need to know about, and that is business. And you know, there are many, many aspects of owning and running a business. To be successful, you have to cover them all. Although not formally educated in any of them, I had honed some skills through my own personal and professional experience.

One of the biggest elements of a successful business is people; hiring, managing, and firing people. I had people skills up the wazoo. Plus, I knew both the oil industry and engineering so I knew what I needed and what standards I would establish and demand – in a kind and socially acceptable manner. From my childhood I was that kid that could talk anyone into or out of anything. That was the gold in my back pocket now.

Second, I was good, no, *great*, at sales. Part of my sales success was knowing the products inside and out. I knew the specifications of each one. I knew how it worked, what it needed to work optimally, how to install it, how to run it and, very importantly, how to repair it. In fact, I could jump in and do that job myself. I had a passion for the industry and the product. Also, I had to know my competitors this much as well. Then I could explain to potential clients where and how we were better. That strategy worked the majority of the time.

What I didn't have in my portfolio were some other big elements such as finance (read: money), and other administrative necessities. I was smart enough to know that what I did not have myself, I had to find others who excelled in those areas. Even if I had had all the skills and knowledge, no one can do everything in a business and definitely not in the size of business I wanted to build. I would need help and I wanted the best help I could find – or at least the best help that was willing to join me on this ride.

In the end, I sold my company five times. And I bought it back four times. With each transaction, I learned a lot. No, I mean I learned B-I-G lessons. The truth of the matter is that every one of those experiences taught me something not just about the nature of some businesspeople, but about myself, too.

Like many other times in my life, I discovered that my gut decisions, those I made without specific, formally educated knowledge, worked out for me. Most of them were driven by my own ethics and the honesty by which I wanted to be known. I just did what I thought was right.

Before we get to those transactions and the lessons I learned, I need to tell you about how I went about building the business that was worthy of selling for millions of dollars.

Part II - Business No. 1 – Pado Ocean Systems

Previously, while I was working on getting the Brunei Shell contract for Oceaneering, I made a friend of George Cundiff. I met him in the small village called Seria, which was in the middle of the jungle on the island of Borneo. The town was officially known as Pekan Seria in the Bruneian district of Belait.

Seria was a town literally cut out of the jungle and the location of the original discovery of oil in the country. It was where about 2,000 of the people employed by Shell lived, having become the center of the oil and gas industries in the nation. Most of the Shell employees were tribal headhunters of the Iban and Dyak tribes.

Many of the tribal peoples lived in long houses on the outskirts of the town. Some lived in town, too. They were good people, who shared the stories of how their people used blow pipes to hunt for animals as well as the heads they were famous for collecting. Rumors were that there were still enclaves of Iban and Dyak people deep in the jungles living in the same way as their ancestors and still hunting heads.

They were hardworking, intelligent, and spoke English well. Although they had moved into modern life, they still sported the prominent blue tattoos that was a significant part of their heritage and culture. I enjoyed meals with them and loved the foods they prepared and shared made from jungle vegetation and a wide variety of spices. It was a truly unique culinary experience.

Shell Oil had hired George's consulting company, Underwater Specialists, Inc., to oversee the contracting and tendering process. The firm was known as one of the best in the industry. I was impressed by George, what he had accomplished, and the kind of person he was. What I didn't know was that George ran with some pretty influential people. Being two of a handful of westerners in the area, we had become drinking buddies and good friends, remaining so to this day.

It was after I won the Australian contract with Chevron that I received a call from George. He knew that I was overseeing the construction of the submersible for the project at Perry Submarine Builders in Florida. He said he was with a guy named John McMillian and they were flying to Palm Beach, near where I was working in Riviera Beach. He wanted John to see the submarine I was building and to talk to me. He said they would be landing in an hour. I asked where they were since I had no idea how they could be arriving in an hour. He said they were calling from one of John's private planes and I was to meet them at the airport.

I did as he asked. Before I left, I alerted the Perry people about who would be visiting. I thought it important since John McMillian was well known in the oil industry. At the time the Alaskan Oil Pipeline was a huge topic in the news, and the talk of the oil world. John McMillian was the owner of the Alaskan Pipeline.

When they landed, I brought them straight to the shop to see the submersible. They arrived just in time for the first test drive in the river behind the shop. I offered John the opportunity to join me in the sub for its maiden test. I assured him that there aren't many people in the world that would ever have this experience and he jumped on it for himself.

I could not believe that I was sitting side by side with one of the most prominent men in the business world. Everything on the sub was working perfectly as we dove when all of a sudden, one of the Perry underwater robots flew by the front of the sub. John was impressed with the sub, the robot, and the experience overall.

Figure 81 George Cundiff, me, and John McMillian on the day I took John under the sea.

Afterward, I took George and John back to the airport where they climbed aboard the private jet and flew off. George called a couple of days later to tell me just how impressed John had been. He talked about it the entire flight home.

This was another of those turning points in life for me. While I was still working for Ocean Systems I had been talking with George. I told him about my desire to start my own business. Come to find out, that was exactly why he had brought John to Florida to see the sub and meet me. George was eager to tell me that he had been talking with John about funding my venture and they had decided they would do just that. I was now going to be in business with some of the most influential oilmen in the world and people I could trust.

I was directed that once I was back in Australia, I was to go into town and set up a meeting at the Arthur Anderson accounting firm to put together a business plan. When I got to Arthur Anderson, they were expecting me and led me to the office of Frank Cooper. John had paved the way, virtually giving them an open checkbook to make sure I got everything I needed. Frank looked exactly as you would expect an accountant to look. After working with him for a while, I began to call him Little Big Man, because although he was slight in stature, he was an incredibly knowledgeable and professional man.

Part of what I needed for the business plan had to come from an engineering firm, so Frank directed me a little further down the street to Worley Engineering. Again, I was working with one of the best firms in the industry and it felt great.

Then it happened. I got another significant phone call from George. He told me that the Williams Company had bought out one of John McMillian's companies. It was John's company that owned the Alaskan Oil Pipeline called Northwest Energy. Apparently in the original tender process to purchase the pipeline, John had beat out Williams Company and they still wanted it. I thought, "OK, that's fine." Then he told me that my little company, Pado Ocean Systems, was also part of the deal. He told me that neither he nor John could continue to work with me. I had to fend for myself with the new owners, the Williams Company. That quickly deflated the high I'd been riding. I decided I would not let it crush me.

I immediately went to see Frank at Arthur Anderson to explain what had happened. He told me to hang tight and wait to hear from Williams. I sat on it for about a week until the representative called. The representative said he saw that Pado Ocean Systems was part of their company now. He said they did not know anything about what I did, and that Williams did not want to be in that type of business anyway. Now I was feeling crushed. Everything was going right down the proverbial tube. My next thought was wondering if they were going to let me have my company. Were they going to charge me something to get it back? I did not have any money, so I once again was in the position of explaining my situation. Here I was in a foreign country with no savings except the equity in my house. I was scared. He listened to me quietly and then told me he would call me back in two days' time. I knew that waiting for two more days would feel like waiting a million years. Once again, I was not sure what was going to happen to me and my family. My nerves were stretched thin.

After two days he did indeed call me back. He told me they wanted nothing to do with what I was doing and that I could have it all free and clear. He would send me the papers to sign. I said thank you and he said good-bye. That was the last conversation we ever had.

Again, I went straight away to Frank's office at Arthur Anderson and told him the outcome of the situation with the Williams Company. The business plan was far from done and I had no money to continue working on it. Frank said they would just hang for a while to see if I could come up with another sponsor or partner. Later I was told they really felt it was over for me just did not want to hit me with that news right then.

During the several months I had been working with Arthur Anderson on the business plan, I had also visited the Western Australia government's office called the Department of Industrial Development. I met with Nick DeGresevich, John Symes, Pat Marney, and Steve Beer, among others there. I explained briefly what I had in mind. They had been encouraging so after the news from the Williams Company, I went back there to talk to them. I fully explained the company I was trying to build and the high-tech industry I was trying to bring to the area. They said they loved my project and would like to have that kind of industry locally. They would work with me the best way they could. They really were amazing people.

I reorganized my finances and took out a loan against the equity in my house. I figured that $50,000 would keep us afloat for about a year while I continued to work on getting my company established. Arthur Anderson said they would keep working on the business plan – slowly – and they did not send me bills in the hopes that I would pick up a business partner that would fund the project.

The people at the Department of Industrial Development provided me with a list of names of the most prominent businesspeople in the area. I called every name on that list trying to make appointments to meet face-to-face, which is how I made the best impression. Several of them told me to 'just tell me what you want' over the phone. I made contact with three or four people every day over the next several months and spoke to each and every one of them with the same energy and positivity as the very first person on the list. I was not dissuaded. I think I must have spoken to at least a hundred people over that time. I got to visit a few, but never got a yes from any of them.

During that time, I heard about an underwater robot project at the West Australia Institute of Technology (WAIT). Of course, I had to check it out. It was there that I met Tom Dockerty, the professor who was in charge of the project. We hit it off right from the beginning. He was a great man getting students interested and teaching them how to put together an underwater ROV. After meeting the students and looking at the ROV, I saw it was really well done. The students were knowledgeable and energetic. With a bounty of nerves and free time, I found myself at WAIT quite often.

In the months of talking, talking, talking to people, I also spoke with the Minister of Science and Technology, Mr. John Button. I did not know much about politics at that point. I had heard about him from television, so I contacted him. Later I found out that his position in Australia was much akin to a cabinet member in the United States. He was an important figure in the government, although I did not realize it at the time. I told him I would like to meet and speak with him about me and what I wanted to build in Australia. I gave him a brief overview and he told me he was coming to Perth, West Australia for a business luncheon and he could meet with me there.

When I explained to Nick at the Department of Industrial Development that I was meeting with Mr. John Button at the luncheon in Perth, his jaw dropped. He wanted to know how I managed to get a meeting with Button because Button was, essentially, his boss. Nick and his team immediately started planning. It was decided that representatives of the Department would go with me to the luncheon and facilitate the meeting. I was grateful after I heard that the luncheon would be attended by several hundred businesspeople and I had no idea where I was going or who I should be looking for when I got there.

I was late in arriving the day of the luncheon and the parking lot was full. Outside stood a single, lone man from the Department of Industrial Development who ushered me through the entrance telling me to hurry up because the event was beginning. We went through a door, which opened right up next to the stage where the podium stood, and several hundred businesspeople turned to watch me enter. What an entrance!

I was steered to the front table set off by itself on the left of the stage. I realized just how serious this was when I recognized Senator Button, the Western Australia Premier, Brian Burke, and the Chancellor to the Exchequer of England, all seated at the table. There were big spotlights pointed at the table and several TV cameras scanning the faces at the table. The government officer introduced me to everyone, and they welcomed me to sit next to Senator Button. Waiters began serving the food, which was a relief to me. Senator Button asked some questions which I was able to answer with ease. He appeared happy with my answers. I don't remember all the speeches. It ended and that was that. It had been a whirlwind day. I went home feeling good about it. Still, I did not know where it would lead. I could only hope.

What I did not realize I was doing was putting money in the bank. I had had meetings with Arthur Anderson and Worley Engineering. I had worked with the governmental agency, and now a government minister. They were all in support of what I was doing. I was ready for somebody that would bring big help.

Returning to my daily routine, I found myself back at WAIT talking with Tom Dockerty as I always did over lunch. During one of our lunches, he told me he wanted me to meet someone. The man was from the Department of Science and Technology and his name was Dr. George Melville. We met and I showed him a movie I had about making a dive with a very sophisticated manipulator. I explained that I realized the only thing in Australia were agencies like his, not the actual industries that could build this kind of high-tech equipment. I said if he would let me, I would start a subsea manufacturing industry in Australia. He asked me what I needed. I explained I was not a permanent resident of the country and would soon be deported, so I needed to be sponsored in the country. That was not problem, he said. Then he asked how much money I needed. I told him I needed several million dollars upfront and at the end of the day, the industry could produce a hundred million dollars a year over time. He told me that that was the exact type of projects they were looking for in Western Australia. It was then that I figured that man I had heard months ago on television was right. I gave Dr. Melville all my contact information and said I hoped to hear from him. He said he would definitely get back with me.

Figure 82 Me and Tom Dockerty

Once again, I made jaws drop when I went back to the Department of Industrial Development and told them I had just met with Dr. George Melville. Instead of questioning how I did it, this time they were just very excited. They explained that the Department for Science and Technology was a federal government agency overseeing the entire nation. They said that if that department would back me, I would be good to go, which is Australian slang telling me I was winning and that things would be all right. It seems they thought I was doing a good job in my own efforts to start my project and get my business underway.

It was only a few days later that Dr. Melville called to say he was bringing a few people to Western Australia to meet with me. One of those people was Dr. Neville Byrne. After hanging up I called the Department of Industrial Development to tell them what had just transpired. They told me we would have the meeting at my house. I told them I didn't have any money to supply food and drinks to cater a party for fifteen people. They said to not worry, just order up the food and drinks and they would take care of it. So that was what I did.

Now here is what you need to know. Senator John Button was Dr. Neville Byrne's boss. Byrne was the head of the Department of Science and Technology. The support I was getting was not because I had followed up the chain of command reaching higher and higher. It was because I had put money in the bank with relationships with Tom Dockerty and others and because I took the initiative to just make calls to people who I thought could help me. It was all done without thought to the status or position of anyone in particular. It was serendipitous the way everyone began to cross connect and come together.

The day came for the party and everyone arrived. I had lots of food and beer. I opened a few of the beers, but no one ate or drank much. We mostly sat around and talked about what I had in mind. In the end, they said they wanted to support me. I could hardly believe it when they said they would be contacting me shortly. I was overcome. I knew I was making good headway.

After everyone from the federal government left, I had lots of food and beer left over. As the local people were getting ready to leave, I asked them what they wanted me to do with all the leftovers. They told me to eat it and drink it and enjoy it. There was enough food to last me and my family for about a week. It was their way of helping me out when they had no way of giving me money to live. It is just one example of the kind hearts of the Australian people.

Part of the generosity shown by the staff at the Department of Industrial Development was spawned by their knowledge of what was going on in my home at the time. You see, the home equity loan had dried up. We were really down and out. By that I meant we had no money to put food on the table or gas in the car. Talk about being nervous as a cat. I was one jumpy guy.

I decided to go and try my luck at getting food stamps. I was not sure I would qualify with my citizenship status – or really, my lack of citizenship or even a visa status. I called and made an appointment. When I walked in the door, I was dressed in my one and only suit, including a tie, and carried my briefcase, even though it was empty. I proceeded to the receptionist's desk and told her the name of the person I wanted to see. She obviously thought I was a salesman because she mentioned that the only place available for me to wait was in a room with all the people who were there to apply for food stamps. I assured her that was not a problem for me.

I scanned the room as I entered. It seemed to be filled with single mothers and lots of little kids running around and playing with toys. Despite all the activity, it was quiet, even somber. I noticed that I was the only one dressed in business attire. And when they looked at me, I knew I was not in the norm. In my mind, these were the only clothes I had to attend to business like this and it sure didn't seem appropriate to dress down for the occasion.

When they announced my name, just like they did for everyone else, they all looked at me in disbelief. I could see the question in the thought bubbles rising above their heads. What is this well-dressed man doing here looking for food stamps? If they had actually voiced the question, I could have easily replied that I, and my family, could get just as hungry as they do with no money.

My uncertainty grew even more intense when we began to discuss my citizenship status. I had none. I explained what I was working on with the government departments. I made particular mention that I was getting ready to start this enterprise. Her face relaxed when I said I literally had no money to provide for my family. She told me that because of my affiliation with the government and how it looked like I would be working with them, she could give me two weeks' worth of food stamps that was worth a total of $60. I readily agreed, thanking her for her consideration over and over.

It felt good to be able to go home with money in my pocket that would, I hoped, stock the pantry for two weeks. My wife and I gathered up my son and turned toward the market. It was a challenge to me to see how much I could purchase with the limited funds. I marched up and down aisles filling the trolley with spaghetti, cereal, milk and more. Our trolley was fairly full by the time we got up to the cashier. When we got there, I realized I was alone. My wife was nowhere to be seen. I paid for our purchases and went to find her.

As I left the store, I found her slumped on the curb, crying. I then understood the way she felt. We had fallen far, and she was helpless in the whole deal. She could do nothing but wait to see what I would achieve – or pull out of my hat.

So, after two weeks and all the groceries were gone, I went back to the food stamp office to ask for another $60 worth of food stamps. I was told this payment was the last I would be given, and, on top of that, I would have to pay back the $120 I received when I got up and running. I prayed another two weeks would be sufficient and assured her I could be relied upon to pay the money back.

The food stamps bridged the gap between poverty and a path to employment. I was a lucky man to have the opportunity to get that relief. I now have greater empathy for people who have to accept food stamps on a regular basis. The experience laid another brick in the wall of my character. I felt by the time I got my project – my business – up and running, I would have a brick wall that a tank would never penetrate. I was grateful.

When I got a call from the Department of Science and Technology it was explained what I had to do next. My project would be one of several that would be presented to a review board. This was the last hurdle I would face and needed to be more than prepared. I needed to have my big guns loaded.

First, I had to finish the business plan with Arthur Anderson. That would include the financial picture for the project including showing all the cash flows in place.

Next, me, the talker, would have to prepare a speech. I knew I could talk the leg off a turkey. Instead, I went to see my friend Tom Dockerty. He and his students helped me put together a video. I wanted to go the extra mile since I knew that always paid off.

In addition, I needed to compile a portfolio of references out in the industry that would support me and use the equipment I would manufacture.

John McDonald, the head of the Australian diving union wrote that my business would put people to work in the diving industry. He had been especially concerned about older divers being assimilated into the new high-tech developments. I had explained how their expertise and hands-on skills would be invaluable as the new robotic technology came into play. While engineers and builders would be on the front lines building, the older divers had an edge because they knew the equipment that would be worked on with the new technology. Once he understood he was excited to be part of supporting my company. It would be helping divers continue their careers successfully.

Bob Baker, who was the head of Shell Oil's offshore drilling program, had worked with me previously. He knew my work ethic as well as my expertise and skills. He came personally all the way from Perth, some 3,000 miles away, which had surprised me. We stayed at the same hotel and had dinner and drinks the night before my presentation. Never once did he say anything about the surprise in his briefcase that he would spring on me in front of the review board.

Unbeknownst to me, he had led a contingent that reviewed my ROV plans and then presented documentation that if I built the equipment, Shell would definitely buy it. He bluntly told the review board, "We support what this man is doing. We would buy his gear." I was flabbergasted and delighted. Nothing could have made me prouder in that moment.

Relationships, my money in the bank, were paying dividends. The experience revealed to me that when people got on board with me, they went the extra mile for me. Whatever it was that I brought to them, it was definitely appreciated. I see now how so many went to bat for me and ran the bases right alongside me when they did not have to do so. For that, I am immensely grateful and indebted.

Shell Oil did indeed lease the first ROV my company built and many more after that. As a result, I made sure that we never disappointed them. I think that made our relationship stronger. Their first contract was in 1990 and even as I write this they still work with my company.

I knew that one of the biggest points I had to make to the review board addressed what the federal people referred to as the "multiplier effect." That is how when you employ 300 hundred people in your company, you are probably supporting several thousand people in the community. This happens because you pay your employees and they spend their money on homes, cars, clothing, food, and other products in local businesses. By employing many people and paying them well, an individual business can support, and even transform, the surrounding community. I knew we would have a good multiplier effect and included that in my presentation.

The day came and I was ready to present myself and my project to the review board. I had it together and working. They laughed when they saw me, saying that the first fledgling entrepreneur coming in front of them was a Yank. After hearing what that man on television said about wanting Australians to be more like American entrepreneurs, I knew that was a good thing. I gave my presentation and walked out into the hall feeling good.

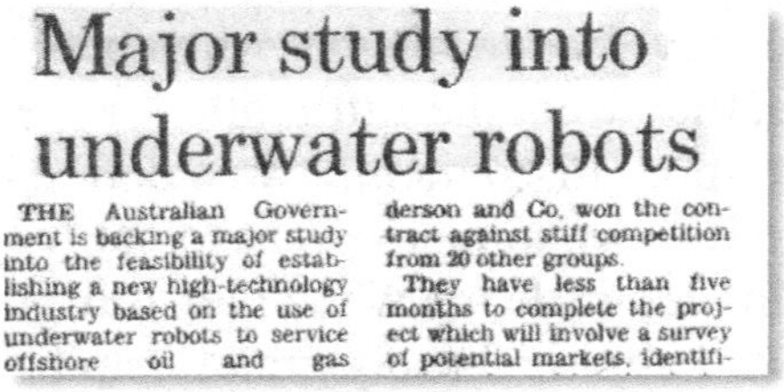

Major study into underwater robots

THE Australian Government is backing a major study into the feasibility of establishing a new high-technology industry based on the use of underwater robots to service offshore oil and gas

derson and Co. won the contract against stiff competition from 20 other groups.

They have less than five months to complete the project which will involve a survey of potential markets, identifi-

Figure 83 August 4, 1964 The Weekend Australian published a story about the feasibility study for my ROV.

After only about ten or fifteen minutes, both Dr. Byrne and Dr. Melville came outside and sat down beside me. They said it went well and the board had decided to spend $350,000 to push this project – or at least a feasibility study – forward. I could not believe what I had just heard. They hired me to work with the people in Canberra (the federal capitol) at a rate of $500 per day. Dr. Byrne had told the review board that that was the kind of money they had to pay to get good people to do the best work. I was OK with that.

One more time in my life I felt I had been in several of the right places at the right times to get to this day. Yes, I put in the blood, sweat, and tears. Australia was the right place and my experience with high-tech gave me the edge to make it the right time. It couldn't have been more perfect.

I never thought I was anything special. I always thought I was the underdog scratching to get to the top of the heap. Because of that, I never quit. In retrospect I now realize what a crazy journey I have had simply because I was tenacious. I often felt I was the underdog. What made the difference is that I was a tenacious underdog –

with my bone. Everything fit together into a wonderful mosaic of persistence, relationships, determination, and commitment to what I knew was good and right. Yes, it all fits together.

At the time, the government of Australia was asking if what I was saying was feasible. And I had to give them the answer.

It took six months to complete the feasibility study. My team and I flew around the world and spoke to as many oil companies as we felt would use the equipment. Although the initial ROV would be simple to operate and repair, future ROV systems would be robotic and autonomous. We spoke to universities in the country to determine if the courses they offered were capable of teaching people to build and operate the high-tech robots the company would eventually produce. We also talked with local businesses to see if they had the capability to provide the services to support the enterprise such as machining, electronics, welding, and trucking.

At the end of the study, we had all the boxes checked. The oil companies said they would use the product. The universities had the courses to train engineers. And the local industries could provide all the skilled trades and services needed to support manufacture of the robots. We were there. We had it all. The only difference was that instead of building the ROV for drilling support operations, for which I had the plans and patents, the government's recommendation was that we mass produce a small, low-cost version of the ROV for leisure and military applications. In my mind, it was a toy.

Because of that, no one would invest in my original plan. I switched focus to the low-cost mini ROV, even though it wasn't my heart's desire.

So, what was the next step? I was thrown on the street with a magnificent business plan, credibility from the oil companies, the Australian government behind me, and all the knowledge needed to make a product. A toy product.

Business 101 in the School of Hard Knocks

This stretch of time was challenging and emotionally exhausting. One day I would be feeling hopeful with possibility and the next my hopes were dashed. There was no way I was giving up or in. I knew what I had was useful for the oil industry and valuable to the country. And with no other options for work, my goal of building my own ROVs was the only future I could see or choose to see. While some might say that single-minded focus was foolhardy, it was the only thing I could envision for my future.

With a vision as big as the one I had, I realized that I could not do it all myself. In fact, no one can do it all by themselves. No one has all the skills and knowledge, or the time, to successfully build a business. I learned to seek out others who had the skills, knowledge, and expertise that I lacked. I authentically and honestly related to them what they needed to understand about me and what I was trying to do. Those personal connections once again supported my efforts, taking up for me in ways I never expected.

To get started and in order to survive, I often did what someone else wanted me to do; from meeting specific people to having a party in my home when I could not afford it. Then, in the end, I went along with the recommendation and started building mini ROVs. That option had never even crossed my mind. At the time, I had no viable alternative to stay afloat. So that was what I did. However, that big ROV was still in the back of my mind.

By this time, my mind was focused on my life and what I was trying to do. When I would share with my family in Indiana what I was working on and achieving, no one believed me. Whatever was going on in Indiana had very little relevance to me. In fact, I seldom thought about the family back home. I guess to be honest, I learned to not think about it. You know, I don't care how much negativity you have about your family, they're still your family. I think my parent's negativity came from the fact that I was such a poor student, and in their minds once a poor student, always a poor student. Just like it would be for a lot of people, it was hard for them to consider I could ever do well and go as far as I did.

Part III - Business No. 2 - Parry Corporation

At this time in Australia, the buzz was all about high-tech and those leading the stock market were looking for high-tech companies to bring into their fold. It took about a week to get a meeting with one of the top entrepreneurs in the country, Kevin Parry.

Parry's company, Parry Corporation, owned a satellite television network; NBN Newcastle, which was a television station; a home appliance chain, and they were a housing developer. Now I wanted to get them into the underwater robot business. As odd as that sounds, it seemed they were interested.

On the day of the meeting, I was led into a boardroom where Mr. Parry and several of the members of the board of directors for the company were seated. I saw they were checking me out just like I was checking them out. It was a comfort to receive the warm welcome they offered. We chatted a bit. Then it was time to get down to business.

As I proceeded through the presentation, I noticed their body language. I could tell I was doing a good job and they were receptive. When I finished, and asked for questions, I was a bit taken aback with the first question out of the gate. They wanted to know what I wanted to get my project rolling.

I handed them the business plan and they were impressed with the depth and breadth. They thumbed through it quickly and then looked back at me and started asking questions. I realized that the questions they were asking were questions you ask when you want to close a deal. I started to get excited. I really felt I was winning.

After my meeting with Kevin and his directors, there were lots of smiles and positive comments going around the table. Kevin told me he was interested, and that, I later discovered, meant that the team was interested. They would go along with whatever he said because he was the boss.

He said they wanted to digest a bit more of what I had presented to them and he walked me to the door. He shook my hand and said he looked forward to seeing me again soon and that they would call me.

My first thought was that here we were again with that "I'll call you" line. Even still, I walked out to my car with a big smile on my face. When I got home, I told my wife about the great meeting I had had with Kevin and the Parry Corporation group of people. I don't think she was that excited. How could I blame her?

Over the year I had told her about everything in a positive way. I think she was desensitized to the gravity of my undertakings by the stories I told her. What I did not know was that she was somewhat depressed. Later I discovered that before we met, she had had bouts of depression. I believe that being dragged around the world, never owning a house or having a grounded home until that time in our lives had been hard on her. For her, rental homes in cities around the world with different languages and cultures had been difficult. So, when I got home with this wonderful news, it was very much anti-climactic. I did not have a lot of people to share the news with or celebrate with. I felt that things were going to start to be good again.

Well, it seems the Aussies are true to their word and good at calling back. It only took one day, and Dr. Jim Chute was on the phone saying he wanted to make a deal. Jim Chute was the high-tech director for Parry Corporation. He asked me to come in to talk.

I had called Kevin Parry because Parry Corporation was one of the most prominent companies in Western Australia. Kevin was a hands-on entrepreneur who was also known as a bit of a rough diamond. I figured because of that he and I would get along well.

Parry seeks oil robot deal

Figure 84 I landed my first partner with the help of the Australian government.

I found Kevin and his people understood that with the government supporting me, there was a real reason to listen to what I had to say. Not just that, I could show that there was a market for the high-tech product I wanted to manufacture – or at least credible evidence of a market.

When I met with Dr. Chute, I carefully explained my situation. Basically, I needed an income and fast. The deal was that Parry could have 50 percent of the company if they paid me $20,000 now and a salary of $60,000 per year. They agreed and I was overjoyed.

After that meeting things moved quickly. They gave me an office in a building at their corporate complex. I came to work every day and we registered a company name, Underwater Systems Australia, Ltd. (USAL) showing the fifty/fifty ownership and I went to work. We needed to hire people and create a plan to get the company rolling. We needed space to work and money to buy parts, machines, hire people, and for marketing.

There was no pressure from Parry to fire up the business and although I appreciated being given the room to work on my own, an uneasy feeling sat on my shoulder during this time. I started wondering what we were really doing here. Progress was slow, really slow, and there was no push to get things rolling faster.

Other than that slight feeling of unease, I thought I was on my way and everything was working out well. I saved my house from being repossessed and reduced the bank loan to a manageable amount. I had regular income and I had a future as the CEO of my very own company. Or at least 50 percent of a company. Even if everyone else was lackadaisical, I was excited and ready to go at it every single day.

As I got to learn the lay of the land at Parry Corporation, I found the people to be friendly. The corporate headquarters was a complex of several buildings just outside of town. In three of the buildings, there were boardrooms, and in true Australian fashion, each contained a bar. At the end of the day, someone poked their head into my office and told me to join them in the boardroom. The bartender asked what I drank. I said vodka and Coke. They did not have vodka, so I had a beer. As the afternoon wore on, more and more executives and their secretaries joined us. I soon learned this was a daily ritual. It was more like a pub atmosphere than a board room.

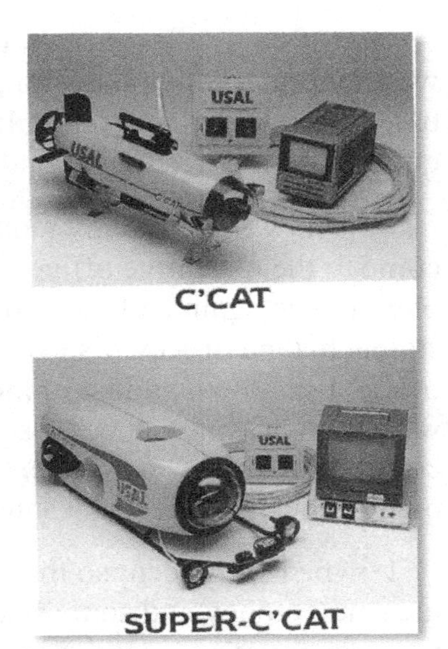

Figure 85 These were the first mass produced ROVs. We sold thousands of them around the world.

That description wasn't quite right, though. Kevin always came in a bit later than everyone else and the secretaries were chased out of the room. He used the bars as an extension to the workday. I did not mind. I found it productive. The only thing I worried about was driving home afterward on the freeway. I tried to watch my drinking because of that. I had about a five-minute run home and knew that the police were out there waiting for me on the highway.

One afternoon I went into the boardroom bar and there was my preferred vodka sitting front and center on the bar. The person stocking the liquor told me it was requested for me and that meant I had arrived.

Several weeks into my tenure, I got a call asking me to come to the executive offices. On the trek across the complex, I once again had that good feeling in the pit of my stomach. One of Kevin's executives ushered me into his office. I sat down and he immediately told me that Kevin wanted to buy me out because he wanted to float our company, Underwater Systems Australia, Ltd., (USAL) on the stock market. He wanted to take USAL public!

I owned 50 percent so the idea was that he would offer me some money and some shares of stock. The next thing to come out of his mouth was that Kevin would give me $100,000. If you remember all of my struggles, you can probably understand how gob smacked I was and why I couldn't say a word. While I was tongue tied, he immediately upped it to $150,000. I thought if he is willing to jump that quickly, there is more money in this bag. I told him I had to think about it. He said that was no problem.

It wasn't a problem for me to think about it, but there was a deadline looming. The tax law on capital gains was changing and in order for the deal to work, we had to finalize everything before that change date which was coming quickly. The pressure pushed the deal along and eventually we settled on a package that was worth about a half million dollars. I received $250,000 in cash and $250,000 in $1 shares in the new public company. We closed on it before the tax change date.

After the deal was done, I went home and told my wife. She did not respond the way I thought she would to the news. I could not understand why she could not enjoy the moment. Not too long after that the check arrived, along with a brand-new car that the company provided. They also raised my salary to $80,000. Things were good and I was happy.

The focus of my work changed at this new juncture. I was now out pursuing contracts and other ways to grow the company and increase its value by developing other products and services that were complimentary to the underwater business.

What we had to begin with was a well-connected business in Australia through Parry Corporation. It was an unspoken practice norm that Australian businesses support other local businesses. Therefore, Australian businesses made a practice of partnering with companies outside the country that had the technology and resources needed to do jobs. In that way, Australian businesses benefited and grew bringing technology into the country. The Australian businesses were the conduit to the rest of the world.

Two companies, one in Canada and one in America, were eager to create joint venture agreements with us. Those agreements would get our service line into the military and the oil industries in Australia. We would bring income and value to the company through securing upcoming Australian contracts. Our company began to accrue value through these contracts, which

$25m plan boosts Mandurah

High-tech park has link with Australia II

Figure 86 We were creating a buzz in Australia with ROVs.

were in addition to the manufacture of the mini ROV toy line.

It didn't take long for me to realize that I had been integrated into the upper echelons of Parry Corporation. Kevin was owner or partial owner of several different companies under the larger umbrella. His other partners were considered executive directors and formed his team. As co-owner of USAL I was a part of that group. Not only was I a part of the group, Kevin sincerely liked me.

I found I was attending a lot of meetings with him. Mostly I did a lot of listening. We visited with a lot of influential people around the country. One day, Kevin mentioned he was going to compete in the America's Cup in Rhode Island. I knew it was a sailboat race for only the very wealthy of the world. Kevin pledged $31 million for the campaign. I was in awe and hoped my mouth was not hanging open.

As part of the America's Cup race, Kevin got a lot of publicity on Australian television and in the international news. He was becoming world famous, and it opened a lot of doors for him. I knew this firsthand because I accompanied him on many overseas trips.

He always took a few of his executive directors on these trips and it was always first class all the way. On a trip to California, we stayed at the Beverly Hilton. The next trip we stayed at the Beverly Wilshire for three entire weeks. While we were there, we ate at every restaurant on Rodeo Drive.

One of his favorite restaurants was a place called Jimmy's. When we were there, we were surrounded by Rolls Royce cars, mink coats, and people in tuxedoes and gowns. What I did not see there were Hollywood celebrities. The reason was that Jimmy's was the place for directors, producers, and studio owners, not the actors.

During these trips, I got to rub elbows with some of the most famous people in America including Glenn Campbell, Andy Williams, Jack Lemmon, and even Ringo Starr. I ran into Ringo on an elevator. I asked him if the rumor about the Beatles getting back together was true and he tersely told me that it would never happen. The Beatles were done. The rest of that elevator ride was in silence.

The day finally came for the meeting with Kevin and the board of directors to discuss the actual IPO for USAL. Kevin said that my company by itself was not worth much. It was his name and his reputation that gave it its worth. He said that without him, by myself, I could not float the company on the stock market. Any IPO I tried would fail. I agreed with him. The plan was to meet again tomorrow to re-evaluate the company and give it a new value. He reiterated that without him, USAL was not worth much and I could never initiate an IPO for the company on the stock market. He also told me not to be shocked at the new valuation of USAL.

The next day we all met in the boardroom again at a formal Board meeting. A motion was made to float the company on the stock market with an Initial Public Offering. A lot of work had already been done by accountants and other professionals to prepare for the offering. Then Kevin stood up and announced the new company valuation. It was $24 million. I was told later that Kevin had been prepared to pay me up to $1 million dollars;

$500,000 cash and $500,000 in shares. Although a shock, I was glad to get what I had gotten.

USAL surfaces for another issue

Figure 87 After the initial IPO, Kevin Parry tried it again.

The company went public on the stock market and the IPO raised $12 million. I could not believe that all the legwork and paperwork I had done had resulted in one $300 plastic robotic toy and now it was worth $24 million. I was not sure how that had come to be. I was happy that I had 250,000 shares that I hoped would rise in value.

We took the $12 million raised in the IPO and put it back into the company. We purchased property down on the water in Fremantle, remodeled the buildings and hired people to start manufacturing.

In the feasibility survey, the Australian government felt there was no market for a large drilling support ROV. What they did recommend and suggest was that there was a market for a small ROV weighing about ten pounds. A personal ROV, if you will. One that could be used by the military for mine hunting. The factory down on the water began manufacturing, for lack of better words, toy underwater robots. We became the largest purchaser of color CCD cameras out of Japan. We placed an order for 4,500 cameras along with 200 km of umbilical cable. We also purchased $500,000 worth of rechargeable batteries. Then we began building the Mini ROVs.

We continued to travel to America because Kevin had companies and business dealings in the United States. All the executives of the companies and other guests would meet in one of the restaurants on Rodeo Drive. There were usually about fifteen people. Kevin and I had developed a good relationship and I usually sat next to, or near him, during these meetings. Kevin would introduce everyone and when he got to me, not only did he introduce me, he told my story, too.

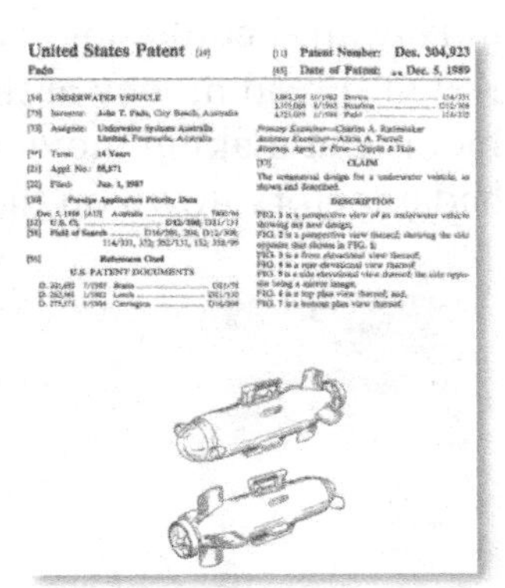
United States Patent
Pado
Patent Number: Des. 304,923
Date of Patent: Dec. 5, 1989

UNDERWATER VEHICLE

Term: 14 Years

CLAIM

DESCRIPTION

Figure 88 My second patent for small robots.

At one of the gatherings, a guy chimed in at the end asking if I would like to meet Jacques Cousteau. I was surprised and said, “You’re kidding me!” He told me that he knew him because he had done business with his company for years and they had become friends. He said Cousteau had an office just down the road from him and he would take me down there if I wanted to go. I almost peed my pants. A few days later, I found myself in Cousteau’s Los Angeles office talking with his son, John Michelle Cousteau.

John Michelle explained the company, how it worked, what they were doing, and their timelines. Afterward, I went back to Kevin and casually told him about the meeting we had had with John Michelle. Kevin saw an opportunity for my company. He asked the executive who had introduced me to Cousteau to set up a meeting between Kevin and John Michelle. At the end of the meeting, Kevin offered to build a $25 million facility for Cousteau in Hawaii. I could not believe it. How quickly and easily Kevin spread money around. Cousteau said they were looking at making movies in Australia. I told him that we had a factory down on the water in Australia. I also said that his big boats could stay for free on the water, with utilities and dock rentals at no charge. The payback was that I could use his name and have my robots featured in the movies. They accepted and came to Australia to moor behind my factory for a year. I was awed by this fact. I could not believe it was happening.

Figure 89 John Michelle Cousteau and me.

What I did not know and found out later was that when my company was floated on the stock market, Parry Corporation was strapped for cash. The plan for the money taken in was that it would be loaned to Parry Corporation. The loan would be paid back over the next twelve years. The interest and term were set so that nobody would complain about the loan to Parry. As it turns out, it would never last twelve years.

Over the next five years we tried to build the business. Cash flow was a problem. In 1987 when the markets crashed, Parry Corporation began collapsing. The banks came in for their money. Finally, an outside group from Hong Kong called Hang Lung Development Co., bought the corporation. Because it was purchased through a stock acquisition, there was no due diligence performed. Once they got into the company to see the books and assess the strength of the companies, they were not happy. When the banks and creditors came calling, it cost Hang Lung something in the area of $165 million. They paid it all and liquidated a lot of the companies, including mine.

Hang Lung hangs out white flag

Figure 90 I wasn't the only one impacted in the Parry Corp. collapse.

Toward the end of Parry's ownership, I had made noises that we should get into the oil drilling support business. That had always been my original intention. No one ever agreed with me. Then I got a call from Oceaneering Singapore asking me if I wanted my old submarine to sit in my front yard. I asked what they wanted for it. We went back and forth casually over several months while the value of the sub declined. Finally, in the end, I traded them two small ROVs for all the guts of the submarine. I got everything except the hull.

This was exactly what I wanted and needed to build the ROV I always wanted to build. The corporate office didn't bother me because I was using these old junk parts and pieces and it was not costing the company any money. I was definitely getting back to my old tricks of using things around me, trading for stuff, and making things work while people around me laughed at me or ridiculed my project. They really did not care one way or another about it.

Returning to the way I had worked as a kid with no money and working all by myself made me feel like I was at home again. It did not take long before I was wheeling and dealing to get cable, borrow a winch, and happily scrounge for parts. Once I had enough parts, I built a functional ROV according to my patent design. I tested it in the ocean and showed all the Parry Corporation Directors including the new Hang Lung executives. I explained this is the direction we should go. I still got lots of resistance. They did not understand the drilling support business. All they saw was the retail business and the mass production of little ROVs. No one wanted to listen to me about the drilling support business. No one. They wanted to sell the business and leave it behind them.

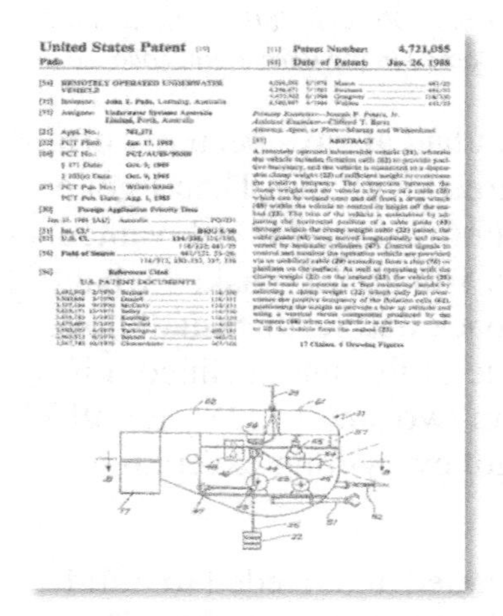
United States Patent

Patent Number: 4,721,055

Date of Patent: Jan. 26, 1988

ABSTRACT

17 Claims, 4 Drawing Figures

Figure 91 My patent for a work class ROV.

My wife was under a lot of stress. She was feeling anxious about all the problems with Parry. It was not just Parry; the entire world was crashing. And part of that crash was our marriage. Divorce was appearing inevitable.

As October 1987 went by, then 1988 and 1989 came with the selling off of all the businesses under the Parry Corporation umbrella now owned by Hang Lung. The television station, NBN Newcastle, went first, all the rest of the properties followed. Hang Lung sold the mini ROV division and the building where we manufactured the toys. My drilling support business was still on hold. I could see me sitting out in the cold – again.

Although I felt down in so many ways, I was not out. I started scrambling. By this time in my career, I knew how to take action to try to make things happen. I was not giving in or giving up.

There were a couple managers at Elders Resources named Bob and Dave that knew my story. I had explained to them what the big ROV was for and what I wanted to do with it. When the liquidator was finally selling everything out of USAL, Elders Resources fronted the money for me to purchase my ad hoc hobby ROV from the company for $250,000.

At the end when I left the Parry Corporation, I felt I was leaving with the equivalent of a reverse Harvard Business degree. I had learned a lot of things NOT to do in a business. I was walking away with the ROV and my ideas. I knew I had a future, I just had to figure out what it would be and how to build it.

Business 101 in the School of Hard Knocks

From my experiences with Parry Corporation, I learned that what I saw as a straight-forward business – designing and building ROVs for drilling support in the oil industry – was not what others would see in my business. Parry saw my business, no matter what I did in that business, as a means to bolster the larger corporation. Taking my company public was just another way to make money for the operations of the umbrella organization.

All the businesses under the Parry Corporation umbrella were in the same situation. Money was being made and shifted around to keep the whole enterprise afloat, until the bubble burst. At that point there was not enough left in any of the companies to salvage the wreck.

In retrospect, I recognize that I was cheated by the way I was bought out and then the company floated on the market at a much greater value. Also, in retrospect, I see that the improved value was a paper value, so I was, honestly, happy with what I got from the deal.

Following my gut, I had already started down the path I originally intended by acquiring and building my design “on the side” as I ran USAL. Therefore, when the end came, I still had something tangible to hold onto. It might not have been much, but it was something that revealed what I wanted to do and where I still wanted to go.

I had passion for what I wanted to do in my own business, even while the people I partnered with saw my company completely differently. That was a lesson I have not forgotten since.

Part IV - The Importance of Paul

I first met Paul when we hired him as an electronics technician at USAL. At the time, I was 40 years old and he was 20 years old. Over the time we worked together at USAL, I got to know him pretty well. Our work together at Drill Support International is what really brought to light what we could do together.

Figure 92 Paul Colley, the best partner I could ever have.

At first glance, he did not appear to be what he really was. He was a tall, gangly young man with long hair. He looked like a hippie who was more likely to say, "Cool, man," and saunter away with his head in the clouds. In reality, he is extremely smart and very quiet. I had to work with him a while to see the man he was inside. When I did, I saw so much potential. I came to see he was technically and personally brilliant and performed his work diligently. It was the complete opposite of what anyone would expect at first glance. I understood how that is because I had been told that I was not what I appeared to be, either.

In addition to that common ground, we had skills that overlapped. When we combined what I knew and what he knew, we created bigger and better things together than we could have achieved individually. The two of us together were impressive and people took note.

In fact, we started to hear comparisons of us to other partnerships such as Captain Kirk and Dr. Spock and even Steve Jobs and Steve Wozniak. At first, I was taken aback. After I thought about it a bit, I had to agree with the comparisons.

One aspect of our work together that was exceptional was the way we interacted with the staff. The best way to describe it was that we were like parents, a mom and a dad. Paul was the father figure who made people come to work on time and toe the line to get their work done. I was the mother figure who made sure everyone had a social life and was happy. He had them working hard and I would organize barbecues and take the engineers and others in shifts to enjoy a late lunch in the afternoons. It worked really well. Paul made them feel like someone cared about the company business that needed to get done. He was a quiet achiever. I made them feel happy about working for the company. The result was that we retained more than ninety percent of our workers. We grew from just the two of us to an employee roster of more than 300, with many of the original employees dedicating 28 or more years of their work lives to our company. We were like a giant family and with our aligned efforts, we built incredible machines.

The way we worked together to build and sustain the company was important, too. Paul and I never argued. When we had disagreements, and we did, we would always solve them by talking through them. We built a mutual trust between us and we both knew we could rely on the other to do what was best and right for the company. At any time either of us could go on vacation and completely unwind and relax because we knew the business was in good hands back home.

When people would come through the shop, I would tell them that it was all Paul's doing. He was the man. Paul would tell people it was all my doing. I was the man. In reality, we did not care who was THE man. What we looked at was the bottom line. When the money came in every month, we split it up and were happy. The earnings of the company started out to be about $1.4 million a year and today, it is as high as $100 million per year. It was good.

It was not just how we worked within the company that was good, it was how we interacted with prospects and clients, too. When we would meet with a potential client, I would start the spiel and Paul would listen. Then I would stop so Paul could chime in with his expertise and fill in anything I had forgotten. We would go back and forth like that to be certain every client's questions were answered before they knew what to ask. We alternated speaking not just to inform the client. We alternated to keep their attention on what we had to say to them. We were a very effective sales team and our customers knew we would be there from the initial sale to the completion of the project as well. When we left the presentation, the client had all the information needed to make an informed decision.

It was very important to us both that when we told clients we would do something, we did it, and we did it right away. The oil community is very small, and it didn't take long for us to develop a reputation. We were the guys to go to when you needed something done. We were proud to be known as ambitious, talented, and reliable.

Figure 93 Our skills and personalities complemented each other. Paul and I were a great team.

It was not just a sales pitch to us. It was how we worked from day one. I remember one job when we were on an oil rig called Ocean General. Our ROV had just been placed on the helicopter deck and the head of the rig, a man named Jimmy Watson, came up to see what it looked like. Paul and I explained what the ROV was, how it worked, and why we had built it the way we did. He was impressed and told us that this was the first ROV he ever understood how it worked. He commented that he was "in the presence of geniuses." Wow, what a compliment from an oil man.

Together, Paul and I built equipment that was cheaper, smaller, and could get more work done than other company's gear. We paid attention to all the negatives that were out there and designed underwater robots that solved all those problems. And it worked. Now today, our company has ROVs working 10,000 feet below the sea day in and day out around the world.

Now TMT is making an ROV that will go to 6,000 meters under the sea; that is 19,500 feet, or 3.7 miles. This new ROV can withstand a pressure of 4.5 tons PSI. It is amazing how far we have gone with the technology over the years.

The business model we developed worked really well for us. In light of the results we got, it was, in fact, about as good a model as anyone could ever get. We were a great team. I have watched other people fight with their partners and threaten each other with words and violence. Egos erupt and arguments ensue over who is working harder or doing more. These people spent their valuable time in fighting amongst themselves instead of building their businesses. We watched many businesses go down the tubes in this way.

Ours did not go down the tubes and part of the reason is that we were of one mindset. We viewed building a team and a business like putting together a rock star band. The greatest bands of all times are composed of people from different backgrounds and with different talents that are brought together to let their excellence shine individually and collectively. We could recognize potential in people and actively cultivated that potential. Every individual in our band made an integral contribution. And just like the greatest bands, we made beautiful music and it was a joy to come to work.

Choosing a partner in business is just like choosing a partner in marriage. You have to really get to know a person and want to build a good life with them. Oh, and one other thing, there is no kissing with the business partner.

Paul and I had a synergy that worked and worked exceedingly well. No one would ever guess that these two seemingly polar opposite men would run one of the greatest high-tech companies in Australia (I think the world). Now, more than thirty years later, I know I was not wrong, he was the perfect partner for me.

Part V - Business No. 3 Drill Support International

Our new partners were not just managers at Elders Resources, they were accountants. The good thing about that situation was that they lived in Melbourne, 3,400 kilometers away. I was my own boss and could run the business how I saw best. All there was to get started was me, Paul, and this big old ROV in a small shed.

Drill Support International was the name of the new company and I was determined we would make a name for ourselves in the oil industry.

When I worked the deal with Bob and Dave, they had 49.5 percent of the ownership and I had 49.5 percent. I made sure that Paul got one percent of the company, and his vote was often the deciding vote. After working with him in the oil industry, which was completely new for him, I saw that he was invaluable. I felt that his contributions and how we worked together was important and I wanted him to know I appreciated him, so within the first year, I gave him an additional eight percent from my shares.

PADO hits PAY DIRT

Figure 94 The first ROV produced by DSI. We hit the market with a contract with Shell Oil.

The first two jobs Drill Support International did were for Shell Oil. My relationship with Shell was paying off and I knew that if we performed well and met their expectations time and again, they would continue to support us. We told them what we could and would do and we did it.

As the years went on, the company got bigger and bigger. That wasn't by chance. I kept a close eye on our competitors. You have to know what your competitors are doing. In fact, I would call and visit their offices and shops unannounced and just walk in their back door to find out what they were doing. I guess you could say I was doing my own version of secret shopping. It was good-natured, but serious, when I would pull into their shops, walk around, talk to people, and take notes. I would use my name when questioned and get chased out. We all laughed about the unorthodox and ballsy way I approached the market research I did.

The downside to all our success was that in order to get the original deal done, I had agreed to pay back the original purchase price of $250,000 with compounding interest to Elders Resources. However, when Elders Resources folded as a business, because of the 1987 stock crash, Bob and Dave purchased the company out of the fire sale and so I ended up owing my partners, who already owned 49.5 percent of the business. Did I tell you they were accountants – and I am not? At the time I knew it wasn't a good deal. I had agreed because I felt I had no choice in order to keep the business going. Because of the compounding interest, the original purchase price was ballooning out of my reach. I knew I could never make enough to buy it back.

I decided that the only way I could ever make it work was to build a business that was valuable enough to sell before I owed my partners more money than the company was worth. And so that is what Paul and I did. Within a couple of years, a company called Stolt Comex Seaway came along and bought us out.

The sale allowed Dave and Bob to get their money along with a tidy profit. It also allowed Paul and I to make some money, too.

Now Paul and I had new partners.

Business 101 in the School of Hard Knocks

What I learned was that the deal I made to start Drill Support International was set up as a no-win situation for me. There was a very slim chance that I would ever get full control of the business. The more time that passed, the less value I had in the company. Eventually, my partners, who essentially owned half at the start, and then owned the debt, would chip away at my ownership share, leaving me – and Paul – with nothing.

When deals are structured, buyers and sellers both have to look at the long-term implications. In my case, I was just trying to keep the business open. It was the only choice I could see at the time. Because the other option was to shut down the company and take a job working for someone else. I did not want to do that. I had big plans.

Throughout the entire history of building a business, I was facing many different challenges and trying to turn them into positives. One of the biggest challenges was partnerships.

By the time I met Paul and saw the potential we had as a team I also saw that to really be successful, we had to be more independent from moneyed partners. Paul was the first partner that I could see as permanent. The others were a means to an end. I never felt that way about Paul. He was someone who would be alongside me for the long haul. We were two sides of the same coin. We were both good at most all aspects of the business, just in a different way. Between us we were able to relate to all aspects of a potential customer. We shared values: Tell the truth, do what you say, and do it now. You can't wait – it shows you are keen. Neither of us cut down or discounted our opponents.

We both also knew the value of doing our homework before going into a meeting with a potential client. That is the only way to develop the questions you need to ask to further your understanding. We agreed about the need to do the homework both before and after every sales meeting.

As with every stage of my life, I knew to talk as much to the people coming up the ladder as the people on the top rungs. Everyone has insights and can help you achieve your goal.

Part VI - Business No. 4 - Stolt Comex Seaway

Once I determined before Paul and I could ever benefit from the business we had to get out from under the accountant partners, I got to work looking for potential buyers.

Stolt Comex Seaway was a company listed on the NASDAQ and by my best guess, I figured they were valued at about $2 billion. I had heard that they had just won a contract in Australia and I figured they would need a partnership with an Australian business to best complete the job. If they were to buy Drill Support International that would give them an established presence. They would have the capability to not just do the job. They would be able to pursue additional work on the continent as well.

The offshore construction company was a marriage of Stolt Nielson Seaway, a Norwegian shipping company, and Comex, a world-famous French diving company. The Norwegians were the leaders on the board of directors. The French thought they were the most important, and therefore, the controlling element of the business. They acted as if they were in charge. In reality, it was the Scots in Aberdeen that ran the company. There were lots and lots of management conflicts, and that affected operations. It was, in so many aspects, run very poorly.

It did not take much calling around to find out who to talk with at Stolt. His name was Vonder Alameda. I made the call. In the conversation I told him I knew he had just won a $125 million contract for Shell in Australia. I asked if he thought the company might be interested in purchasing a small, established company to get a presence in Australia. He seemed interested and we made an appointment for him to come and visit our business.

When he arrived at Drill Support, I gave him the grand tour (of our small operation). He was very positive and smiling when he said those dreaded words, "I'll call you." Oh, those words I have heard so many times. However, I have to say that in Australia, and especially at this stage in the development of my business, when people told me they would call, they did.

In fact, it was only about two days before I got a call from Mr. Alameda. He informed me that in about a week I could expect a visit from some Stolt vice presidents who were coming to Australia to initiate the Shell job. He reminded me that I had offered to give anyone else from the company a tour. When they arrived, we gave them a grand tour and the V.I.P. treatment. I also told them some of our stories, so they knew we were serious about the business. They learned we had a good reputation because they inquired about us with the people at Shell before they even came to see us. I felt from the beginning that there were synergies between the two companies and we both needed each other.

It took a couple of months of negotiating. We finally came to a deal that made everyone happy. The deal called for half of the purchase price to be paid up front, with the remainder due at the end of three years. This is a common structure for these kinds of deals. There was also a clause that if we worked hard and built income and profits greater than they were when the deal was inked, we would share in that at the three-year point.

I was thrilled because we were going to be part of a big company with offices all around the world. They had large offshore construction vessels, the kind you see with thousand-ton lift cranes, helicopter decks, and several hundred men. They worked across the globe installing oilfields off the shores of a variety of continents.

Paul and I got settled and started working. In addition, I took up golf as part of my networking with oil company executives and to enhance my selling options. I had taken a few lessons and had come to thoroughly enjoy the game.

Every year for the company's annual meeting, they would gather a large portion of the executive and management teams at some exotic location. One year I got a call from the main office in Aberdeen Scotland. They told me I was to come to the yearly manager's meeting, and it was going to be held in Scotland. I do not know if there is a God or not, but when they told me that this year's meeting was to be held at the world-famous St. Andrews Golf Course, I decided that there must be because how else would I get this lucky.

I was thrilled because I knew I would have a once-in-a-lifetime chance to play golf on this premier course over my stay at the club, which I did, and it was amazing.

The rest of the time I mingled with the 33 other managers and a good showing of support staff. In the midst of people from Norway, Brazil, Scotland, France and several other locations, I discovered that once again, I was the only American in the group. It did not take long for me to understand that no one in the party particularly liked Yanks. What is more, they did not like each other, either. It was pretty apparent that they viewed each other as a threat to their own personal advancement. It was an uneasy time. However, getting to play on that golf course made it all worth it.

At the time the company was purchased by Stolt Comex Seaway, we were already working on contracts offshore with Shell Oil, Mobile and others. Our ROVs were actively laboring in seas and oceans around the world. Our work was instrumental on the new frontier of deep-water drilling. We were successfully replacing human divers and eliminating the deaths that had become more and more common. Our ROVs were the eyes, ears, and hands of any of the work to be done in the depths oil companies were pursuing.

Over time I learned a lot about the company under which we worked and got to know the upper management as they came to visit Perth. When they came to Australia, I solidified relationships by treating them well. We went to great restaurants and I took them around the city to show them what a beautiful place it was. I was purposefully putting money in the bank with these relationships. I even took them to meet with oil company executives to see what was happening with them. Remember, networking is money in the bank.

When Stolt Comex Seaway bought Drill Support and hired Paul and I, I would try to talk to the managers that ran their underwater robots in the North Sea. Wow was that a learning experience. Every single person was out for themselves and it was a dog-eat-dog world. Egos drove ambition and no one would share any information in fear of losing out. It was a good thing I was 12,000 miles away from them because I knew I would not be slated for any of the upper management positions. The other good thing was that they were just as happy having us in the outback of Australia beavering away.

I stayed on my toes, very conscious of the three-year anniversary and kept an eye on how the company operated. When the original deal was struck, the shares of Stolt Comex Seaway were at about $18 on the stock exchange. Using some creative accounting and reporting practices over the next couple of years, the stock price rose as high as $75. When the share price went high, the principles began selling off their stock. I sensed that there were others, besides me, who wanted out. After that, the stock price began a steady decline.

Seeing these sell offs and being aware of the poor management, I made the decision that when the three - year anniversary came around, I would take my payout and leave the company. I did not like the way the company was run or the direction it was heading.

When I communicated with the management that I would be leaving and wanted my money, I was told by my boss that I, and my part of the company, was insignificant and they were not going to pay me anything. Yes, I realized that they were a $2 billion company and Drill

Support was a small fry compared to them. I had a contract and knowledge of how they were running their company.

My partners and I filed a lawsuit. We found ourselves preparing for court. My lawyers had told us it could go either way, so we figured we had nothing to lose. We might as well go for it.

My networking had indeed given me money in the bank, and I was going to use it now. In fact, I had five people lined up to testify on our behalf. My attorneys said the other side had no one. I also had something else. The company commonly used transfer pricing.

Transfer pricing is a strategy of getting around paying tax in the country where a company is working. For instance, suppose there is a company based in Europe and they are actually doing work in Asia. They partner with a local company and form a new company. There are taxes due on the revenue they take in on their profits in the new company's country. The goal is to minimize the profit. What they do is this: The European company sells equipment, supplies or parts to the new company. For example, they sell a spare part like an underwater camera. On the open market the camera might cost $2,000. They charge the new company $20,000 for the camera. As an expense to the new company, they reduce the profits and do not have to pay tax on the $20,000. The profit of $18,000 goes to the European company as income. In some situations, similar practices are legal under a tax minimalization strategy. The transfer pricing strategy of inflating costs in this way is not.

Another practice commonly used was paying upper management salaries in foreign countries to avoid taxes in the home country. When I talked with one of their primary attorneys and explained what I knew and wondered what the Australian Tax Department would be interested in knowing, he told me he heard what I was saying and that I had worked hard for the company. He would see what he could do.

The day we went to court I was really nervous. We arrived early to get situated and go over our strategy. I was half listening as our attorneys were giving last minute details and instructions to the friends there to testify for us.

I was too busy watching the door. I knew that when the door opened it was going to either be a cast of thousands ready to fight against us or a single attorney. My attorneys told me that it would be a good sign to see one lawyer facing us because that would mean they wanted to make a deal. Finally, the door opened and in walked one, single man. He sat down next to our entourage and started to chat with my attorneys. I could not hear what they were saying. The perspiration was running down my back, chilling me to the bone. There were so many things on my mind and the outcome of this case would determine which direction my life would take next.

When the two lawyers finished their conversation, my attorney rose and looked at me. For once in my life, I could not read a person's face. He was expressionless and my heart sunk. He sat down beside me, leaned in close, and told me they wanted to make a deal. It took everything inside me not to jump up and give a giant whoop. I swear, I could have kissed him. It was such a relief.

My shirt was wet, and I was exhausted from the stress when the judge entered the courtroom. My attorney announced that we were going to make a deal and that the company was going to pay me. The judge, in his wisdom, said that just to make sure, he would adjourn the proceeding for one month. That would protect us if they reneged and did not pay what we were due. We could carry on the lawsuit at that time.

In the end, the company paid all of us, and all of us, except Paul, ended our three-year relationship with Stolt Comex Seaway and went our separate ways. Paul stayed as an employee.

It seemed like everything was coming to a head that year and all at the same time. I got the payout from Stolt, but everything in the business was gone. I should have seen it coming. Honestly, I never thought it would happen to me. My marriage fell apart completely, and I filed for divorce. The greatest tragedy was the effect it had on my son, John. He was eighteen years old and it was very hard on him.

Here I was at another crossroads. I was done with Stolt Comex Seaway. My marriage was over, the divorce was final, and all my assets had been divided equitably. I had no company. I had no job. I had no wife. I had no house. I was totally untethered.

One of the things I learned first-hand during this time is "He who has the Gold has the Rule." It takes a certain kind of person to navigate through the business minefield. By this time, I had experienced huge egos, bankruptcy, corruption and just plain, simple stupidity. Hopefully, I was learning and wouldn't repeat any of the mistakes I had made or had seen others make.

Now I was looking to start a new company and I had to start from scratch. I felt I was even behind where I was in the beginning. It was a juggling act. I had to make the heart of the ROV business grow while fighting the swamp of unscrupulous people, illegal business practices, and losing my family.

My hands were empty. My mind and heart were still full. I felt I had no choice in my head except to soldier on. They say that women are the best multi-taskers. I think I did a good job of it. Having an occasional drink helped, too.

Something amazing happened at just the perfect moment. I got an email from my first sweetheart, Cindy Robinson. She was the girl I met as a lifeguard and dated throughout high school. I had let her go when she left for college. And yes, I knew she was the love of my life when we went our separate ways. I couldn't believe it when I got that email. At that moment, I knew there was a God. We began to communicate again.

Bolstered by such good fortune and with my heart buoyed, I worked hard to pick up some venture capital. Then the best thing happened. My son, John, came to live with me. Life was getting back on track, and the future was looking hopeful – and happy.

Business 101 in the School of Hard Knocks

The most important thing I learned during this time is one of the most important lessons I have ever learned. When you have a company that you want to build and need to sell in order to continue operations, you do not want to sell it to a company that has a similar business inside it already.

What you find in a well-established company with similar business is that they already have everything they need. In the end, you will eventually get phased out and they end up taking over everything. In this case, you will be left without a business or even a job.

Instead, what you really want is a partner that needs your company as much as you need them. One that will help you build the business. If you find that situation, you can stay and have a major influence in the company. It is possible to achieve your desired goal of staying with the business and growing it. The perfect deal creates a partnership between the two parties that does not absorb your business. Instead the partners and businesses work alongside each other. That is the truest win-win.

You know the saying about not knowing what you don't know? Well, I was starting to know a lot more and build the repertoire of business practices to NOT follow. It was never more evident that sticking to the values of honesty, integrity, and dependability would be the best way to conduct my own business, if I ever had control of my own business.

Part VII - Business No. 5 - Total Marine Technology

By this time, I had learned that trying to capitalize my company by selling it to similar operations was not the way to go. I had to take a new tack. I began my search and met Mal Wardle. He had a company called Total Marine Services (TMS). I liked that his company had nothing in it like ROVs. I explained what I wanted to do and that I was bringing in another guy who was an integral part of the company. I convinced him to invest $1 million. He also gave us a shop from which to work. My contribution was the technology and knowledge of the business. We formed a new company called Total Marine Technology (TMT). We were partners, each holding fifty percent of the company. The partnership was done despite his friends, other businesspeople, telling him he was nuts.

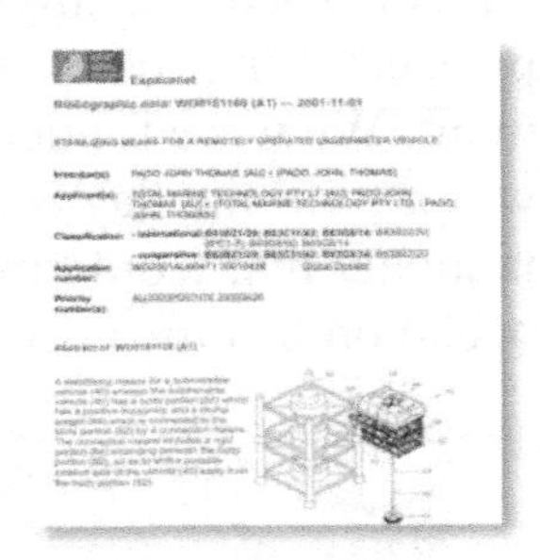

Figure 95 New design that was square instead of rounded and had a new anchoring system.

The next thing I knew I had to do was get Paul back by my side. He had stayed at Stolt Comex Seaway and it took a good bit of coaxing, and, I will admit, harassment, to lure him to Total Marine Technology. I explained the deal I had struck with Mal Wardle to put up the money so we could build a brand new ROV. I willingly offered Paul fifty percent of my shares and a vision of what we could do together. He left Stolt and was my equal partner.

Mal had oceanfront property in Fremantle at Total Marine Services. We moved into a large facility there. We revisited the ROV design and made a few changes including changing the shape to a rectangle. We did not have to cut corners physically or figuratively this time. It was a pleasure to not be constricted by materials and equipment. We were funded to do the very best we could. It was a thrill the day we took possession of an A-frame launcher that would pick up the ROV and set it into the ocean on a crane arm.

Figure 96 THE ROVs we built were Not small. When properly maintained, they can last 20 years.

We hired a couple of people who had been with me for the last twenty years in the various iterations of my businesses. We built our first ROV and got our first contract with a Japanese company called IMPEX. At first, the geologists at Woodside laughed at IMPEX for buying this one particular offshore lease. Woodside had previously held the lease on the ocean site IMPEX was going to drill. Woodside had found nothing there. In the decade since they had shuttered the project, technology had advanced and IMPEX discovered a way to access the oil there. IMPEX started drilling and found about eight billion barrels of oil. Now, today, as I write this, I can say that the first job serviced by TMT is still producing and I expect will continue for many decades to come.

The first year neither Paul nor I took a salary. We were building and everything we got we put back into the business. Once we started rolling, we knew it would pay off.

During this time, we were competing with Stolt for jobs and we were winning the bids out from under them. As fast as we were growing, they were falling behind. I saw that we could put more ROVs to work, so I started calling the people at Stolt who had taken my and Paul's jobs. I wanted to know if they would sell us the three ROVs we had built there. They were arrogant and wanted to stick it to us, which I guess I could understand. They said they would sell them for $20 million. We all knew it wasn't a realistic price. That didn't deter me. Every few months I would contact them again either with a letter or a phone call. I would goad them saying things like I could put them back to work since we were beating them on all the bids. Things didn't change with their willingness to sell. I kept watching the company shares drop like a lead weight. I stayed with it, starting to make offers of my own. The last offer I made was a nominal $250,000. I knew the ROVs were worth a lot more than that, and so did they. My goal was to just keep chipping away at them. I could feel they were going down. One day I called and learned that the two divers who were running the ROV division had been fired. Share prices were down to a dollar or two. Shortly after that the company went into bankruptcy. When I heard that, I thought maybe I had lost my chance.

It was a couple of months later that I got a call from the liquidators' representative. They had come across my correspondence and asked if I was still interested in the rusty old hunks of metal sitting in the yard. They would take my offer of $250,000. This was the call I had prayed about getting. Inside I was jumping up and down and cheering. On the outside I was cool. I told him, yes, I would still pay the $250,000 if they would also give me everything that went with them. I wanted the tools, the workshop equipment and all the spare parts. They really had no idea what they had and, I figured, did not really care. They were just trying to get rid of it all. He told us to come down and take whatever we wanted. They were liquidating everything.

Figure 97 We built one of the only 4-arm ROVs in the market. This Nomad is 5.5 tons and rated to go to 10,000 feet.

Paul and I jumped on it and immediately went there and packed up everything we had lost and more. While he got it organized in the shop and starting cleaning it up, I went out and got two jobs within a week. We put the ROVs to work. In the first six weeks, we made $1.5 million and went on to make many more millions off these ROVs in the next years. Again, as of today, these original ROVs are still in service deep, deep under the waves.

Mal and I traveled first class around the globe selling our wares and inking deals. We grew the company and it was thriving. We were getting a lot of attention and our company had brand recognition and a reputation that was credible and solid in the industry.

As we were growing sales, we also had to grow the manufacturing side of the business. It was during the expansion part of the growth that I learned a very important lesson about venture capitalists, which is the role Mal

Wardle had in our deal. It came time to expand our manufacturing and we determined we needed another million dollars to make it happen. We were fifty-fifty partners so that meant we each had to come up with $500,000. Of course, Paul and I didn't have that kind of money to invest. It is discouraging to be sitting at the door to success and you can't go in because you cannot afford it. Mal offered to put the entire $1 million in – in exchange for 90-95 percent of our shares. I was looking to expand something I felt passionately about, and he saw dollar signs and a way to get more money out of the business.

By this time, I had already seen the handwriting on the wall. I knew this was what was coming. We stood our ground because we felt his offer was unfair and we were keeping up our side of the business in spades. We told Mal that without us and the knowledge we had he wouldn't be able to operate the business on his own. I suggested he would lose his shirt, in fact, he would lose everything. Mal had put one of his houses up as collateral for a loan and he saw that he ran the risk of losing it, too.

Mal understood where I was coming from and the position he was in at the time. When the dust settled, Paul and I each retained twenty percent of the company, giving Mal sixty percent. He invested the money and we built the company pretty quickly to the point that cash flows were always positive. We had a lot of work and we were ready for the next step.

Our business caught the attention of a Malaysian company called Sapura. They called and wanted to know if we were interested in selling to them. By this time in my career, I knew exactly the kind of partner I did not want. Sapura was an offshore construction company and did not have an ROV division and that appealed to me. TMT would be a complement to their services and a partnership would be beneficial for everyone.

I was energetic about this new opportunity. Mal, having experience in wheeling and dealing and hoping to increase his return, suggested we put feelers out to the industry to see if anyone else would be interested in buying us. If we could find another buyer, we might be able to generate a bidding war. In the end, there were three companies bidding to buy TMT, two of them were Oceaneering and Sapura. Everyone started putting in their bids.

After the bidding process ended, Sapura made the best offer. It took a year to finalize the deal. In the end, they completely bought out Mal and a portion of the shares that Paul and I owned. After the contract was signed, I was able to write Mal a check for $9 million. Not a bad return on his original two million dollars three years earlier, especially when all his buddies told him not to do the deal. Mal went on to do other deals and Paul and I were going to run TMT under the Sapura umbrella.

It had been a struggle doing business with western companies and now we were embarking on something completely new. We were getting into bed with a Malaysian company and I honestly did not know what to brace myself for in the future.

As I was preparing myself for this new challenge, it occurred to me that here was another instance of the connections between my father's life and mine. During WWII he had been based in Fremantle, outside Perth, patrolling the Malaysian coast in a submarine to prevent the Japanese from invading Malaysia. Now I was living in Perth, working in Fremantle and going into business with a group of Malay businesspeople. His service under the sea saved the country. I was going into a partnership to work under the sea to help them build the country.

Business 101 in the School of Hard Knocks

Nothing came home more in the deal with Mal than the truth that "He who has the gold has the rule."

Sometimes it is a hard lesson to learn and accept that for many in the business world, gold is what they seek. My desire was to create something new and useful in the world. I was passionate about ROVs and I needed a company to build them. I knew that others were only interested in my business as a product in itself. It did not matter if I was making ROVs or ice cream.

This is especially true of venture capitalists. They see businesses as cards in a game. Each one is a commodity meant to be bought, sold, or traded. If the product or service is the passion of a business owner, knowing the goal of a partner is essential in order for it to work for the long-term.

I once had a teacher tell me that no one can ever take your learning away from you. By the time I was dealing with Mal Wardle, I saw the value in all the learning I had accumulated in the business world. I was able to see what was happening and be proactive to protect myself and those who depended on me.

Never a shrinking violet to begin with, I had the confidence, or perhaps, the bravado, to stand up and stand my ground by this point.

Part VIII - The Final Step with Sapura

It wasn't just that Sapura had made the best offer. I had a good feeling about doing business with them. I had done work for or with people in the company over the previous decade. It was great to work with the new Malaysian owners. I found them to be honest, hard-working, smart, and I could see in their heart they were kind and people with class and style. After more than two decades of our association, I can say I pegged it correctly.

The morning we signed on the bottom line, Paul and I were standing in a hallway in the headquarters going over the contract. Everything we had agreed to was in the contract and there was nothing we had not agreed to slipped in. We gladly signed it.

We had heard they had a big event planned to celebrate the deal. Paul and I were dressed in our usual attire, jeans and polo shirts. Definitely no suit or shirt and tie since neither of us owned anything like that at all. We walked into the hall and every one of the fifty people turned to look at us, revealing fifty suits and fifty ties. As soon as they saw how we were dressed, they, without a word or question, immediately removed their ties and suit jackets. Talk about class. It was a wonderful experience and a great day.

As part of the deal, Paul and I became employees of the company. I was the Chief Executive Officer and Paul was the Chief Operating Officer. Our salaries and the benefits were generous. It was certainly a far cry from food stamps. The best part of the deal, which was different from all the other business partnerships I had had in the past was that they believed what I said and trusted me to do what I said I could do. We had resources and we were not in any way constrained. It was up to me and Paul to change the way the oil industry worked now.

We were personally stable and ready to get to work. We moved the manufacturing operation into an expanded facility. That allowed us to increase production of ROVs and pursue more contracts. The ROVs took time to build. As soon as each one was produced, we quickly put it to work. We grew at a strong and steady pace.

Sapura did not bring in any of their people for the first three or four years. The leaders would come to Perth or we would go to Malaysia for status meetings. At one of the meetings the owners of the company joined us to ask a question. They wanted to know how big we thought we could grow if there was an infusion of say, $60 million. It was a dream come true.

The construction division had made a deal to build off-shore work vessels in Brazil. We would build ROVs and place two of them on each of these vessels. Once completed, those ships and our ROVs went to work in 10,000 feet of ocean water. Sapura expanded, building more ships around the world and putting our ROV systems on them. We ended up with 38 ROVs and a great engineering division employing more than three hundred engineers.

We worked our way up to $100 million in revenue per year and continued to grow. My dream of building ROVs that would become the workhorses of the ocean had come true. I was proud that I had helped others improve their lives, and especially that I had helped such a talented man as Paul become such a success and happy in his life and he helped me as well.

Not only was TMT growing and thriving, I was truly happy at home, too. Cindy had been my first romantic love and I discovered she had never truly left my heart.

Cindy had married right after college and moved with her husband, a farmer, to Danville, Indiana. Together, they had three children. All the children were grown and out of the house when she and her husband divorced. Cindy was a single woman again.

After lots and lots emails and phone calls, we had picked up on the relationship, albeit long distance. The point finally came that I flew to America to see her. We met in Texas and then went to give me my first taste of Danville, Indiana. Later she would visit me in Australia. We enjoyed being together and it was not easy being apart.

My father had always told me I would never find another Cindy and you know what, he was right. I had never been happier having her in my life again. She agreed to move to Australia in 1999. By October 2000 we were married and settled into a happy life. I was so happy to have found her again.

Around this time, I got a call from my mother to tell me that my father had died. One of the last things he ever said to me was that I had achieved what I did all on my own. I knew then that he did understand and know how far I had gone. I was happy he said that. He gave me recognition for what I had achieved before he died. In 2000, when Mom called, the truth of that statement really hit home. He was right, I did do most everything in my life without the support of a family.

Even still, I offered to make the arrangements for the burial. The Burnes Funeral Home was still there in Gary, and I knew I could take the time and money to do that. Mom told me to not bother. Her attitude was very cold, and I felt it through the phone line. That was it. I didn't bother and only spoke to my mother again once in the next thirteen years. I did not attend Dad's funeral, nor did I go to Mom's in 2013. I have not visited their gravesites, either. I understood that I was well and truly on my own in life.

I stepped back into my life. I loved taking Cindy everywhere and to see everything that Australia had to offer. The town of Perth had about 1.5 million people and was on the same latitude as San Diego, California. There were hills along the back of the town with a desert behind them. Perth was a destination and the pathway to Rottnest, a holiday island just about ten miles off the coast. On the weekends there would be up to 10,000 visitors to the island because no one could live full-time on the island. The island was named Rottnest by Dutch explorers because marsupials nested on the island and they said they looked just like 25-pound rats. It is a beautiful place with white sands and turquoise waters.

Figure 98 The beach on Rottnest was one of our favorite places.

Perth was a wonderful place to live. It had everything anyone could want. There were great multi-cultural restaurants because of its close proximity to Asia. There is a spectacular football stadium, world-class museums, and the availability of one of my favorite pastimes: four-wheel driving and camping.

Australia is populated on the coasts and hardly anyone lives in the center of the continent. We went off road everywhere. One trip was called the Canning Stock Route. It was a trail made in the 1800s. In America, it would compare to a trip leaving San Diego and then five weeks later ending up in North Dakota, all on dirt roads and without any towns in between. Participants had to bring everything. The only exception was help from a fuel truck that would meet up at certain designated times and locations. If anyone arrived late, they were in a world of hurt.

When Cindy and I got married, I had promised her that she could go back home to Indiana twice a year for two months each time. In addition, if any of her children got married or had children, Cindy would be able to return for those occasions as well. It became apparent to me that Cindy was longing to be closer to them all.

Things were changing. I was seeing a new direction.

Business 101 in the School of Hard Knocks

Persistence pays off. I had spent almost twenty years trying to build a company that was doing the things that we did with the Sapura owners. I never gave up and eventually, through all the trials and tribulations, dishonest players, greed, and everything else found in the business world, it worked out. Through the years a lot of people made a lot of money and Paul and I built something new for the benefit of the world.

On a personal note, the heart knows what the heart knows and needs. Getting a divorce was one of the most difficult things I ever did. I truly felt marriage was a forever deal. From this experience I learned to look at every situation as an opportunity for something new, different, and better.

You have heard the saying, "When one door closes, another one opens." You can see that it holds true throughout my story. What you have to realize is that you have to go and knock on the door to get it open. Then, once you get a door open, you have to work to keep it open.

Even though our investors squeezed Paul and me for what they could, we still managed to grow the company in size, technology, and income. In the end, we won. Today, I am happily semi-retired, and Paul is successfully running a $600 million company.

Section Eight - Time to Let Go

Part I – When You Know

Business was booming and everything was great, but I was tired, and I felt my health was suffering. I would soon be turning 65 years old and started to think about retiring. I knew that Paul had the business well in hand.

What I did not know is that I had developed a heart condition called atrial fibrillation. I guess heart disease does run in the family because here I was, in the soup just like my dad. That is where the heart beats too fast and does not pump blood correctly. I was told it came from snoring. If I would have stayed in Australia, it would not have been long before I died. When I got back to the good old USA, the doctor here found the problem and fixed it. Now I am back and at it again. Lesson for readers: if you snore and hold your breath while sleeping, you will die. Get it fixed immediately. It is an easy fix, so just do it.

I could see my time in Perth Australia was coming to a close. I had been there for 30 years. I had made promises and it was important to me to keep those promises.

Because we, mostly Cindy, traveled a lot to Danville, we had purchased a house there over the years. During the time we were absent, a cousin lived in the house. When the cousin moved out and into a new chapter of her life, there was no one to stay and keep watch on it. The grandchildren were growing. I saw the time was right for us to go home.

I talked with Paul and told him I was ready to step away. He accepted my decision and we set about making the arrangements for me to sell my shares in the company when I turned 65 years old.

I had a year before I would retire and there was a lot to be done on both sides of the globe. Cindy went back to Indiana to take care of things in Danville and I stayed to finish my work and tie up all the loose ends in Perth.

I had already started the process of selling the rest of my company to the majority shareholders. Our house was another story.

It was a beautiful home on five acres overlooking the city with a view out to the west coast and the Indian Ocean. It had a Koi fishpond, a large greenhouse, a heated pool, a hot tub and was surrounded by the wild kangaroos, snakes, and the ever-present Redback spiders. It was like living in the Hollywood Hills.

Because we were asking $1.5 million for the house, buyers were scarce. It took a while to sell it. When it did sell, I was tasked with emptying it. I gave away a lot and packed what I could fit into a forty-foot shipping container. It would have been impossible to bring everything I had back to the United States. I made arrangements to ship the container overseas to Danville. It was a job.

I had lived in Australia for more than half of my life. Perth was very difficult to leave. I had great friends and many, many wonderful memories. I had had the opportunity to explore my passion and build businesses. I had started the sub-sea manufacturing industry in the country with the help of the Australian government and a few local entrepreneurs.

Today, Total Marine Technology, Ltd. (TMT) is a leader in its industry. There are 300 engineers building

Figure 99 TMT facility, ROVs, and staff when I left to retire and return to the United States in 2011.

the most high-tech underwater equipment in the world. TMT is turning revenues of more than $100 million a year. I am so proud of what the company has become through the efforts Paul and I had put into it.

It took days to say good-bye to all the great friends and wonderful people that had become as close as family to me. On September 12, 2011, almost exactly 30 years after I arrived in August 1981, I left Australia.

Figure 100 My colleagues had some life-size cutouts of me made so they could keep my "happy face" around.

I was headed to a little Midwestern town of 10,000 people called Danville, Indiana. I didn't realize as I was closing one door, another was opening.

Part II – Final Recollections

Here I am sitting in a Qantas A-380. Qantas is my favorite carrier and the A-380 is my favorite airplane ever. I am getting ready to take off from Perth, Australia and begin the thirty-plus hours of travel back to the United States. I am on the last leg of my working life journey – the last road trip to home and retirement. I am going to have a nice long think and a nice tall drink.

I remember the first flight I ever took. It was paid for by my employer and, in fact, so were all the rest of the flights I took over the following forty years. The first one was from Houston, Texas to Los Angeles, California on Continental Airways. I cannot remember the designation of the aircraft. It was way back in the 1970s and the plane was likely small. Not like this plane today, the A-380. No, this one carries five hundred people with two decks, upper and lower, running the length of the plane.

In the old days I sat in the back of the plane where it was noisy and cramped. I did not care about the noise or being a bit cramped up. No, I was thrilled to be able to travel and see the world with such a great job. Now, these days I sit in the front where it is quiet, luxurious, and the food is great. I have to tell you that the overseas airlines are well-run and clean. The staff truly treats passengers here like we belong in these seats.

It is not the same as when you travel today with other carriers. They put the seats out to the highest bidder and pack passengers in like cattle to planes that are not cleaned often enough the way they should be. Through the years I have discovered that a lot of airplane staff tend to carry a chip on their shoulders. Sad to say, in my opinion, many carriers cannot hold a candle to the foreign airlines.

I have thirty hours stretching out in front of me. It should give me some time to reflect on where I have been and what I have done over the last forty years. My first thought, obviously, is about all the planes I have been on and how many miles I have traveled. When I add up the number of miles I have flown and accumulated I think it roughly comes up to about 1,300,000 miles. That equates to about fifty-two times around the globe. I have seen most of the world. The only place left out of my travels has been Africa.

Let me go back to the beginning. In the beginning, it was all new to me and I was young and single, just like when I was in the Navy. We would do our work. We would also be on the lookout for bars, music, and girls. And, unlike my Navy days, I had money in my pocket this go around. Not only did I visit many of these cities and countries, I got to live in some, as well.

After the initial thrill of the bars and nightlife, I always started to venture out and learn about the culture and the people of whatever place I landed in at the time. There are so many differences in geography, history, language, and culture. And that makes for a rich experience. Unlike others I worked with, I tried to learn a bit of the language. I am proud to say that I can at least say hello and thank you in at least fifteen different languages. In some, like Chinese, Malaysian, Indonesian, Spanish, and Polish, I can manage a small, very short, conversation. I loved trying to learn from people who became friends.

I had worked in Canada, on both coasts. My favorite Canadian place was Vancouver. In fact, it was my second choice for a place to live and work. Perth, my very favorite place in the world, was first. I had been to Mexico and I went to Brazil. I worked down the coast there from Vitoria and Rio to Maceio. It was beautiful.

One of the unwritten rules in the oil industry was to not send married men to Scotland or Brazil on their first trip. Why? It was because so many got divorced and married a local girl. Look at me. My first posting was in Scotland, and I married a Scottish girl. The difference was that I went there a single man.

I stayed in Scotland for all of about two years. I traveled all over Scotland and England. I also made a trip over to the Shetland Islands. The people there consider themselves Vikings, not Scots. The weather in Scotland was always bad. Gray houses and pubs everywhere. The pubs are the center of Scottish life just like in England. England's weather was a bit better, but I found it gray and drab, too. I knew it was not a place I wanted to stay long term.

I went on to spend time in Northern Europe; a bit in Holland, three months in Norway, six months in Sweden. It was in 1977 that I was working with the Swedish Aircraft company SAAB building the first Work Class ROV with an anthropomorphic manipulator on it. Norway and Sweden were similar to me. I discovered the people of each nation were not too keen on the people of the other nation. They were all clean, well-educated people. The negative was that there was also a great deal of alcoholism. Every time I flew into Sweden, they wanted me to bring Everclear 190 proof alcohol. It was not very affordable in country because the government was trying to curb drinking in Sweden. They were doing this by raising the cost of alcohol. To lower the cost of their drink, the residents all began to make their own wine at home.

The amount of alcohol was governed by volume, not proof. I was allowed to bring in one liter of Everclear and my Swedish friends loved it. They would mix together one liter of Everclear with five gallons of their wine.

You might think that drinking and getting drunk was the same around the world. In my experience, it was not. I noticed that when some drank, they would get drunk, but somebody was home inside their heads. When others drank, there was nobody home. They would get this blank stare on their faces.

At one time, I spent three months in Spain. One thing I had heard about but never experienced was the concept of siesta. It was really interesting. The town basically shut its doors at noon and reopened at three p.m. All of us Americans did not know what to do during the siesta time until we found a restaurant that stayed open and spent our time there. After reopening, the businesses would then stay open late into the evening. The climate was wonderful, and the people were friendly.

The food was fantastic. There were lots of promenades with alfresco dining. It would be ten o'clock at night and whole families would be around the table. The children would be running around playing and the adults would sit and socialize. The towns I stayed in were not places for nightclubbing. They were traditional Spanish towns centered around the Catholic church and family life. I liked the Spanish way of life. It made sense to me.

Italy was very similar in this practice of eating with family on the promenades. I spent about six months in Italy living up and down the coast along with spending time in Rome, Sicily, and Malta.

I stayed for a month in a chalet in Sardinia. I was there fleet racing with all the America's Cup participants as they prepared for the big 1987 race in Australia. Paul and I were Channel 9's underwater TV crew. We came over from Australia with our Kookaburra sailing team. I filmed the winged keels for the first time and got them on the international news. We worked in and out of the Yacht Club Costa Esmeralda. It was amazing. It is known as the most exclusive yacht club in the world. Everything was exceedingly expensive. It was 1986 and drinks were between $25 and $50 each. They definitely meant to keep out the riffraff.

We all have preconceived notions about people and places. I had always thought that Italy was full of dark-haired people. I did not know that the northern Italians were blonde and blue-eyed much like the countries adjacent to northern Italy. The southern Italians were dark-haired much like the people of Spain and the Middle East. Even the architecture had a middle eastern flair. Just like in America with Union and Confederate supporters during the Civil War, the northern and southern Italians did not see eye-to-eye a lot of the time.

Italy also had a tradition of a siesta time just like in Spain. The doors closed at noon and reopened at three o'clock. Then families spent time out on the promenades together late into the evening. If I had to live in Europe, I would live in Italy. It is my favorite European country.

I visited Dubai and Bahrain for shorter periods. It was very different from anywhere else in the world, although I found the people very clean and friendly like most everywhere else. However, because of all the talk about terrorism I had had it drilled into my head that it might not be safe. When I visited, I always felt uneasy there. Several times when I was asked to go to that part of the world, I declined. Just like I declined to work in Nigeria. There was a problem with oil workers being killed in Nigeria and I just decided I would not take the chance. I felt lucky to be able to make the choice. I guess you could call me a coward. I felt I just wanted to live a longer life.

Although Indian food is one of my favorite kinds of foods, I found Bombay as a city to be dirty. So dirty that I often did not want to eat there. However, I had to eat to survive and much to my delight, everything I ate was fabulous and delicious.

I was working with ONGC (Oil and Natural Gas Company of India) during my time there. I toured the area with a guide, and it was an eye-opening experience. The caste system is very much alive. Of course, my viewpoint is colored by my life and experiences. What I came away with was interesting to me.

Superficially looking at the towns and region, there were lots and lots of people. It was chaotic, dirty. I saw people eating garbage and beggars lining every street. We judge places by our own experiences and what we know. After thinking about it, I concluded that this was their culture and their way of life. This is their experience, what they know, and how they expect to live. People living within this culture are generally happy. Some may have to sleep on the streets where others might have a cardboard box home in a shanty village. Those with cardboard houses in a shanty town were happy to not be sleeping on the streets. I felt it was just like the difference between some people in America living in the urban projects or a suburban house or a mansion. For the Indians, they felt their cup was full, and they were happy for what they had. They are as content with their lives as we are with ours.

The last trip I made to India was around the time that the name of Bombay was changed to Mumbai. All of my experiences in India were generally in the crowded metropolis of Mumbai. I know there are places in India that are considered beautiful. My time there was limited to the dirty chaos of an overpopulated city.

The first stop I ever made in Asia was in Singapore. My wife and I lived there for a year and that is where one of the most wonderful events of my life happened. My son John was born in Singapore in 1979. In order that he could be born there, we had to sign an agreement stating that he would be born an American citizen and that he would not claim Singapore citizenship.

Singapore is a small island that is twenty-six miles long and fourteen miles wide. It has few natural resources. The population of Singapore is about 3.5 million people. The people of Singapore are primarily of Chinese ancestry. In 1965 the Malaysian government encouraged Singapore to be its own country. It is the hub of Asia and steeped with deep history. It seems that everything coming in or out of Asia goes through Singapore, including me. Singapore was the hub of many of my travels around the globe through the years.

The country of Singapore was run by a benevolent dictator named Lee Kuan Yew. Over the thirty or so years of his rule, he turned Singapore into a developed country. He was good for this tiny country.

I have also lived in Brunei, which is at the northern tip of the island of Borneo. The country is governed by the Sultan of Brunei who is one of the richest men in the world. Today Brunei is still oil-rich, and Shell Oil is the primary oil company in the country. Brunei's population is made up of indigenous people who are headhunters. A lot of the headhunters have assimilated into modern society there and work successfully for the Shell Oil Company.

During my travels, I have visited Malaysia, Thailand, Vietnam, the Philippines, New Zealand, Indonesia, Sumatra, Java, Sulawesi, Bali, Borneo, Japan, China, Hong Kong, Russia and then ventured to Hawaii, Fiji and Tahiti. I also flew over the North Pole twice, which was an experience!

I have many great stories to share and tried so many great foods. One of the most unusual foods I have ever eaten was fried rice with fruit bats. That was in Vietnam. And those bats were the size of cats. They lived in the treese, hanging upside down as you expect. I thought they were like flying rats. They were huge. That being said, they were also delicious. I have seen other kinds of foods in my travels like dog, snakes, various types of insects, grasshoppers, scorpions, and more. It is just what people are used to eating where they live. It might surprise you that I did not eat many of these foods.

For instance, I stayed in the town of Manado on the island of Sulawesi, which is in Indonesia. In downtown

Manado I was told that you could eat anything there. I saw people eating rats as if it were chicken. I was told if we went inland a bit, I could experience eating a human being. I considered it politely, but graciously declined. It stayed in my thoughts for days afterward. Who was the human I would have eaten, and would I have been the next meal for someone else? Remember, this part of the world is known for headhunting and Papua New Guinea, well known for cannibalism, was just next door.

I was in Manado with the watch company Jaeger-LeCoultre as one of their diving sportsmen. I was there to promote their new diving watch, "The Master Compressor." It is known to be one of the best diving watches in the world. They were bringing me and the watch to one of the best places on the globe to dive. I worked for them for five years. A few times a year I would fly away for a couple of weeks to stay in some exotic diving locale and take people out of the shops to go with me to have some fun and showcase the watch. It was amazing work. I loved it and so did the people who went diving with me.

Over the years I had grown to love Asia; its people, foods, and its cultures. What they all seemed to have in common was that the people are all hard-working, smart, and believe it or not, very friendly. They came to remind me of a huge anthill, where everyone works hard toward the same goal.

As you know, I ended up in Perth, Australia for thirty years. I flew out of Australia to all of the countries I mentioned. I also visited the United States many times over those years, too. However, the trips were mostly for work and I spent very little time seeing the sites in America.

Now I am heading to Danville, Indiana to retire with my childhood sweetheart, Cindy, by my side. I am looking forward to living in this quintessential Midwestern American town. It happens to be the county seat with a great big old courthouse in the town square. Very picturesque.

I know Cindy and I are going to take off to see America. Now I can see it from a more worldly point of view, and I have the time to really enjoy it. I have thought about how we are going to do this. First thing that comes to mind is an RV. When you live in an RV, you have to also tow a car behind it. Then you have to find a place to park each night, which can get costly. The pantry has to be stocked and meals cooked and cleaned up after. I figure it is just too much work. Anyway, I feel an RV is more like driving around your badge of success.

Instead, Cindy and I are going to buy an SUV and stay at Hampton Inns. They have good beds and a great breakfast. When we get up in the morning we just walk out, all fed and let someone else take care of our room. We will be free to explore.

I think how different our lives are from my parents' lives. After I got out of the Navy and left to go to school in Florida, my parents were robbed at gunpoint by a 14-year-old at their home in Gary. The kid had a .38 and he held the revolver to my dad's head. The next day, my parents put our house up for sale. It took some time for it to sell. No one wanted to live in Gary. They kept dropping the price until, finally when it did sell, it was worth only $6,000. That meant they only had enough money to move into a trailer park in Valparaiso, Indiana. They lived there for more than thirty years. After my dad died in 2000,

Mom stayed for a few more years until she got to the point where she needed to be in a home. My sister, Debbie, traveled from Florida to Indiana and brought Mom to Florida. Debbie moved her into a retirement home near her house in Port St. Lucie. My mom died there in 2013.

The reason my parents waited so long was because my mother would not sign the papers to sell the house. She felt if she did, my dad would run off with the money. My parents were the last original homeowners of that subdivision from the 1950s to leave. My mom was so headstrong it took a gun to get her out!

While I write this, I think the main influence in my life was my dad and the impact his submarine service had on me. He planted the seed to a career path that I pursued with zest and found more success than I ever dreamed possible. No matter what happened in the past, I wish he were here to see what I have become built and the success I have found.

I know I learned some lessons from my mom, especially about being social and the center of attention. I think most of the lessons from her were mostly about how not to live and how not to treat people you're supposed to love. Even though he had faults like gambling, my father had given me passion and focus. I do not know where I got the tenacity to stay on my path. The only thing I can think of is it is like when you buy a new car that is red. All of a sudden you begin to take notice of how many red cars are on the road like yours. They had been there all along. You are just now noticing them. It was the same way with me. I began to notice anything that had to do with submarines, underwater adventures, or the ocean. I paid attention and those things fed my passion.

Part III - The Real Hero of My Story

Yes, my father planted seeds. It was Sister Isabel that gave me the tools, clarity, and belief in myself that served me on my journey.

When I first met her at St. Luke's Catholic School in the late 1950s, I was a kid full of lots of nervous habits. I bit my lip, twirled my hair and flicked my eyelashes. She took me under her wing with all my faults and tics and problems and we had a love affair for five years, even though I was not aware of it at the time. It was a love affair with learning. Being her student saved my life.

I had flunked out of third grade at Emerson public school and changing schools to St. Luke's was what my parents considered my last hope. All of us kids at Emerson called St. Luke's a prison because all we saw was discipline, straight lines, and uniforms. However, I know that my parents enrolling me in St. Luke's was the one thing they did right by me in my childhood.

Sister Isabel and I met daily after school in the old church choir room. The school recognized that I needed tutoring in almost all subjects. I was really behind. And I could tell, too, because the kids in my class were way ahead of me, and I had already done third grade once. That is why they assigned me to her.

Math and handwriting came relatively easily, though I had to make a big jump from counting one to ten to counting into the thousands. And my handwriting still looks a bit like chicken scratches now. My main problems were reading, composition, and spelling, which would take five years of extra help. After the first year I no longer had to stay after school, the teacher just made a daily announcement in front of the class, "Tom, you can go to Sister Isabel's for remedial reading now." That surely pulled the rug out from under my self-esteem. Especially by seventh grade when I was starting to get interested in girls.

In the first year when I stayed after for reading, I hated it. For one, it was hard for me, and it was exacerbated because I could hear the other kids having fun outside. Sister Isabel would demand that I read ten pages. I would try to get by with less by sneakily turning two pages at a time. She always knew what was up. I was looking at the number of pages, and Sister Isabel just wanted me to read for the half hour. Of course, she got her way.

Figure 101 Sister Isabel was all business all the time.

We never chatted. It was always business with her. I can't even remember if she smiled at me, mostly because she was always looking over my shoulder from behind. Sister Isabel wore a formal habit with a large wingspan and the traditional head stocking, so I do not even know what color hair she had. All I really saw of her was her face, and there was always a hint of garlic in the air. It was intimidating.

And all that reading. Now, decades later, I understand what she did for me. Her stern attitude and tenacity not only forced me to learn to read but turned my life around.

Maybe she did not know what led up to our years of relationship. Surely, she knew I had failed at Emerson. I was convinced I was stupid. Furthermore, my parents were not very good at being parents. They never nurtured or praised me. I thought I never did anything praiseworthy. I got in trouble for everything I did, so I felt I was a burden that kept them from living their lives.

I was what has been termed a latchkey kid. After school every day, I came home to an empty house where I was alone and unsupervised. I liked it that way. I would play with my friends on the block. I would also get into everything in the house, especially the stuff under the kitchen sink. Boy, did I mix up some dangerous concoctions. I almost burned the house down a couple times. My toys were a fascination too. I took them apart to figure out how they worked. What angered my parents was that I never could get them back together again.

When all the other kids at school could answer the nuns' questions, it reinforced my belief that they were smart, and I was just dumb. When my report card was full of Ds and Fs, my dad would say that I would end up digging ditches. That thought spurred me, alright, like a bruise in the ribs.

Sister Isabel's spurring had belief behind it. I felt she believed I could read, and over those five years I did read. And, what's more, I started to believe in myself. I started to realize that I wasn't stupid, and I wasn't a waste of space. She never insulted me or made me feel bad, she was always patient. That made all the difference.

She probably never knew what I had been up to since our daily meetings ended. She more than likely never knew that after I graduated from high school, I enlisted in the Navy where I went to electronics and diving school, studying eight years in total, mastering engineering, oceanography and diving. I'm not sure what she would have said to learn I was stationed on a submarine, and eventually landed a two-year internship at the Smithsonian Institute which led to managerial positions in high tech underwater companies. I would have liked to see her face when she learned that, in the end, I became one of the leading inventors and entrepreneurs of underwater robots in the world.

Figure 102 Because Sister Isabel was all business, I am better for it.
Drawing by Gary Varvel

She would understand that I started at the bottom and worked my way up to the top. She would know I started a company from nothing, and then learn that after 30 years I had a multimillion-dollar corporation with more than three hundred engineers.

Total Marine Technology still provides cutting-edge technology in underwater robots to the offshore oil and gas industry around the world, installing oil fields as deep as two miles under the sea. I have made my mark in life, with a lot of work and some luck. In the end, it was the unique understanding that I was not measured by tests or book learning but by my success.

Thinking of Sister Isabel reminds me of my beginnings. It's a funny thing that I started out in Indiana where I grew up and dated Cindy. Now 55 years later, I'm going back home to Indiana, married to her. I have come full circle and feel happy believing I have had the best life possible and knowing there is still more to come.

I look forward to this new chapter because I am returning to Indiana a different person. A better person. I am a changed man.

After five decades, I have come to learn that there are many different kinds of love in this world. Romantic love like I feel for Cindy. The love and caring between partners and colleagues who work side-by-side toward a specific goal. The love of friends who support and encourage you through the rough and ragged times.

There is another kind of love I have experienced. It began at a table with a book opened wide. It is the selfless kind of love when someone reaches out and takes your hand to give you something, expecting nothing in return. It was the kind of love Sister Isabel gave to a wary, nervous, and distracted boy.

I never would have found the success I have found if it were not for Sister Isabel's selfless hard work to get me through building the foundations of learning. There had been no one else who saw fit to invest in me at that time in my life. She took me on as a duty and with sacrifice to teach me skills over and above just reading and writing.

Years later, after I truly understood the importance of what she gave me, and the grace with which she did it, I went to seek her out to tell her what she had meant for me and the impact she had made on my life. I discovered she had died. In that moment I wished I could have been there at her side when she passed.

I went to her grave site. I knelt down in the cool earth and told her my feelings. My heart was broken. The lump in my throat was so big I could hardly breathe. Tears rolled down my cheeks as I sobbed. I was humbled by the life of this great woman and teacher and sad because I had lost the chance to tell her so. I had lost the chance to thank her.

Now, I believe I serve her best by telling her story to the world. I know that her beauty shines like the sun in my heart and reminds me to always strive to be a better person in everything I do and for everyone I meet. She taught me it is our duty and greatest purpose in life to do our best and to give to others, without expectations.

Her story is one of the most important parts of my story and will always be memorialized in this book. I want everyone to know that to me, and for me, she was one of God's angels on earth.

May God bless you, my Sister Isabel, as you have blessed me. You taught me about the kind of love that truly makes the world a better place. You were one of the truest loves I ever had in my life.

ABOUT THE AUTHOR

Tom Pado has settled into life in the midwestern town of Danville, Indiana with the love of his life, Cindy. Perhaps not quite settled as you might think. After all, it is hard to do that after living the life he has lived. Instead, he is forging new paths and experiences as he becomes active in the community and local government.

Part of what compelled him to write this book was the responses he received from people as he shared the stories of his life in conversations and speaking engagements around the world. He speaks on entrepreneurship, technology, business, salesmanship, and marketing. As with all areas of Tom's life, there are more stories than what would fit into the book.

Don't worry, you won't miss out. If you are interested in hearing more from Tom, about his work, adventures, and ideas about the world, go to his website at www.tompado.com and explore.

Tom is always interested in meeting new friends. If you have something to share, or questions to ask, you can reach him through email at DiveDeeper@TomPado.com. He'd love to hear from you.

Please feel free to share your thoughts in a review about his book at Amazon.com.

VOICES FROM THE PAST

SPEAK UP TODAY

"Tom Pado was a next-door neighbor friend from Gary, Indiana on Louisiana Street. We knew each other and were fast friends from the word "go." Along with other friends, we played together masterfully whether it was baseball or looking for flies, lightening bugs or grasshoppers. Tom stood out because of his love of the neighborhood wildlife.

We didn't realize at the time; Tom would have a much-distinguished place in business and science. His talent in deep sea diving and science was developed in those happy days in Gary where he had the will to know and understand the animals as well as the science. Who would guess a simple boy, raised and educated at St. Luke's and Emerson Schools developed into a much-admired person in his marine based field?"
Genie Skrivan, childhood friend
Crown Point, Indiana

"As a shipmate on the *U.S.S. Becuna*, I definitely witnessed the shipyard escapade. I think the biggest thought we all had regarding that incident was that Tom Pado had the biggest set of balls of anyone else we knew in the Navy, plus the confidence to actually pull it off. He, and that incident are one of my fondest memories of my time in the Navy."
Dave Graversen, Town Manager, ret.
Topeka, Kansas

"I had been there for so many successful launches, but I will never forget the launch that fateful day. Preparing to launch. Weather is a Go. Rocket on launch pad is a Go. Tom Pado (mission control) is a Go. Countdown 3,2,1 BOOM! Houston, we have a problem. One crewman DOWN with what looks like a gunshot wound to the abdomen. I told my parents my brother, Jim had fallen into the hedges and poked a hole into his stomach. The burnt powder residue and the metal ragments the doctor removed from my brother's abdomen told another. The truth came out. My brother Jim still bears the scar to this day and wears it as a badge of courage. Life growing up with Tom is remembered fondly with wonder we made it through!"
Louis Grosdanis, childhood friend
Lowell, Indiana

"I can't remember the time before Tom was my good friend, and he still is today, more than six decades later. He was always sociable and offered his great smile to everyone he met. I was there in Gary as he built rockets and radios. I experienced the launches and even traded some of my stuff for his intercom radio. We sang in the Bishop's Choir together and were half of the four horsemen on the football team. After high school when he left for the Navy, I knew he'd make his way through the world. Because what I liked about Tom was that I never knew what was around the corner. But I did know it would be an adventure!"
Ron Kazmerski, childhood friend
Danville, Indiana

"One night as a teen hanging out with friends at Calvin's Drive-In, I heard tires screeching followed by a very loud thud. We then saw a convertible sliding into the end of the parking lot upside down. It settled on a concrete support for the Calvin's sign, which saved the driver's life. Sitting there stunned, I see Tom Pado jump out of his car and running over to the crashed vehicle, hollering at everyone within earshot, to help him flip the car over. I was amazed by Tom's presence of mind while the rest of us were sitting there frozen. The vivid memory is a testament to the man of action Tom was then and continued to be throughout his life and career."
Joe Cerda, childhood friend
Carmel, Indiana

"Tom Pado proves once again he's a man of endless talents - now an author. As his friend and neighbor, I wasn't sure if he was a genius or would end up blowing up our house with his experiments. He's attained tremendous success and this book is filled with life lessons, how he overcame never-ending obstacles, his formula for success, and love stories that will touch your heart."
Barb Warus Bruno, CPC, CTS, Author
Merrillville, Indiana

"I have known Tom for more than 45 years and from the first time we spoke I knew he was a leader. From the jungles of Borneo to the boardroom where he, I, and John McMillian became partners in a deal to build underwater robots, I learned being around Tom would always be an adventure."
George Cundiff, CEO Underwater Specialists, Inc., ret.
Boca Raton, Florida

"While we were in college Tom was always the organizer, from arranging diving trips in the dark of night to hunt for stone crabs under the Jupiter Inlet Bridge, to journeying up to Titusville and climbing to the roof of my Dad's boat plant to marvel at Apollo moon rocket launches. Tom was the idea guy. All our projects were baby steps toward the phenomenal accomplishments that Tom would later achieve in the global world of underwater remotely operated vehicles. Who knew then what the future would hold for Captain Fireplug!"
Laurilee Thompson, Owner, Dixie Crossroads Seafood RestaurantTitusville, Florida

"I had so much fun and it was such a pleasure to work with Tom for 15 years. His interesting life stories and passion for people and life kept everyone around him inspired and in fits of laughter. He is well known for being a pioneer in underwater technology down under. He is a great salesman and entrepreneur, with a heart of gold. Tom was always generous with his time, money and personality. There was always a BBQ to be had where he'd cook the best ribs. He won the lotto a few times and with his windfall he always gave me (and others) a gift.Tom is easily the centre of attention with his wicked sense of humour and stories, but always humble and never fails to ask about the people around him. We loved him so much we were gutted when he retired to the States. I had a life-sized cardboard cutout of him printed and that has hung around the office for years. We take him to the BBQs, parties, and set him up in obscure places. His influence and spirit live on at Total Marine Technology."
Denise Danks, Tom's Personal Assistant, Total Marine Technology
Perth, Australia

“I first met Tom about five years before I went into business with him in 2000. We got along great. Tom was known as one of the best underwater robot guys in the oil industry and for winning the lottery three times. When Tom approached me to go into business, I jumped at it. But Tom didn’t come alone. He had a partner, Paul Colley. They were an odd-looking couple of blokes. One was short and wide and the other tall and gangly looking. I referred to them as Captain Kurt and Dr. Spock. We worked well together, and we all made money."
Mal Wardle, Director, Total Marine Technology, ret.
Perth, Australia

"Tom is one of those unique individuals that can relate as easily to shop floor workers as corporate executives - and everything in between. I found that he had a rare EQ coupled with an insatiable need to know how things worked and overlaid with a down-home, genuinely transparent way of dealing with people. What you saw was what you got! You could trust him. To top it off, he has an unbelievable sense of humor and can tell jokes for hours! Tom is one of our industry’s great pioneers."
Kevin McEvoy, Oceaneering President, ret.
Houston, Texas

“This book written by Tom Pado is a true example of how someone’s persistence and determination to overcome diversity resulted in becoming a well-respected leader in his industry and his community. His desire to excel in spite of a difficult childhood translated into success and worldwide respect.”
Marcia Lynch, Danville City Councilor and
Chamber of Commerce Executive Director, ret.
Danville, Indian